STAPLES AND BEYOND

CARLETON LIBRARY SERIES

The Carleton Library Series, funded by Carleton University under the general editorship of the dean of the School of Graduate Studies and Research, publishes books about Canadian economics, geography, history, politics, society, and related subjects. It includes important new works as well as reprints of classics in the fields. The editorial committee welcomes manuscripts and suggestions, which should be sent to the dean of the School of Graduate Studies and Research, Carleton University.

Staples and Beyond

Selected Writings of Mel Watkins

Edited by
HUGH GRANT
DAVID WOLFE

Introduction by
WALLACE CLEMENT

Carleton Library Series 210

McGill-Queen's University Press
Montreal & Kingston · London · Ithaca

© McGill-Queen's University Press 2006
    ISBN-13: 978-0-7735-3144-4   ISBN-10: 0-7735-3144-0 (cloth)
    ISBN-13: 978-0-7735-3145-1   ISBN-10: 0-7735-3145-9 (paper)

Legal deposit third quarter 2006
Bibliothèque nationale du Québec

Printed in Canada on acid-free paper

McGill-Queen's University Press acknowledges the support of the Canada
Council for the Arts for our publishing program. We also acknowledge
the financial support of the Government of Canada through the Book
Publishing Industry Development Program (BPIDP) for our publishing
activities.

Library and Archives Canada Cataloguing in Publication

Watkins, M. H. (Melville Henry), 1932–
    Staples and beyond: selected writings of Mel Watkins / edited
    by Hugh Grant, David Wolfe; introduction by Wallace Clement.

    (Carleton Library Series; 210)
    Includes bibliographical references and index.
    ISBN-13: 978-0-7735-3144-4   ISBN-10: 0-7735-3144-0 (bnd)
    ISBN-13: 978-0-7735-3145-1   ISBN-10: 0-7735-3145-9 (pbk)

    1. Canada – Economic policy – 1945–. I. Grant, Hugh M. K.
    (Hugh Murray Kenneth), 1956–. II. Wolfe, David. III. Title.

    HC115.W289 2006   338.971   C2006-901917-7

This book was typeset by Interscript in 10.5/13 Baskerville.

Contents

Preface

For anyone first exposed to Canadian political economy in the 1960s and 1970s, Mel Watkins is an iconic figure. His strong association with the Watkins Report, commissioned by Liberal Cabinet Minister Walter Gordon in the mid-1960s, and his critical role in the drafting of the Waffle Manifesto in 1969 (documented in Dave Godfrey's *Gordon to Watkins to You*) earned him instant recognition among a generation of students and activists deeply concerned with the growing degree of foreign control over the Canadian economy and the inadequate response to the issue by the mainstream political parties of the day. Political activism, through his subsequent involvement with the Berger Inquiry in the 1970s and his passionate opposition to the Free Trade Agreement and the NAFTA in the 1980s and 1990s, remains a central part of Mel's contribution to Canadian society and politics.

Along with his continuing engagement in Canadian political life, Mel has always been an active scholar. Born in the Innis tradition of Canadian political economy, his thinking was shaped by the work of his contemporaries, including Kari Levitt, Jim Laxer, Tom Naylor, Wallace Clement, Stephen Hymer, and, above all, Abraham Rotstein. Through his many contributions to magazine columns, government reports, and books and scholarly journals, Mel profoundly influenced the intellectual development of Canadian political economy over the course of more than four decades. However, because of the diverse range of publications in which this body of work first appeared, many of his more academic contributions to political economy are less well known than his political contributions. This collection brings together for the first time his most important contributions to academic scholarship. It is organized to reflect the scope of his work, which includes theoretical writings on the staple thesis; analysis of foreign investment, the multinational corporation, and international trade; observations on the state of Canadian economics and political economy; commentaries on a range of political issues; and reflections on technology. Papers are ordered chronologically within each section with the year of publication highlighted to provide the appropriate historical context. But these papers are not mere historical artifacts or "period pieces": the themes addressed and the arguments made continue to resonate and offer important insights into the nature of Canadian political economy today.

The range of topics and the even wider range of approaches may help explain why this collection is so long overdue. The editors faced two imposing barriers. The first was that Mel has written so much and influenced so many: the task of winnowing down his extensive writings was complicated by frequent objections over what was being excluded. The publication of some of Mel's columns from *This Magazine* in *Madness and Ruin: Politics and the Economy in the Neo-Conservative Age* (Toronto: Between the Lines, 1992) may provide solace to some, but to others we send an apology for being unable to accommodate their recommendations. The second barrier was that Mel continues to write so much and continues to influence so many. Just as one version of the manuscript reached an almost final stage of preparation, a new paper would appear that recast his thinking on a topic or that addressed a new issue.

Several people have contributed to putting this collection together. Daniel Drache helped to get the project started, David Wolfe's initiative in organizing a conference dedicated to Mel's scholarly work kept it rolling, and Janice Macauley and Denise Maharaj provided the valuable editorial assistance needed to ensure that it reached fruition.

We have attempted to limit our editorial intrusions to a minimum. Some papers have been edited for length in order to include as many papers as possible and in a few instances material has been rearranged to eliminate possible redundancies. Any editorial changes made to the original paper are noted in the first footnote, which also provides a reference to the original publication. We have also provided short introductions to each section to help put the material that follows in context.

We will, however, avail ourselves of the opportunity – as editors of the volume and long-time colleagues of Mel's – to reflect upon our own association with him. His contribution to Canadian political economy is, or will be, apparent to those who have an opportunity to read his work. Less well known, except to those who had the good fortune to enrol in one of his courses, is his influence as a teacher and mentor to undergraduate and graduate students at the University of Toronto.

Our association with Mel dates from the early 1970s, at a time when the Department of Political Economy was a rarefied, if not rather strange, place. In the politically charged atmosphere of the Vietnam War period, it was not unusual for incoming undergraduates to be familiar with the Waffle Movement, the Committee for an Independent Canada, and the findings of the Watkins and Gray Reports on foreign ownership, or to read *Canadian Dimension* and *The Canadian Forum* regularly. Eager first-year students in search of their lecture room in Sidney Smith Hall ran the gamut of newspaper sellers from a wide range of political parties and factions of the day. Most of the writings of Marx, Lenin, Mao, and Tim Buck were available for purchase. Rare times indeed.

Once acclimatized to the University of Toronto, it was possible to find a number of courses scattered through various academic departments that dealt with the issues pertaining to the New Left. This was less true in Economics; however, Ian Parker was a source of inspiration and two faculty members had definite name recognition: Abe Rotstein and Mel Watkins.

Despite the presence of Parker, Rotstein, Watkins, and others, pursuing an "alternative" program of study in economics grew more difficult as the neo-classical orthodoxy extended its grip on the former home of Innis and Easterbrook and the Keynesian consensus crumbled. The "Political Economy Course Critique" for 1973/74, published by the students' association, observed that "Numerous students emphasized the need for courses on 'the exploitation of multi-national corporations' or on 'Marxist economic theory.'" Lest students' criticisms be shrugged off by faculty and

administrators, they were accompanied by a warning: "We, the editors, sincerely hope that this course critique will aid in pinpointing
some of the inadequacies in each individual course. This, however,
is not enough. Words must be followed by action."

In a curious act of pluralism, or perhaps product differentiation,
the department responded by creating two versions of a course on
Canadian economic issues, one taught by Ed Safarian and the
other, not recommended for commerce students, by Mel Watkins.
As the latter was presumably designed to assuage the small band of
dissident students, the department was doubtless surprised when it
was consistently over-subscribed and the overwhelming choice of
commerce majors seeking to complete their economics require-
ment. The "Course Critique" for "Eco 337: Contemporary Issues in
the Canadian Economy" reported that: "Professor Watkins' course
is one of the few, if not the only economics course to follow the
Marxist viewpoint of economics. Watkins is, in addition, not afraid
to point out the shortcomings of the Keynesian school of economics." Despite this blessing, he did not escape criticism, "because he
spoke for practically the entire two hours each lecture." When Mel
was seconded to work for the Dene during the Berger Inquiry, the
course's popularity forced the department to arrange a last-minute
replacement. The best it could come up with was an equally witty
and urbane, if less renowned, academic from the Hautes Etudes
Commerciales, Jacques Parizeau.

As the opportunity to study political economy within Economics
slowly disintegrated, Mel took refuge in the undergraduate Canadian studies program at University College and in teaching a graduate course in Canadian political economy with colleagues David
Wolfe and Stephen Clarkson in political science, distancing himself, both physically and intellectually, from his colleagues in economics. Despite this, his courses – whether offered in economics,
political science, or Canadian studies – became a rite of passage for
those concerned with political economy, drawing students from every discipline and interdisciplinary program. Whatever else his students learned, it was clear that political economy could be a
strongly grounded theoretical discipline while still commenting on
the immediate issues of the day. The former required an acute
awareness of the "intuition," or "vision" that informed the theoretical model, while the latter demanded a personal engagement in
the current issues.

For his part, Mel was never far removed from the important political issues of the day, whether through his principal authorship of the Watkins' Report on Foreign Ownership, his involvement in party politics (from the Waffle Group to his candidacy in two federal elections under the NDP banner in the Beaches-East York riding), as an advisor to the Dene Nation during the Berger Inquiry hearings, as an anti-free trade advocate for the Canadian Labour Congress during the FTA debates, as a columnist and contributing editor at *This Magazine,* or through his work for Science for Peace. Yet throughout these various activities, Mel could almost always be found in his office and the lecture halls at University College, University of Toronto, where he stimulated the intellectual development of successive generations of students until his retirement in the 1990s.

Throughout this period he continued his scholarly activities, contributing new papers to academic conferences, participating in several versions of edited collections on the development of Canadian political economy, and writing for academic journals. As scholarly trends evolved over the course of these decades and the dominant academic issues of the day changed, Mel remained firmly committed to two critical values: the seminal contribution of the Innis tradition for an understanding of the development of the Canadian economy, society, and the polity and the need to analyse the factors contributing to, and the political implications of, a growing loss of Canadian sovereignty. His intellectual contribution to understanding these issues remains as critical today as when he first started writing about them in the 1960s. It is our fervent hope that this collection will expose his work to a new generation of students and scholars for whom these issues are as pressing today as they were when Mel joined his first anti-war teach-in at the University of Toronto.

Hugh Grant, University of Winnipeg
David A. Wolfe, University of Toronto

May, 2005

Mel Watkins and the Foundations of the New Canadian Political Economy[*]

WALLACE CLEMENT

It is my privilege to introduce this collection of papers written by Mel Watkins. I will concentrate on the formative period of Mel's intellectual life up to the point I came to know Mel personally, leaving the past two decades for others. I will then make a few remarks about our personal association.

THE BEGINNINGS

Melville H. Watkins comes from what he describes as "Bobby Orr Country" (that is, McKellar, Ontario, just north of Parry Sound). He entered the University of Toronto in 1948 with the intention of being an accountant. Mel tells us that "It was still possible, when I was an undergraduate studying economics, to feel that it was Canadian economics. That is not possible now." He attended some of the last lectures by Harold Adam Innis but felt that by the time Innis died in 1952, he was already becoming irrelevant and an impediment to the development of American-style economics in Canada. Mel went on to graduate school in the United States, studying at the Massachusetts Institute of Technology, noting that

---

[*] This introduction is based on the opening address at "Speaking Out: A Conference in Honour of Mel Watkins," University College, University of Toronto, 17–18 April 1998.

when he returned to Canada in 1958, he was "a well-trained technocrat and an American left democrat."[1]

Professor Watkins began his career as a fairly conventional economist. Circumstances, however, were to transform him into a bellwether for the new Canadian political economy. The "other" boy from Perry Sound became a professor of political economy at the University of Toronto where he made quite a conventional start, publishing an important text in economics with D.F. Foster, called simply *Economics: Canada*.[2] It contains fifty articles, none by H.A. Innis, but two attributed to the Bank of Canada, one to the Bank of Nova Scotia, and one to the *Financial Post*, as well as one to John Kenneth Galbraith, whom the editors say "blends insight and iconoclasm." The only piece by the young Professor Watkins is adventurously entitled "The National Accounts." I will spare you the details, except to note that this is one of the few places where you will find four statistical tables in a Watkins article (three of which contain residual errors of an estimate and the last two are adjusted for grain transactions). We all start somewhere.

The same year he published his signature piece for the *Canadian Journal of Economics and Political Science*, "A Staple Theory of Economic Growth," eventually gathering this paper and others into what became a standard collection on *Approaches to Canadian Economic History*.[3] (Has anyone else noticed that the book contained a "grateful acknowledgement" for financial assistance from the Ford Foundation?) The subject of that early paper was Harold Adams Innis. Following a systematic review of Innis's staples approach, Watkins says, "the fundamental fact is the pervasive interdependence with the North Atlantic community, and particularly with the United States. Canada is a small and open economy, a marginal area responding to the exogenous impact of the international economy. The basic determinants of Canadian growth are the volume and character of her staple exports." It would take several years before he would return to this insight.

July 1964 finds Melville H. Watkins celebrating the publication of Harry G. Johnson's *The Canadian Quandary* in the pages of *The Canadian Forum*. Johnson subtly contends that "Canadian nationalism as it has developed in recent years has been diverting Canada into a narrow and garbage-cluttered cul-de-sac." Watkins argues, "Those who have put nationalism behind them can see free trade as a meaningful manifestation of more responsible international behaviour."[4] In the same issue, arguing the counterpoint, Abraham Rotstein tears a few strips off Johnson's book, arguing "For those not mesmerized by the market, debate on public policy might centre on weighing real economic benefits against equally real political costs. No one can be indifferent to the problems of unemployment and lagging economic growth in this country."[5] Thank goodness the views of Rotstein prevailed between these two longtime colleagues. A little over a year later they were writing together in the same publication, this time extending the work of Marx and McLuhan in a creative discussion of "The Outer Man: Technology and Alienation."[6] In 1965, Melville H. Watkins writes an article called "Canadian Economic Policy: A Proposal" in an important collection edited by Abraham Rotstein, adopting the voice of "the Average Economist" (in reality the voice of Harry Johnson) "correcting" the average Canadian's misconceptions. Watkins writes: "Canada is less of a special case than many Canadians seem to believe ... In straightforward language, then, Canada is a very rich country, with no BUTS permitted." He goes so far as to claim Canada "should flourish under free trade." Two of his proposals are: "Move toward free trade by lowering the tariff multilaterally" and "Stop harassing foreign investors."[7]

A year later Watkins is back on the pages of the *Canadian Forum* asking "Is Gordon's Game Worth the Candle?" In 1970 he looked back on this publication saying "in '66 I reviewed Walter Gordon's *A Choice for Canada* for the *Canadian Forum* – and favourably on the whole, which put me in a distinct minority among Canadian economists."[8] The memory plays strange tricks. At the time he actually said: "With no desire to impugn Mr. Gordon's motives, his nationalism reflects too much of the mentality of the petty bourgeoisie; he is suspicious of large corporations – they do not provide 'the best training for future heroes' – but he largely accepts the ideology of liberalism which permits them to thrive. His recommendations for reform run too heavily toward gimmickry – the usual failing of tax accountants – and not enough toward broadgauged policies which are prepared to challenge the assumptions on which society – both American and Canadian – operates."[9] Maybe for someone who once aspired to be an accountant that's considered "favourable."

TASK FORCE ON THE STRUCTURE
OF CANADIAN INDUSTRY

Walter Gordon had a broad mind and sense of humour. This was some tax accountant. In *A Choice for Canada* he cites a speech made in 1965 to an American audience where he said: "There are those, of course, including many economists in academic circles, who see no problem for Canada in the snowballing of foreign investment, even between our two countries. These people cite in their support the classical theory of free trade and the desirability of international specializations ... The formulation of public policy cannot occur in neat conventional compartments – economics, political science, sociology, etc. Everyone knows – and everyone in government knows this instinctively – that all economic policies have political and social consequences."[10] Walter Gordon seemed to be a man ahead of his time.

Mel speaks most fondly of Walter Gordon. Reflecting back from 1987, he said "When I first went to work for him in the mid-1960s as an advisor on foreign ownership, I told him I was not a Liberal but a New Democrat. He said not to worry, that many of his strongest supporters were similarly misguided and that he couldn't afford to be choosy."[11] Must have been heady times for Mel. The Task Force he was asked to lead included such luminaries as Stephen Hymer, Gideon Rosenbluth, Abraham Rotstein, and A.E. Safarian. The first line of the Report, issued to the Privy Council Office in January 1968, read, "The extent of foreign control of Canadian industry is unique among the industrialized nations of the world." It concluded with the statement: "Foreign direct investment makes a positive contribution to Canadian economic growth by creating economic benefits for Canada. But foreign investment also creates costs."[12] A spectre was haunting the members of the Task Force and the country.

The engagement had a transformative effect on Mel. He was struck by what he called the "gutless" quality of those holding high office in Ottawa. Back at the University of Toronto while drafting the Report, he was drawn into the Dow Chemical protests taking place there and was becoming an activist. The response to the Report itself was cause for reflection. Its release by Cabinet was delayed by US President Johnson's New Year's message on monetary controls. Mel noted the irony: "A situation created by US control of the Canadian economy precluded issuing a report analysing US control of the Canadian economy." Only a short time after the Report was released he said, "the Report – I'm saying it now, I saw it then – was really not a radical document. It said the multinational corporations run this country, so why don't we get them to run it better? Why don't we leave them the power but get more benefit for Canadians?"[13] The Cabinet reception was frigid. As Walter Gordon recalls: "The Pearson cabinet rejected the Watkins Report out of hand. The then Minister of Finance [Mitchell Sharp] commented that it represented only the personal views of a few academics and had no bearing upon government policy. Other ministers thought the report should not be made public, although in the leaky Pearson Cabinet little could be kept secret for long. Eventually, it was decided to table the report but to make it clear the government took no responsibility whatsoever for its proposals. This was done. As I had been personally responsible for the creation of the task force and as I agreed with its conclusions, I felt compelled to resign in protest."[14]

Although Cabinet swept the Report under the rug, foreign control would not go away. Obvious problems led to a mandate in the spring of 1970 for the Honourable Herb Gray to "bring forward proposals on foreign investment." A few years later the Gray Report, *Foreign Direct Investment in Canada* (1972), was released, providing a thorough-going indictment of Canadian government policies, business practices, and social structure.[15]

TRANSFORMATION

As was true for so many intellectuals, the late 1960s marked a tremendous transformation in Mel Watkins. He embraced socialism before he embraced nationalism. His 1966 piece on "Technology in Our Past and Present" already indicated a major change in his economic thinking.[16] He reflected that "the greatest potential for Canada as a national society may lie in a substantial rejection of the market economy as the cornerstone of the market society and the market mentality." The same paper contends "to place significant impediments on foreign ownership and to do nothing else risks turning Canada into a technological backwater" and asserts that we must transcend "nationalism in any form." We have a few clues about the intellectual influences on him at this time through his

1970s reflection. He wrote: "For a couple of years I immersed myself pretty deeply in McLuhanism, and what it really did was liber-
ate me, sweep the cobwebs out of my mind ... Then Innis became
meaningful to me again, much more than before. I stopped being
simply sentimental about Innis, and rediscovered Canadian political economy as a defence against Americanized economics."[17]

There were other influences. Stephen Hymer, who had served
with Mel on the task force and was a professor at The New School
for Social Research until his untimely death, had been a close
friend and influence. Hymer is remembered for his penetrating observations about multinational corporations. In a piece written in
1970, he claimed, "Multinational corporations are a substitute for
the market as a method of organizing international exchange." He
concludes by saying that the multinational corporation "will create
grave social and political problems and will be very uneven in exploiting and distributing the benefits of modern science and technology. In a word, the multinational corporation reveals the power
of size and the danger of leaving it uncontrolled."[18] Mel was also
influenced by the writings of John Kenneth Galbraith, a fellow
Canadian (albeit ex-patriot) economist, who was also engaging
professional economists from the margins. Writing in *Economics and
the Public Purpose*, for example, Galbraith observed: "Left to themselves, economic forces do not work out for the best except perhaps
for the powerful."[19]

Mel was beginning to find his intellectual cadence. A key
marker is his paper "Economics and Mystification," published in
the *Journal of Canadian Studies* in 1969 and reprinted that same
year in the remarkable final section of a book called *Business and
Government*. The section is entitled "Toward a New Political Economy" and includes pieces by Karl Polanyi, Charles E. Lindblom,
and Robert L. Heilbroner. The editorial introduction to the section by K.J. Rea and J.T. McLeod includes an extensive discussion
of C.B. Macpherson, a colleague of Mel's at the University of Toronto. Of the Watkins piece they say: "Professor Watkins reminds
us that the analytical model of the free market is by no means
philosophically neutral. He sounds the call for a more sensitive
political and social approach to economic questions, and under-
lines the need for a reaffirmation of nonmarket values by students
of the social sciences. If a sharper challenge has been issued to

Canadian scholars, we have not heard it."[20] The piece is about "mysteries and mystifications." For Watkins, "it is the failure of economists to deal with power, analytically and theoretically, that constitutes the mystification. By ignoring power the economist claims to be apolitical." The piece is hard hitting, contending that "the critical point is that the theory economists use has been emptied of the political. The economist has a trained incapacity to understand power: his innocence is not accidental." Economics ignores "that the market is not a neutral mechanism that can be allowed free reign in a society without the most profound political and social implications which then constrain the solutions which economists can put forward. The market creates the market society and thereby a set of institutions and values which are anything but neutral."[21]

The profound failure of economics pushed Watkins back to Innis, via McLuhan, at a time when Harry Johnson reigned over Canadian economics – from London and Chicago. It was not far to the conviction that would mark Mel's place in Canadian intellectual life. In 1970 he declared in the clearest of terms: "Canadian nationalism was impossible without democratic socialism just as socialism cannot be achieved without independence."[22]

NEW CANADIAN POLITICAL ECONOMY

The decade of the 1970s brought a coming of age for the new Canadian political economy. In 1970, the University League for Social Reform published *Close the 49th parallel etc: The Americanization of Canada*, edited by Ian Lumsden.[23] This was the first in a series of primers that established the coming of age for the new Canadian political economy: *Capitalism and the national question*, edited by Gary Teeple in 1972; *The Canadian State: Political Economy and Political Power*, edited by Leo Panitch in 1977; *A Practical Guide to Canadian Political Economy*, by Wallace Clement and Daniel Drache in 1978; and the start of the journal *Studies in Political Economy: A Socialist Review* in 1979. Mel Watkins was a force behind all these developments. His contribution to the Lumsden collection was "The Dismal State of Economics in Canada" where he returned to Innis, characterizing him as "a liberal nationalist" and claiming that "Innis's anti-imperialism argues for the necessity of a Canadian nationalism of the left." Another important marker was the publication, also in 1970, of Kari Levitt's influential study, *Silent Surrender*.[24] Mel Watkins wrote the Preface for that book.

Reconsideration of the writings of Harold Innis has been Mel's main scholarly contribution to the revival of Canadian political economy. As he says: "the large questions which Innis asked about the nature of Canada – about staples bias and the risk of dependency – did not go away. Rather, circumstances, notably the nationalist, New Left ferment of the 1960s, and the long shadow it was to cast within the universities, put them on the agenda in an unprecedented way."[25] Mel used a revamped Innisian paradigm to challenge the hegemony of his economist colleagues and has been a conservator, interpreter, and extender of Innis's dedication to the big questions of political economy, their holistic quality, and the dimensions of time and space. This is not the place to provide a primer on Innis but a few citations illustrate the power of his thoughts. In the opening essay (written in 1929) in his most famous collection he says at the end of the first paragraph: "the application of economic theories of old countries to the problems of new countries results in a new form of exploitation with dangerous consequences. The only escape can come from an intensive study of Canadian economic problems and from the development of a philosophy of economic history or an economic theory suited to Canadian needs."[26] In the final essay in the collection (originally written in 1948), Innis asserts that "Canada has had no alternative but to serve as an instrument of British imperialism and then of American imperialism ... American imperialism ... has been made plausible and attractive in part by the insistence that it is not imperialistic."[27]

Mel wrote several pieces systematically reinterpreting Innis for a new age. In his piece "The Staples Theory Revisited" he claimed, "Innis in particular was a liberal with a difference, who saw the dark underside and the gross contradictions and this makes him susceptible to an approach that specializes in such matters."[28] He concludes there are at least two liberal versions of the staple's theory and perhaps two Marxist versions; Innis had become a contested terrain. A little later he engages even more deeply the "power of paradigms" and how "the disciplines discipline" as he maps the contested views characteristic of Canadian political economy and Innis's place in them.[29] I can only mention his modes of production application of the staple's insights as most evident in his paper

"From Underdevelopment to Development" in the 1977 collection he edited under the auspices of the University League for Social Reform entitled *Dene Nation:The Colony Within*.

PERSONAL REFLECTIONS

My first personal encounter with Professor Watkins was on a panel of the first Political Economy session at the Learned Society meetings in Quebec City in 1976. He flew into the meetings from Yellowknife. He critiqued my first book in *Ontario Report*[30] and was soon to be appointed the external examiner for my PhD thesis. What would you think about an external examiner who had accused you of being limited by the "terrible blinders" imposed by the discipline of sociology? Instead of the prevailing left-nationalist image of unmediated domination by American capitalism, I had brought to attention the persistence of an indigenous elite concentrated in finance, transportation, and utilities that had entered into a partnership with foreign capital in manufacturing and resources. Watkins' position was "Surely whoever dominates the goods-producing sector dominates the economy of a capitalist country. To believe otherwise seems simply to defy common sense."

I did have the common sense to be unsure when my committee informed me that Professor Watkins was selected as my examiner, given his commentary on my Master's thesis. If I was unsure, Dean Gilles Paquet was clear. Watkins had done something to aggravate Paquet. He wanted someone else to be the external and appointed Dennis Wrong, Professor of Sociology, Harvard University, as a second external. This was academic politics well beyond my scope. Dean Paquet and John Porter, my supervisor, were at loggerheads, as was the continentalist economist Paquet with the nationalist economist Watkins. I survived. Then, in January 1978, Mel wrote another review in *Ontario Report*, this time of *Continental Corporate Power*, which he entitled "Unequal Alliance." Instantly I knew that should have been my book's title, but too late. This time, however, I had redeemed myself: "Clement is now unambiguously of the view that the alliance is an unequal one for Canada."[31] I am not sure which of us moved the most.

He and I later became friends while I was teaching at McMaster University in Hamilton. We were on the board of the fledgling *Studies in Political Economy* together and regularly rode to meetings in Kingston where we met with the crew who came from Ottawa. When the board was unable to construct the opening statement for the journal by committee, Mel and I were delegated to draft it. We did it at his dining room table with very little difficulty and no acrimony. The statement appeared in issue Number 1 of the journal as the "Editorial Statement" and declared, "Political economy is alive and flourishing in Canada." It notes political economy's "indigenous liberal, yet unorthodox, tradition" with Innis and its "highly creative Marxist tradition" with Macpherson, Pentland, and Ryerson.

Subsequent association with Mel has been close, both intellectually and personally. He wrote the first chapters in both of the collections I have edited on the new Canadian political economy: "The Political Economy of Growth" in 1989 and "Canadian Capitalism in Transition" in 1997.[32] He subsequently wrote the first chapter entitled "Politics in the Time and Space of Globalization" in *Changing Canada*, published in 2003.These papers are his most developed expositions of the linkages between the old and new schools of Canadian political economy. He is a brilliant observer. He is well known as a speaker, columnist, and activist. But his greatest quality is as an observer, a quality that gives the special edge to his other activities. Mel has helped to "bring me out" somewhat. I am basically a researcher – someone who is constantly doing homework. I thought public intervention was simple – write a Master's thesis, have it published, have Ed Broadbent use it in the House of Commons to criticize the government of the day, and a Royal Commission would follow. Since then I have learned that the public process is usually a bit more complicated. Mel has been the activist – from his days on the task force to his work with the Dene around the Berger Inquiry to his work with the Canadian Labour Congress (CLC) against Free Trade.

I was fortunate enough to experience his CLC work first hand. Mel spent the CLC/Free Trade period living with Elsie and me in Ottawa while Kelly, his wife, was in London heading the CBC's European Bureau. One could not have asked for a more congenial houseguest – one who rose early to join our youngest son Jeff for breakfast. Jeff still talks fondly of those discussions. Elsie and I often say it was like he had always been with us – quite a compliment from her – slipping comfortably into our oldest son's room while he was away at university. Mel reviewed the original OCGS proposal for the Institute of Political Economy's Master's program at Carleton University (along with Liora Salter) where he has twice taught in the Summer School, spreading the neo-Innisian word to a receptive audience. To cite Duncan Cameron from a recent conference we attended, Mel has been most important for nourishing "public debate and public discussion." To cite Kari Levitt's comment from the same occasion, Mel Watkins has earned our respect. He has certainly gained mine. His rich legacy is an insightful and independent scholarship for the new Canadian political economy.

NOTES

1 See Mel Watkins, "Getting to Democratic Socialism," in *Gordon to Watkins to You, A Documentary: The Battle for Control of Our Economy*, edited by Dave Godfrey and Mel Watkins (Toronto: New Press, 1970), 3–5.

2 M.H. Watkins and D.F. Foster, eds., *Economics: Canada* (Toronto: McGraw-Hill, 1963).

3 W.T. Easterbrook and M.H. Watkins, eds., *Approaches to Canadian Economic History* (Toronto: Carleton Library, McClelland and Stewart, 1967). "A Staple Theory of Economic Growth" is the only piece he chose to include in his 1993 update of this collection, *Canadian Economic History: Classic and Contemporary Approaches*, edited by M.H. Watkins and H.M. Grant (Ottawa: Carleton University Press, 1993).

4 J.K. Granatstein and Peter Stevens, eds., *Forum: Canadian Life and Letters, 1920–1970. Selections from the Canadian Forum* (Toronto: University of Toronto Press, 1972), 372.

5 Granatstein and Stevens, *Forum*, 376.

6 Abraham Rotstein and Melville H. Watkins, "The Outer Man: Technology and Alienation," *Canadian Forum* (August 1965): 384–6.

7 Melville H. Watkins, "Canadian Economic Policy: A Proposal" in *The Prospect of Change: Proposals for Canada's Future*, edited by Abraham Rotstein for the University League for Social Reform (Toronto: McGraw-Hill, 1965), 64–5, 82.

8 Watkins, "Getting to Democratic Socialism," 7.

9 Melville H. Watkins, "Is Gordon's Game Worth the Candle?" *Canadian Forum* (July 1966): 400.

10 Walter L. Gordon, *A Choice for Canada* (Toronto: McClelland and Stewart, 1966), 91–2.

11 Mel Watkins, *Madness and Ruin: Politics and the Economy in the Neo-Conservative Age* (Toronto: Between the Lines, 1992), 27.

12 Privy Council Office, *Foreign Ownership and the Structure of Canadian Industry* (January 1968), 1, 121.

13 Watkins, "Getting to Democratic Socialism," 61, 84.

14 Walter L. Gordon, *Storm Signals: New Economic Policies for Canada* (Toronto: McClelland and Stewart, 1975), 93.

15 See Wallace Clement, *The Canadian Corporate Elite* (Toronto: McClelland and Stewart, 1975), 116–17.

16 Melville Watkins, "Technology in Our Past and Present" in *Canada: A Guide to the Peaceable Kingdom*, edited by William Kilbourn (Toronto: Macmillan of Canada, 1970), 290–1.

17 Watkins, "Getting to Democratic Socialism," 6.

18 Stephen Hymer, "The Efficiency (Contradictions) of Multinational Corporations" in *The Multinational Firm and the Nation State*, edited by Gilles Paquet (Toronto: Collier-Macmillan Canada, 1972), 49, 64.

19 John Kenneth Galbraith, *Economics and the Public Purpose* (Boston: Houghton Mifflin Company, 1973), xiii.

20 K.J. Rea and J.T. McLeod, eds., *Business and Government* (Toronto: Methuen, 1969), 362.

21 Melville H. Watkins, "Economics and Mystification" in *Business and Government*, 391–2; original in the *Journal of Canadian Studies* 4, 1 (February 1969).

22 Watkins, "Getting to Democratic Socialism," 2.

23 Melville H. Watkins, "The Dismal State of Economics in Canada" in *Close the 49th parallel etc: The Americanization of Canada*, edited by Ian Lumsden (Toronto: University of Toronto Press, 1970).

24 Kari Levitt, *Silent Surrender: The Multinational Corporation in Canada* (Toronto: Macmillan, 1970).

25 Mel Watkins, "Innis at 100: Reflections on His Legacy for Canadian Studies," *Canadian Issues/Thèmes Canadiens* 17 (1995): 176.

26 Harold Adam Innis, "The Teaching of Economic History in Canada" in *Essays in Canadian Economic History*, edited by Mary Q. Innis (Toronto: University of Toronto Press, 1956), 3.

27 Innis, "Great Britain, the United States and Canada" in ibid., 405, 407.

28 Mel Watkins, "The Staple Theory Revisited," *Journal of Canadian Studies* 12, 5 (Winter 1977): 83.

29 Mel Watkins, "The Innis Tradition in Political Economy," *Canadian Journal of Political and Social Thought* 6 (Winter/Spring 1982): 1–2.

30 Mel Watkins, "Review of *The Canadian Corporate Elite: An Analysis of Economic Power*," *Ontario Report* 1, 5 (June 1976): 39.

31 Mel Watkins, "Unequal Alliance," *Ontario Report* 2, 5 (January 1978): 38.

32 Mel Watkins, "The Political Economy of Growth" in *The New Canadian Political Economy*, edited by Wallace Clement and Glen Williams (Montreal: McGill-Queen's University Press, 1989) and Mel Watkins, "Canadian Capitalism in Transition" in *Understanding Canada: Building on the New Canadian Political Economy*, edited by Wallace Clement (Montreal: McGill-Queen's University Press, 1997).

STAPLES AND BEYOND

PART ONE

The Staple Theory of Development

The four papers in this section, taken together, provide a comprehensive and compelling presentation of the staple thesis. As such,
they form a cornerstone of the "new political economy" in Canada.

The first of these papers, the now classic "Staple Theory of Economic Growth," brings the pioneering work of Harold Innis and
W.A. Mackintosh within the orbit of a Keynesian aggregate demand
model. The natural resource export becomes the potential source
of exogenous growth if it triggers activity in associated industries.
Borrowing Hirshman's technical concepts of forward and backward linkages – or how the production function in the export sector may generate associated economic activity within the country –
it adds the innovation of the "final-demand linkage." The importance of this third linkage cannot be overstated: by focusing
attention on the magnitude and distribution of income in the
export sector, both the degree of foreign ownership and the role
of the state become critical to determining the pace and pattern of
economic development.[*]

The paper received high praise and crops up in a remarkable
number and range of university reading lists both inside and

_____

[*] Hirschman acknowledges the importance of this contribution: see A.O.
Hirschman, *Essays in Trespassing: Economics to Politics and Beyond* (New York:
Cambridge University Press, 1981).

outside Canada. Its harshest critic, however, proved to be the author himself. The "Staple Thesis Revisited" elaborates on several earlier themes, but particularly on the nature of class relations and the role of the state in dictating the direction of development. The paper acknowledges the important distinction drawn by Naylor and Clement between the factions of the capitalist class and goes further by inquiring into the primary conflicts – between merchant and independent commodity producer and between capital and labour – throughout the early staple trades and later phases of industrialization.

The third paper, "Dene Nation," is a masterful application of the staples thesis to a contemporary issue in Canadian political economy. In the context of the hearings of the Berger Commission into the appropriateness of a natural gas pipeline through the Mackenzie Valley, the Dene noted that this was another in a series of incursions on their land and their right to self-determination. Each staple had different implications for the Dene economy. The fur trade, which relied upon Dene trappers as primary commodity producers, was more compatible with other subsistence pursuits, in contrast to mineral exploitation, which relied upon the commodification of labour and land. If the fur trade created the conditions for the reproduction of a viable Dene economy, the oil and natural gas exploitation, in the absence of a land settlement that recognized their right to self-determination, promised only its destruction.

The fourth paper, "Transitions," situates the Canadian economy within the appropriate international context. The contradictions of being a "dependent capitalist" country are apparent in the seeming paradoxes of the simultaneous inflows of foreign investment and Canadian investment abroad, and the high average standard of living in Canada despite the lack of economic diversification and the lack of autonomy in crucial aspects of economic and political decision making.

1

A Staple Theory
of Economic Growth (1963)

The staple approach to the study of economic history is primarily a
Canadian innovation; indeed, it is Canada's most distinctive contribution to political economy. It is undeveloped in any explicit form
in most countries where the export sector of the economy is or was
dominant.[1] The specific terminology – staple or staples approach,
or theory, or thesis – is Canadian, and the persistence with which
the theory has been applied by Canadian social scientists and historians is unique.

The leading innovator was the late Harold Innis in his brilliant
pioneering historical studies, notably of the cod fisheries and the
fur trade; others tilled the same vineyard but it is his work that has
stamped the "school."[2] His concern was with the general impact
on the economy and society of staple production. His method was
to cast the net widely. The staple approach became a unifying
theme of diffuse application rather than an analytic tool fash-
ioned for specific uses. There was little attempt to limit its application by the use of an explicit framework.[3] Methodologically,

Reprinted from *Canadian Journal of Economics and Political Science* 29 (1963):
141–58. In the original paper, "Financial assistance for the Summer of
1961 is gratefully acknowledged from the Ford Foundation," as are the
comments on an earlier draft provided by J.H. Dales, W.T. Easterbrook,
C.P. Kindleberger, J.I. McDonald, A. Rotstein, and S.G. Triantis.

Innis' staple approach was more technological history writ large than a theory of economic growth in the conventional sense.[4]

Once solidly entrenched in Canadian studies, the staple approach has now fallen on more uncertain days as its relevance has come to be questioned by Canadian economic historians.[5] The strongest attack has come from Kenneth Buckley who maintains that it is "practical and efficacious" as a theory of economic growth to 1820, but that thereafter "other sources of national economic growth and change" are impossible to ignore; he concludes that Canadian economic historians should "replace the notion of an opportunity structure determined by geography and natural resources with a general concept of economic opportunity without specifying determinants."[6] Vernon C. Fowke's emphasis on agriculture serving the domestic market as an impetus to investment and hence to economic growth in central Canada prior to Confederation involves a devaluation of the role of staple exports; while W.T. Easterbrook has argued, after extensive review of the literature, that the staple theory no longer constitutes – and apparently ought not to – an adequate unifying theme for the study of Canadian development.[7] On the other hand, Hugh G.J. Aitken has remained satisfied with the approach. His own recent writings have been focussed on the new resource industries of the twentieth century; in commenting on Buckley's paper he suggested that the staple approach is relevant at least to 1914; and has subsequently maintained that "it is still true that the pace of development in Canada is determined fundamentally by the exports that enable Canada to pay its way in the world."[8]

The sample is small, but so too is the number of practising Canadian economic historians. There would appear to be declining confidence in the relevance of the staple approach, especially if consideration is given to what has been said as well as what has been written. But, curiously, the decline has been parallelled by rising interest among non-Canadians who may or may not refer to Innis and Canada. The leading advocate of the staple approach today is Douglass C. North, whose work may well have set the stage for a reconsideration of the causes of American economic growth from the American Revolution to the Civil War.[9] Two American economists, Richard E. Caves and Richard H. Holton, have critically reexamine the staple approach from the viewpoint of modern economic theory as a prelude to forecasting the state of the

Canadian economy in 1970, and have given it a surprisingly clean bill of health.[10] R.E. Baldwin has provided a brilliant theoretical article on the impact of staple production on an economy, and both North and Caves and Holton have acknowledged their indebtedness to him.[11] Mention must also be made of the analytical approach used by Jonathan V. Levin in his study of the role of primary product exports in Peru and Burma; of the implications for the staple approach of the application of modern income and growth theory to the classic problem of the transfer mechanism for capital imports in the Canadian balance of payments, particularly in the great boom before the First World War; and of the distinction made by Harvey S. Perloff and Lowdon Wingo, Jr., between "good" and "bad" resource exports in the context of American regional growth.[12]

The simultaneous waning of the reputation of the staple approach among Canadians and its rise elsewhere has created a gap in the literature which this paper will attempt to bridge. It will be argued that the staple theory can fruitfully be limited to a distinct type of economic growth; restate a staple theory so constrained in more rigorous form, primarily by drawing on the literature cited in the paragraph above; contrast this staple theory with other models of economic development; and finally, consider again the relevance of a staple approach to the Canadian case.

I

The linking of economic history and the theory of economic growth is a prerequisite to further advance in both fields. One obvious link lies in the development of theories appropriate to particular types of economic growth. The staple theory is presented here not as a general theory of economic growth, nor even a general theory about the growth of export-oriented economies, but rather as applicable to the atypical case of the new country.

The phenomenon of the new country, of the "empty" land or region overrun by Europeans in the past four centuries, is, of course, well known. The leading examples are the United States and the British dominions. These countries had two distinctive characteristics as they began their economic growth: a favourable man/land ratio and an absence of inhibiting traditions.[13] From these initial features flow some highly probable consequences for the growth process, at least in the early phase: staple exports are the leading sector, setting the pace for economic growth and leaving their peculiar imprint on economy and society; the importation of scarce factors of production is essential; and growth, if it is to be sustained, requires an ability to shift resources that may be hindered by excessive reliance on exports in general, and, in particular, on a small number of staple exports. These conditions and consequences are not customarily identified with underdeveloped countries, and hence are not the typical building blocks of a theory of economic growth. Rather, the theory derived from them is limited, but consciously so in order to cast light on a special type of economic growth. Because of the key role of staple exports, it can be called a staple theory of economic growth.

II

The fundamental assumption of the staple theory is that staple exports are the leading sector of the economy and set the pace for economic growth. The limited – at first possibly non-existent – domestic market, and the factor proportions – an abundance of land relative to labour and capital – create a comparative advantage in resource-intensive exports, or staples. Economic development will be a process of diversification around an export base. The central concept of a staple theory, therefore, is the spread effects of the export sector, that is, the impact of export activity on domestic economy and society. To construct a staple theory, then, it is necessary to classify these spread effects and indicate their determinants.

Let us begin with the determinants. Assume to be given the resource base of the new country and the rest-of-the-world environment – the international demand for the supply of goods and factors, the international transportation and communications networks, the international power structure. The sole remaining determinant can then be isolated, namely, the character of the particular staple or staples being exported.

A focus on the character of the staple distinguished Innis' work. C.R. Fay expresses the point most succinctly: "the emphasis is on the commodity itself: its significance for policy; the tying in of one activity with another; the way in which a basic commodity sets the general pace, creates new activities and is itself strengthened or perhaps dethroned, by its own creation."[14] The essence of the technique has been thrown into sharp relief by Baldwin. Using the method of ideal types, he contrasts the implications of reliance on a plantation crop and a family farm crop respectively for the economic development of an area exporting primary products. The important determinant is the technology of the industry, that is, the production function, which defines the degree of factor substitutability and the nature of returns to scale. With the production function specified and the necessary *ceteris paribus* assumptions – including the demand for goods and the supply of factors – a number of things follow: demand for factors; demand for intermediate inputs; possibility of further processing; and the distribution of income.

These determine the range of investment opportunities in domestic markets, or the extent of diversification around the export base. If the demand for the export staple increases, the quantity supplied by the new country will increase. This export expansion means a rise in income in the export sector. The spending of this income generates investment opportunities in other sectors, both at home and abroad. By classifying these income flows, we can state the staple theory in the form of a disaggregated multiplier-accelerator mechanism. In Hirschman's terms, the inducement to domestic investment resulting from the increased activity of the export sector can be broken down into three linkage effects: backward linkage, forward linkage, and what we shall call final demand linkage.[15] The staple theory then becomes a theory of capital formation; the suggestion has been made but not yet elaborated that it is such.

Backward linkage is a measure of the inducement to invest in the home-production of inputs, including capital goods, for expanding export sectors. The export good's production function and the relative prices of inputs will determine the types and quantities of inputs required. Diversification will be the greatest where the input requirements involve resources and technologies which permit of home-production. The emphasis usually placed in studies of economic development on barriers to entry into machinery production suggests a high import content for capital-intensive staples, and hence a small backward linkage effect. Caves and Holton, however, emphasize the importance of capital-intensive agriculture in supplying linkage to domestic agricultural machinery production.

Theory and history suggest that the most important example of backward linkage is the building of transport systems for collection of the staple, for that can have further and powerful spread effects.

Forward linkage is a measure of the inducement to invest in industries using the output of the export industry as an input. The most obvious, and typically most important, example is the increasing value added in the export sector; the economic possibilities of further processing and the nature of foreign tariffs will be the prime determinants.

Final demand linkage is a measure of the inducement to invest in domestic industries producing consumer goods for factors in the export sector. Its prime determinant is the size of the domestic market, which is in turn dependent on the level of income – aggregate and average – and its distribution.

The size of the aggregate income will vary directly with the absolute size of the export sector. But a portion of the income may be received by what Levin has called "foreign factors" – factors which remit their income abroad – rather than "domestic factors." To the extent that income received by foreign factors is not taxed away domestically, final demand linkage will be lessened. The servicing of capital imports is a case in point. Primary producers are notoriously susceptible to indebtedness, and the burden will be greater the more capital-intensive the staple. Leakage can also result from wages paid to migratory labour and from immigrants' remittances.

The average level of income, that is, the per capita income of the domestic factors, depends on the productivity of "land" or the resource content of the staple export, for other factors are importable. The distribution of income, on present assumptions, is determined by the nature of the production function of the staple, in Baldwin's models being relatively unequal for the plantation crop and relatively equal for the family farm crop.

The impact of these two market dimensions on final demand linkage can be seen by classifying consumer spending in two ways. First, consumer spending may be either on home-produced goods or on imports, and the higher the marginal propensity to import the lower the final demand linkage. Second, it may be either on subsistence goods and luxuries, or on a broad range of goods and services; the latter are more likely to lend themselves to those economies of mass production which lie at the heart of on-going industrialization, while luxury spending – other than for labour-intensive services – is likely, given the tendency to ape the tastes of more advanced countries, to be directed toward imported goods, that is, to create in Levin's terminology "luxury importers."

Final demand linkage will tend to be higher, the higher the average level of income and the more equal its distribution. At a higher level of income, consumers are likely to be able to buy a range of goods and services which lend themselves to domestic production by advanced industrial techniques. Where the distribution is relatively unequal, the demand will be for subsistence goods at the lower end of the income scales and for luxuries at the upper end. The more equal the distribution the less likelihood of opulent luxury importers and the greater the likelihood of a broadly based market for mass-produced goods.

The discussion of the linkages so far has assumed that investment is induced solely by demand factors. But on the supply side the expansion of the export sector creates opportunities for domestic investment which may or may not be exploited. Consideration must be given to the relationship between staple production and the supply of entrepreneurship and complementary inputs, including technology.

The key factor is entrepreneurship, the ability to perceive and exploit market opportunities. Entrepreneurial functions can be fulfilled by foreigners, and to the extent that this makes available technical and marketing skills the result can be advantageous to the new country. But the literature on economic development, and particularly on the dual economy, raises many doubts as to the adequacy of foreign entrepreneurship. It may flow freely into the export and import trades, but fail to exploit domestic opportunities. Exports may be regarded as safer, in part because they earn directly the foreign exchange necessary to reimburse foreign factors, but largely because export markets are better organized and better known than domestic markets. Foreign domination of entrepreneurship may militate against its general diffusion.

An adequate supply of domestic entrepreneurship, both private and governmental, is crucial. Its existence depends on the institutions and values of society, about which the economist generalizes at his peril. But the character of the staple is clearly relevant. Consider, for example, Baldwin's polar cases. In the plantation case, the dominant group with its rentier mentality on the one hand, and the mass of slaves who are prevented from bettering themselves on the other, can produce a set of institutions as inimical to entrepreneurial activity as is to be found in any tradition-ridden society. Business pursuits may be castigated as "money grubbing"; education – which, as North emphasizes, is very important – is likely to be confined to the elite and to slight the development of technical and business skills; political activity tends to be devoted to the defence of the status quo. On the other hand, in the family-farm case, as in wheat areas, the more equal distribution of income can result in attitudes toward social mobility, business activities, education, and the role of government which are more favourable to diversified domestic growth. These are gross differences; the more subtle ones could be worked out for specific staples.

Even where domestic entrepreneurship is forthcoming, its effectiveness rests on the availability of labour and capital, both foreign and domestic. The "push" from the old countries has in the past created a highly elastic supply of labour, although not, as the slave trade attests, without some resort to the use of force. But the individual receiving country has to create conditions sufficiently favourable to the inflow of labour to compete with other receiving countries. The original staple may create a social structure which is unattractive to the immigrant with skills suitable for the development of domestic economic activity. Where the staple is land-intensive, as is fur, the staple producers may find it in their own self-interest to discourage immigration and settlement. The transport technologies associated with particular staples provide varying passenger fares and hence differential stimuli to immigration. The availability of labour domestically will depend on the competing attractions of staple production and the quality of the labour force that has resulted from the exploitation of the particular staple. The staple activity may attract excess labour through non-pecuniary advantages: the romantic life of the fur trader and the aristocratic life of the planter are frequently alleged to have had detrimental consequences for other sectors of the economy. The quality of the labour force is significantly related to education.

Foreign capital, both in substance and in preference for foreign trade over domestic industry, is difficult to distinguish from foreign entrepreneurship, which we have already discussed. The availability of capital domestically will depend on the extent of domestic saving and the biases of the savers in placing their funds. The amount of saving will be determined by the production function for the staple. For example, Baldwin argues that savings will be higher with the skewed income distribution of the plantation crop than with the equal distribution of the family-farm crop. This would be the conventional view, although the opposite would be true if it were assumed that saving was encouraged by greater investment opportunities at home or discouraged by a greater concern with consumption for status in a more hierarchical society. But the amount of saving may not matter greatly. For domestic savers, like foreign capitalists, may be biased against domestic activities; they may prefer to expand the export industry further or to invest in the import trade. They may also prefer to invest abroad, for in an open economy capital can flow out as well as in. It is only when there are abundant opportunities in domestic markets waiting to be exploited that the amount of domestic saving will significantly determine the rate of investment.

The technology applied in domestic sectors is likely, to the extent that it is up to date, to be substantially borrowed from abroad. The newness of the country will minimize the difficulties of adapting borrowed technology and create a potential minimum growth rate not significantly lower than that achieved by advanced economies. The inflow of foreign technology will be facilitated by the inflow of foreign entrepreneurship and capital. To the extent that innovation is necessary and possible in the export sector, confidence may be gained by domestic entrepreneurs which will facilitate creative responses in domestic sectors. As domestic entrepreneurship emerges, innovations should become more appropriate to domestic factor proportions and the requirements of the domestic market.

A historically relevant theory must allow not only for the differing character of particular staples but also for the impact of the resource base of the new country and the international environment. For any particular new country the initial conditions can vary, and these conditions can change over time, both autonomously and as a result of the actions of the new country consequent on its success in exploiting its particular staple or staples.

Although these points are important, it is difficult to say much in general about them. For any given inducement to invest offered by the market, an appropriate resource base is necessary; the best of all possible staples will do little to encourage development if the resource base is sufficiently bad, and the impact of a particular staple can vary widely depending on the resource base of the particular country.[16] The resource base itself can change through discovery, and success in staple production, at least for some staples, may expedite the process.[17]

So too the international environment can vary in its suitability for the development of new countries. Staple producers begin as colonial outposts of old countries and differences among the latter, in their markets for staples, their supplies of factors for export, their institutions and values, and their colonial policies, will affect growth prospects. Change can take place in any of these dimensions: in foreign demand and foreign supply, which can destroy old staples and create new ones; in transport facilities, which can cheapen internationally traded goods; in the "push" of factors from the old countries and the "pull" from other new countries; in colonial policy and in the frequency of wars which can either encourage or discourage growth. And the new country, to the extent that it is successful, may gain power to mould the environment to suit its needs. It can develop a transport system adequate for both domestic and export requirements; it can pursue a commercial policy by which it can cause further processing of its exports and promote import-competing industry without unduly interfering with the optimal allocation of its resources.

What is the likely growth path of a staple economy? Growth is initiated by an increase in demand for a staple export. If the spread effects are potent, as the export sector grows so too will the domestic sectors. The result will be increasing demand for factors. Domestic slack, if it exists at all, will be quickly absorbed, and the continuation of growth will depend on the ability to import scarce factors. If the supply of foreign factors is elastic, the customary tendency for the expansion of one sector – in this case exports – to affect domestic sectors adversely by driving up factor prices is mitigated. This explains the very strong booms that are a feature of growth in staple economies.[18]

But what of the nature of growth in the long run? In a staple economy, as in any other, sustained growth requires an ability to shift resources at the dictates of the market – what C.P. Kindleberger calls "a capacity to transform." Particular export lines can create prosperity, but typically only for a short time. Over the longer pull they cease to be profitable either because of diminishing returns on the supply side, or adverse shifts in demand consequent on competition from cheaper sources of supply or from synthetics, or because of the income-elasticity of foreign demand, or simply because of changes of taste. This tendency can be slowed up by attempts to improve marketing and by seeking out cost-reducing innovations. The possibility of the latter depends on the character of the staple; for example, because of the physical properties of the plants, cotton production was historically much more resistant to mechanization than wheat-growing. But the law of diminishing returns cannot be checked indefinitely. Sustained growth, then, requires resource flexibility and innovation sufficient to permit shifts into new export lines or into production for the domestic market.

The probability of long-run success for the staple economy is significantly increased by its two distinctive initial features: a favourable man/land ratio and an absence of inhibiting traditions. The first implies a relatively high standard of living which facilitates expanding domestic markets and substantial factor mobility. The fact that new countries do not start their development with population pressing against scarce resources gives them an enormous advantage over the typical underdeveloped country. Specifically, they have neither a large subsistence agricultural sector severely limiting markets for domestic industry, nor a pool of cheap labour permitting industrialization to proceed with only limited impact on the incomes of much of the population. Subsequent population growth, in part by immigration, means that the size of population is closely related to economic opportunity at a relatively high standard of living. The second feature, the lack of traditions, means that institutions and values must be formed anew, and although there will be a substantial carry-over from the old world, the process will be selective and those transferred are likely to take a form more favourable to economic growth.

These are substantial advantages, and go far to explain the extraordinary success of some new countries. But even for the staple economy, historians insist that the process of growth is not without pitfalls. It is frequently alleged, at least implicitly, that the achievement of a high level of national income masks deficiencies in the structural balance of the economy. W.W. Rostow charges that the high levels of welfare achieved in new countries by exploiting land and natural resources will delay their reaching the "take-off" stage.[19] If the concept of take-off is interpreted as meaning simply the growth and diversification of the manufacturing sector, this argument runs counter to the staple theory. Rostow's claim, however, is no more than an untested hypothesis. He has not outlined the specific mechanism by which primary exports delay industrialization. It is not clear that he is saying anything more than that if a country has a comparative advantage in primary exports it will perforce have a comparative disadvantage in manufactures. This static view communicates nothing about the process of growth in a world where factor supply can be highly elastic and the composition of imports can shift radically over time. The first peril, then, is illusory.[20]

A more real difficulty is that the staple exporters – specifically, those exercising political control – will develop an inhibiting "export mentality," resulting in an over concentration of resources in the export sector and a reluctance to promote domestic development. Our previous comments on the social and political structure associated with particular staples are relevant here, but the literature on economic development in general is replete with other hypotheses and examples. Easterbrook, developing a theme of Innis', has commented that bureaucratic institutions concerned with "playing it safe" tend to emerge in the face of the initial uncertainties of a marginal status, and then to persist.[21] In the Cuban case, H.C. Wallich emphasizes the importance of the "sugar mentality" which "gives sugar an economic and political dominance even greater than its true weight in the economy."[22] H.W. Singer has pointed out that, when export earnings are high, the country is able to finance development but lacks the incentive to do so; when the earnings are low, the incentive exists but the means are lacking.[23] In Canada, there is evidence of a boom-and-bust psychology; excessive optimism causes booms to proceed beyond their proper limits,[24] while depressions are met by resort to tariffs which are "second best" in the short run and probably inappropriate in the long run and which persist once introduced.[25] One is led to conclude that staple economies are often believed to be much more at the mercy of destiny than they actually are. As Levin has demonstrated in his study of Burma, planning can alter income flows, thereby strengthening linkages and increasing domestic investment.

The serious pitfall is that the economy may get caught in a "staple trap." Sustained growth requires the capacity to shift attention to new foreign or domestic markets. The former requires a favourable combination of external demand and available resources. The latter requires a population base and level of per capita income that permit taking advantage of the economies of scale in modern industrialism. Both require institutions and values consistent with transformation, and *that* requires the good fortune of having avoided specialization in the wrong kind of staple, such as Baldwin's plantation crop. If the staple is unfavourable or if stagnation persists for any extended period because of a weak resource base, the staple economy can take on the character of the traditional underdeveloped country in both respects stressed by Rostow. Firstly, institutions and values can emerge which are inimical to sustained growth, and the process of remoulding will be difficult. Secondly, a population problem can be encountered as the population initially established through immigration continues to expand through natural increase. Persistent unemployment and underemployment will become characteristic of the economy. Immigration may be replaced by emigration, as resort is had to the Irish solution. In the absence of alternative opportunities, factors will tend to accumulate excessively in the export sector or in subsistence agriculture. In the former case, growth may become "immiserized" as the terms of trade turn against the country.[26] In the latter, the economy will face a problem common to most underdeveloped countries: development will depend on the interdependent growth of agriculture and industry. In any event, the initial opportunities for easy growth will no longer exist.

If the pitfalls are avoided – if the staple or staples generate strong linkage effects which are adequately exploited – then eventually the economy will grow and diversify to the point where the appellation "staple economy" will no longer suffice. Population growth will come to result more from natural increase than from immigration. Per capita income will rise beyond the level consistent with any customary definition of underdevelopment. With the gaining of entrepreneurial confidence and the expanding opportunities of domestic markets, domestic entrepreneurs will persistently usurp markets from foreign suppliers.[27] A well-developed secondary manufacturing sector serving domestic markets and possibly even foreign markets will emerge. Staple exports and imports of manufactured goods may fall as a percent of national income. If "land" remains relatively abundant, this may not happen; that should not be taken as proof of backwardness, however, for it may be no more than the momentary outcome of the operation of the law of comparative advantage.

III

We have taken pains throughout to emphasize the special character of the staple theory. Consideration of the range of relationships possible between foreign trade and economic development will underline the point. In a recent synthesis of the literature, Kindleberger has put forth three models relating foreign trade and economic development; these cover cases where foreign trade is, respectively, a leading, a lagging, and a balancing sector of the economy.[28] In the model in which it leads, autonomous foreign demand, typically accompanied by technological change in the developing country, sets the pace, and economic development is a process of diversification around an export base. The staple economy is clearly a special case of this model.

In the model in which foreign trade lags, domestic investment leads, tending to create pressure on the balance of payments which is met by import-substitution. A large number of underdeveloped countries believe that this is the relevant model. The restrictive nature of the commercial policy of developed countries, combined with the tendency for import demand to expand more rapidly than income in the early stages of development – chiefly because of the need to import capital goods and possibly also industrial raw materials and food – lend credence to this belief. The contrast between the leading and lagging models is that between development based on trade-expansion and development based on trade-contraction.

The model in which foreign trade is the balancing sector covers the case of trade-expansion that is not demand-led, but rather based on autonomous supply pushes in the export sector. It applies to the case where domestic investment leads, creating balance of payments difficulties which are met by pushing exports rather than by limiting imports. A trade pattern based on exporting manufactures, in order to import food and take the strain off domestic agriculture, has been espoused by both W. Arthur Lewis and the late Ragnar Nurske, and is a particular version of the balancing case.[29]

Kindleberger's classification applies to countries already in the process of development. The limitations of the staple theory emerge most clearly when we consider the case where export production is superimposed on a pre-existing subsistence economy. For the staple economy, the export sector can be an engine of growth; for the subsistence economy, the consensus appears to be that the export sector will have either limited or adverse effects on the economy. The linkages effects are likely to be slight, regardless of the character of the export good, because of the internal structure of the underdeveloped country, including the existence of non-competing groups in the domestic and foreign sectors.[30] Even where groups are competing, if there is disguised unemployment in the subsistence sector, increases in productivity in the export industry will not bring increases in real wages; these depend on raising productivity in the subsistence sector and to this exports make little or no contribution.[31] The country might have been better off if it had never exported in the first place. Growth may have become immiserized, as was previously noted. Domestic factors may have been drawn into export production when they could have been more productively applied to domestic manufacture.[32] Investments made complementary to the export sector may generate pecuniary external economies which excessively encourage primary export production.[33] Imports which flood in as a result of exporting may destroy existing handicraft production, and if the export sector does not absorb the labour which is displaced, the gains from trade may be negative.[34] If exports and domestic investment compete for available saving, then a rise in the export volume can directly reduce the rate of growth of income.[35]

IV

The closeness of the link between the staple approach and Canadian historical research makes it unlikely that the application of a more explicit theory will add much to our understanding of Canadian economic development. Nevertheless, a few comments are in order, both to clear up some specific ambiguities and to resolve the issue of the relevance of the staple theory to Canada's economic development, past and present.

1. The cod fisheries and the fur trade were clearly the leading sectors of the early period. Neither staple required much permanent settlement, although as the fur trade came to rely less on aboriginal peoples and penetrated further west and as the cod fisheries

shifted from the green cure to the dry cure – an example of forward linkage – the impetus to settlement increased. In New France
the distribution of income consequent on the fur trade may have
been such as to lower final demand linkage – although it would
hardly bear comparison with that resulting from a plantation crop
– and the aristocracy may have been as much feudal as bourgeois in
its attitudes, although the drive of men such as Jean Talon should
not be forgotten. But neither the character of the staple nor the
Frenchness of the colony explain the slow growth relative to the
American colonies. Rather, what is fundamental was poor location
compared with New England for supplying the West Indies market.
This limited the diversity of exports and thus retarded the development of commercial agriculture, lumbering, and above all the
carrying trade and shipbuilding which were then the keys to development. A small population base, established more for reasons of
imperial design than of economics per se, grew rapidly by natural
increase. In the face of limited economic opportunities, labour
accumulated in subsistence agriculture and New France came to
approximate the dual economy, with a compact agricultural community of habitants and the moving frontier of the fur traders,
which had only limited contacts one with another.[36] By the time of
the Conquest the colony had clearly taken on some of the coloura-
tion of an "old" society and was partly ensnared in the staple trap.

In the Atlantic colonies, New England's success in developing an
aggressive commercial economy around the fisheries shows that
the character of cod as a staple can hardly explain the slow growth
of Nova Scotia and Newfoundland. Rather, proximity to the markets of the West Indies and southern mainland colonies and, to a
lesser extent, good agricultural land and the possibility of a winter
fishery, were the prerequisites that were lacking. The effects of a
poor location and a weak resource base – the latter being particularly applicable to Newfoundland – were intensified by the
frequency of imperial conflict and the commercial and military ag-
gressiveness of New England. The result militated against either
England or France taking the effort that was necessary to create an
environment favourable to further development. The area was not
so much trapped as buffeted about and ignored.

Absence of economic opportunity because of geographic factors
was the crucial constraint on both continental and maritime developments. Innis' method has obscured this point and has led to

exaggerated emphasis on the character of the staples, particularly of fur. But if the nature of the staples is insufficient to explain the absence of rapid growth, lack of diversified development imprints more clearly the character of those staples around which some success is found and increases the probability that their peculiar biases will persist in institutions and values. Thus, with fur came the life of the habitant and the vision of a centralized transcontinental economy; with cod, parochialism and a commitment to the sea.

2. Fowke has argued that commercial agriculture in Upper Canada rose above the subsistence level prior to the 1840s in the absence of substantial external demand. Although allowance must be made for "shanty demand" linked to timber exports, the point is conceded, and with it the implication that some growth is possible without exports as the leading sector. But the quality of the growth that took place was unimpressive. The census of 1851 shows industrial development to be confined to flour mills and sawmills, both of which were on an export basis, and to the small-scale production of the simpler types of manufacture for the local market.[37] The population and income levels that had been attained were not sufficient to sustain a large or technologically sophisticated manufacturing sector. Buckley rightly insists that the economy became more complex after 1820 and that the range of economic opportunity widened, but this does not mean that staple exports ceased to be of critical importance.

3. One of Buckley's criticisms of the staple approach is its tendency "to ignore any section once the staple which created or supported it is no longer expanding," and he cites as an example the slighting of Quebec's economic development since the decline of the fur trade.[38] His point has some validity, at least so far as Quebec is concerned, but the neglect is not inherent in a properly stated staple theory of economic growth. As the new country (or region) ages, whether it be successful or unsuccessful, it takes on the character of an old country and becomes amenable to analysis as such. In Quebec in the nineteenth century, it is clear that the expansion of timber and ships as staple exports, the entrepreneurial drive and accumulated capital of the English commercial class carried over from the fur trade, and emigration which relieved the pressure of population on scarce resources combined to lessen the probability

that the region would become too deeply enmeshed in the staple
trap. Nevertheless, it is the interrelationship between agriculture
and industry in the context of a rapidly growing population that
should be made the focus of study, as one would expect to be done
for any presently underdeveloped country. Statistics on the relative
rates of growth of Ontario and Quebec indicates, incidentally, that
if one gives credence to the alleged anti-commercial attitudes of
the French Canadian, then, given the less favourable man/land ratio Quebec inherited from New France, what needs to be explained
is the remarkable success of Quebec.

4. The period of Canadian economic history on which most controversy has focused recently has been the "Great Depression" of
1873–96. So long as it could be properly regarded as a great depression, it was amenable to the staple approach. Its bad reputation
was based on the slow growth of population and persistent emigration, and this could be linked to the failure of the western wheat
economy to expand in a sustained fashion in the face of a trend decline in the world price of wheat. The absence of rapid extensive
growth made it possible for the period to be passed over quickly in
the history books, and to be remembered more for the attempts
that were made to promote development than for the actual
growth achieved. Recent research, however, particularly the statistical work of Firestone, McDougall, Hartland, and Bertram,[39] makes
it impossible to continue to regard these years as a great depression; they witnessed, in fact, an impressive increase in real per capita income, comparable to that in the United States, considerable
industrial expansion, and substantial capital inflow.

The growth in real income can be attributed partly to the export
sector. Exports did fall as a percentage of national income. Nevertheless, the real value of exports grew absolutely; there were important shifts in the composition of exports which generated new
investment, from wood products to agriculture, and within the latter, from grain to animal products, with cattle and cheese emerging as the new staples; probably exports became more highly
manufactured – the growth of cheese factories is striking – and
more capital-intensive; railway building provided an important
stimulus to growth and its *primum causum* was the expectation of
large exports of western grain.

Exports, then, continued to play their conventional role as a leading sector. They can hardly be given full credit, however, for the increase in real income of this period. Factor increments shifted from export markets to domestic markets with a success inconsistent with a markedly backward economy. Yet the extent to which the adaptation was made to a declining stimulus from the export sector should not be exaggerated. The decade rates of growth of manufacturing after 1870 are not comparable to those of the first decade of the twentieth century when exports were expanding rapidly, and at the end of the century Canadian industry was still backward relative to that of such countries as Britain, the United States, and Germany. There was substantial net emigration in every decade from 1861 to 1901. The Canadian economy was not growing fast enough to generate employment opportunities for increments to the labour force by natural increase; while this may be no cause for concern from an international perspective, contemporary political debate and newspaper comment leaves no doubt that Canadians regarded this steady outflow of population as evidence of an unsatisfactory performance by the economy.

5. A restatement of the staple theory might be expected to cast new light on the hoary issue of the long-run impact of the Canadian tariff. A conventional argument has been that the tariff permanently increases population because export industries are less labour-intensive than import-competing industries.[40] Young would appear to have effectively disposed of this line of reasoning, but there may be some validity to the population sustaining argument for a tariff if one looks at its effect in a boom period, such as 1896 to 1913.[41] It is clear that, by reducing the marginal propensity to import, the tariff increases employment in import-competing industries. At the same time, the fact that factors are in highly elastic supply limits the extent to which costs rise for the export industries, while the sheer strength of the boom, which is being further increased by investment in import-competing industries, keeps imports high in spite of the tariff, thus tending to eliminate foreign repercussion. The tariff would appear to increase employment opportunities, and thereby the population-sustaining capacity of the economy. If, as is probable, the infant industry argument is not valid, however, then the real income has been lowered. We return

to the customary view that the Canadian tariff has increased population while lowering real income. But there is an important qualification, as a result of which population may not be increased in the long-run. The tariff will tend to strengthen a boom which is already excessive and thus to increase the problems of readjustment that have to be faced eventually. To the extent that these problems are not otherwise solved, emigration to the United States with its higher wages is likely to be greater than it would have been in the absence of the tariff.

6. The period 1896 to 1913 was undeniably an example of a classic staple boom. But the industrial development which was achieved in its wake so increased the complexity of the Canadian economy as to make it impossible to continue to use staple industries as the unifying theme of economic growth, or so the implicit reasoning seems to run in the best of the textbooks.[42] The notion of a discontinuity in Canadian economic development in the early twentieth century, though superficially attractive, is difficult to maintain, as Caves and Holton have demonstrated. The manufacturing sector appears to have been filling in slowly over a long period of time, without passing through any critical stage of economic maturity. Patterns of short-run change consistent with the staple theory are to be found in all three periods of rapid growth in this century, 1900–1913, 1920–1929, and 1946–1956: the rate of investment closely reflects the demand for exports, current and prospective; production for domestic markets expands around the export-base, replacing imports; excessive optimism leads to overexpansion in the export sector and complicates the subsequent problems of readjustment; and the quantity of saving adjusts itself to investment demand, in part by inducing capital imports.

Is the staple theory, then, relevant to Canada today, or has it been long irrelevant? Does the evidence adduced by Caves and Holton on the common character of growth patterns in the twentieth century, which could be extended to include the boom of the 1850s, reflect historical necessity or historical accident? Is Canada unable to grow at a satisfactory rate unless exports lead, or able to do so but relieved of the necessity until now by good luck? There is no doubt that luck is a neglected factor in Canadian economic history. Nevertheless, the fundamental fact is the pervasive interdependence with the North Atlantic community, and particularly with the United States. Canada is a small and open economy, a marginal area responding to the exogenous impact of the international economy. The basic determinants of Canadian growth are the volume and character of her staple exports and the ability to borrow, adapt, and marginally supplement foreign technology. These guarantee for Canada a minimum rate of growth that cannot diverge too widely from that achieved elsewhere, particularly in the United States. They create no assurance, however, of a rate of growth sufficient to maintain full employment, even if the expansion of the labour force be limited to a natural increase. The probability that borrowed technology and staple exports will provide a sufficient impetus to the economy has diminished as staples have become more capital-intensive.

That expanding exports and satisfactory economic growth have been correlated in the past is clear. How this is interpreted depends on a judgment as to the freedom of action that Canada possesses. The emphasis increasingly placed by economists on the link between the inefficiency of Canadian secondary manufacturing industry and the Canadian tariff suggests that the major difficulty is an inhibiting export mentality, the elimination of which lies within Canadian control.[43] From this point of view, economic institutions and political values, an inefficient structure of industry combined with an unwillingness to do anything about it, have in the past prevented Canada from growing at a satisfactory rate in the absence of a strong lead from primary exports, but this need not be true for the indefinite future.

NOTES

1 The American economic historian, Guy S. Callender, devoted considerable attention to the importance of international and interregional trade in staples in the United States (*Selections from the Economic History of the United States, 1765–1860* (Boston, 1909)). This aspect of American growth was much neglected until being recently revived by Douglass C. North, *The Economic Growth of the United States, 1790–1860* (Englewood Cliffs, N.J., 1961).

2 See his *The Fur Trade in Canada: An Introduction to Canadian Economic History* (Toronto, 1930; 2nd ed., 1956); *The Cod Fisheries: The History of an International Economy* (Toronto, 1940; 2nd ed., 1954). A collection of his

writings in the Canadian field can be found in *Essays in Canadian Economic History* (Toronto, 1957) and a complete bibliography of his writings is compiled by Jane Ward, *Canadian Journal of Economics and Political Science* (1953) 19: 236–44. W.A. Mackintosh is sometimes given credit as a co-founder of the staple theory; see his "Economic Factors in Canadian History," *Canadian Historical Review* (1923) 4: 12–25, and "Some Aspects of a Pioneer Economy," *Canadian Journal of Economics and Political Science* 2 (1936): 457–63.

3 This point has often been noted; see, for example, Richard E. Caves and Richard H. Holton, *The Canadian Economy: Prospect and Retrospect* (Cambridge, Mass., 1959), 30; and W.T. Easterbrook, "Problems in the Relationship of Communication and Economic History," *Journal of Economic History* 20 (1960): 563.

4 Kenneth Buckley makes this point strongly in "The Role of Staple Industries in Canada's Economic Development," *Journal of Economic History* 18 (1958): 442.

5 For its use in communications study – where, following the later Innis, the media become the resource or staple – see Marshall McLuhan, "Effects of the Improvements of Communication Media," *Journal of Economic History* 20 (1960): 566–75; and *The Gutenberg Galaxy* (Toronto, 1962), particularly 164–6.

6 "Role of Staple Industries," 444, 445.

7 Fowke, *The National Policy and the Wheat Economy* (Toronto, 1957), ch. 2; Easterbrook, "Trends in Canadian Economic Thought," *South Atlantic Quarterly* 58 (1959): 91–107; and "Recent Contributions to Economic History: Canada," *Journal of Economic History* 19 (1959): 76–102.

8 Aitken, "The Changing Structure of the Canadian Economy" in Aitken *et al, The American Economic Impact on Canada* (Durham, N.C., 1959); "Discussion," *Journal of Economic History* 16 (1958): 451; and *American Capital and Canadian Resources* (Cambridge, Mass., 1961), 74.

9 North, "Location Theory and Regional Economic Growth," *Journal of Political Economy* 62 (1955): 243–58; "International Capital Flows and the Development of the American West," *Journal of Economic History* 16 (1956): 493–505; "A Note on Professor Rostow's 'Take-off' into Self-Sustained Growth," *Manchester School of Economic and Social Studies* 26 (1958): 68–75; "Agriculture and Regional Economic Growth," *Journal of Farm Economics* 41 (1959): 943–51; and *Economic Growth of the United States.*

10 *Canadian Economy,* Part I.

11 Baldwin, "Patterns of Development in Newly Settled Regions" *Manchester School of Economic and Social Studies* 24 (1956): 161–79.

12 Levin, *The Export Economies: Their Pattern of Development in Historical Perspective* (Cambridge, Mass., 1960); G.M. Meier, "Economic Development and the Transfer Mechanism: Canada, 1895–1913," *Canadian Journal of Economics and Political Science* 19 (1953): 1–19; J.C. Ingram, "Growth and Canada's Balance of Payments," *American Economic Review* 47 (1957): 93–104; J.A. Stovel, *Canada in the World Economy* (Cambridge, Mass., 1959); and Perloff and Wingo, "Natural Resource Endowment and Regional Economic Growth" in Joseph J. Spengler, ed., *Natural Resources and Economic Growth* (Washington, 1961), 191–212 which draws on Harvey S. Perloff, Edgar S. Dunn Jr., Eric E. Lampard, and Richard F. Muth, *Regions, Resources and Economic Growth* (Baltimore, 1960).

13 Both features are recognized by W.W. Rostow in *The United States in the World Arena* (New York, 1960), 6; the first is also cited by Bert F. Hoselitz, "Patterns of Economic Growth," *Canadian Journal of Economics and Political Science* 21 (1955): 416–31.

14 Fay, "The Toronto School of Economic History," *Economic History* 3 (1934): 168–71. See also Easterbrook, "Problems," 563.

15 Albert O. Hirschman, *The Strategy of Economic Development* (New Haven, 1958), ch. 6.

16 North's book is weakened by his failure adequately to appreciate the importance of the resource base. He applies Baldwin's polar cases to the American South and West in the period prior to the Civil War, but has very probably exaggerated their efficacy in explaining rates and types of development by understating differences in the general resource base which favoured the West.

17 Note the Canadian mineral discoveries consequent on railway building and hence linked ultimately to the development of the western wheat economy.

18 On external diseconomies generated by an expanding sector when factor supplies are inelastic, see Marcus Fleming, "External Economies and the Doctrine of Balanced Growth," *Economic Journal* 65 (1955): 241–56. On the character of export-led booms in Canada, see the literature cited in n. 17.

19 Rostow, *The Stages of Economic Growth* (Cambridge, 1960), 36.

20 North, after appeal to the American case, reaches a similar conclusion.

21 See his "The Climate of Enterprise," *American Economic Review* 39 (1949): 322–35; "Uncertainty and Economic Change," *Journal of Economic History* 14 (1954): 346–60; "Long Period Comparative Study: Some Historical Cases," *Journal of Economic History* 17 (1957): 571–95.

22 Wallich, *Monetary Problems of an Export Economy* (Cambridge, Mass., 1960), 12.

23 Singer, "The Distribution of Gains between Investing and Borrowing Countries," *American Economic Review* 40 (1950): 482.

24 The classic example is the building of two additional transcontinental railways during the wheat boom, 1896–1913. The general phenomenon is noted by A.F.W. Plumptre, "The Nature of Economic Development in the British Dominions," *Canadian Journal of Economics and Political Science* 3 (1937): 489–507.

25 The high correlation between depressions and tariff increases is noted by John H. Young, *Canadian Commercial Policy*, A study for the Royal Commission on Canada's Economic Prospects (Ottawa, 1957).

26 For a formal presentation of the theory of immiserizing growth, see J.Bhagwati, "Immiserizing Growth: A Geometric Note," *Review of Economic Studies* 25 (1958): 201–5, and "International Trade and Economic Expansion," *American Economic Review* 48 (1958): 941–53.

27 This mechanism is emphasized by Hirschman, *Strategy*, 120 ff.

28 C.P. Kindleberger, *Economic Development* (New York, 1958), ch. 14.

29 Lewis, *The Theory of Economic Growth* (Homewood, Ill., 1955); Nurkse, *Patterns of Trade and Development*, Wicksell Lectures, 1959 (Stockholm, 1959).

30 H. Myint, "The Gains from International Trade and the Backward Countries," *Review of Economic Studies* 22 (1954–55): 129–42.

31 W. Arthur Lewis, "Economic Development with Unlimited Supplies of Labour," *Manchester School* 22 (1954): 139–41.

32 Singer, "The Distribution of Gains."

33 Lewis, *The Theory of Economic Growth*, 348.

34 G. Haberler provides a geometric demonstration of a case where free trade is harmful, given rigid factor prices. "Some Problems in the Pure Theory of International Trade," *Economic Journal* 60 (1950): 223–40. The argument is extended in Steffan Burenstam Linder, *An Essay on Trade and Transformation* (New York, Stockholm, 1961), ch. 2.

35 R.J. Ball, "Capital Imports and Economic Development: Paradoxy or Orthodoxy," Kyklos 15 (1962): 610–23.

36 Dietrich Gerhard, "The Frontier in Comparative View," *Comparative Studies in History and Society* 1 (1959): 205–29.

37 O.J. Firestone, "Development of Canada's Economy, 1850–1890," in *Trends in the American Economy in the Nineteenth Century* (Princeton, 1960), 217–52.

38 "The Role of Staple Industries," 447.

39 O.J. Firestone, *Canada's Economic Development, 1867–1953* (London, 1958), and "Development of Canada's Economy, 1850–1900"; Duncan M. McDougall, "Immigration into Canada, 1851–1920," *Canadian Journal of*

Economics and Political Science 27 (1961): 162–75; Penelope Hartland, "Canadian Balance of Payments since 1868" in *Trends in the American Economy in the Nineteenth Century*, 717–55; Gordon W. Bertram, "Historical Statistics on Growth and Structure of Manufacturing in Canada, 1870–1957," Canadian Political Science Association Conference on Statistics, June 10–11, 1962.

40 W.A. Mackintosh, *The Economic Background of Dominion-Provincial Relations, A Study Prepared for the Royal Commission on Dominion-Provincial Relations* (Ottawa, 1939); reprinted in the Carleton Library, 1964, 140 ff; and Clarence L. Barber, "Canadian Tariff Policy," *Canadian Journal of Economics and Political Science* 21 (1955): 513–30.

41 Young, *Canadian Commercial Policy*, 89 ff.

42 W.T. Easterbrook and H.G.J. Aitken, *Canadian Economic History* (Toronto, 1956).

43 See H.E. English, "The Role of International Trade in Canadian Economic Development since the 1920s," (PhD thesis, University of California, 1957); S. Stykolt and H.C. Eastman, "A Model for the Study of Protected Oligopolies," *Economic Journal* 70 (1960): 336–47; R. Dehem, "The Economics of Stunted Growth," *Canadian Journal of Economics and Political Science* 28 (1962): 502–10.

2

The Staple Theory Revisited (1977)

In a paper published on the staples approach in 1963, I attempted to pull out of more diffuse historical writings, notably by Innis, an explicit theory of economic growth appropriate to Canada and other "new" countries.[1] In retrospect, its contribution was to give legitimacy to the staples approach – by showing that it was respectable within orthodox economics – but this was bought at the high price of constraining the theory to the very limiting paradigm of orthodox economics in general and the theory of international trade in particular.

In revisiting the theory, it seems appropriate to review in particular much of the literature that has appeared since 1963 that is of *analytical* interest.[2] This literature can be conveniently classified under four heads: 1) quantitative testing of the staple theory under the influence of the new economic history; 2) studies on the closely related topics of foreign ownership and the structure of Canadian industry, to the extent that they are concerned with the evident bias toward staple export, on the one hand, and a retarded industrial structure on the other hand; 3) historical and contemporary analysis of resource policy, with particular respect

A revised version of a paper by the same title published in the *Journal of Canadian Studies* 12(5) (Winter 1977): 83–94.

to the further processing of staples, the appropriation of economic rents from staple production and the North; and 4) work
based on the Marxist paradigm.

The bias of the paper is toward the Marxist paradigm. This reflects the straightforward fact that, in quantitative terms and, in my
opinion, in qualitative terms as well, it is scholars working out of
the Marxist paradigm who are now predominant in the literature
on the staples approach. This presumably is the result of a general
resurgence of scholarly interest in Marxism that is, of course, not
confined to Canada.

That Marxists should be attracted specifically to the staple approach is wholly understandable and should give no offense.[3]
While its leading proponents were certainly liberals, at least in the
beginning it was clearly political economy and at least in the hands
of Innis it was about dependence – and these latter two characteristics are, of course, central to Marxists. Innis in particular was a liberal with a difference, who saw the dark underside and the gross
contradictions and this makes him susceptible to an approach that
specializes in such matters.[4]

I

Beginning in the late 1950s and thereafter, the postwar quantitative bias of American scholarship spread from economics into economic history, and the resulting new economic history penetrated
the study of Canadian economic history in some part through the
work done by American scholars and Canadian-born scholars resident in the US. The latter is indicative of the difficulties of transplanting the new phenomenon to Canada and suggests that its
contribution is likely to be second-order. Nonetheless, worthwhile
contributions have been made, directly by Bertram and by Caves,
and indirectly by Chambers and Gordon in a joint article so scan-
dalous as to compel reasoned defense of the staples approach.[5]

Bertram's article, appearing simultaneously with my own in 1963,
demonstrates the gradual but steady filling in of the manufacturing
sector around the impetus generated by staples exports. The two
articles have much in common in terms of giving not only the staples
approach but the Canadian staples-oriented economy a relatively
clean bill of health, but Bertram goes further in the second respect.

Drache suggests that there are not one but two (non-Marxist) theories of capitalist development based on the staples theory, the steady-progress view of Mackintosh and the dependency view of Innis.[6] Bertram and other writers in the new economic history, opt wholeheartedly for the more laundered Mackintosh approach.[7] MacDonald in his critique of Naylor (of which more below) makes an analogous distinction between two branches of the staples approach: first, metropolitanism, or the commercial penetration of the hinterland positively viewed, as evidenced by (the early) Creighton and Ouellet; and, second, the entirely different principle that a dominant trade might organize an economy inexorably around itself and lead to stagnation. MacDonald puts my 1963 article in the second category, as well as the writings of Fowke, Pentland, Dubuc and Ryerson.[8]

Caves' first article enhanced the legitimacy of the staple model for orthodox economists by showing its formal similarity with the unlimited-supply-of-labour model in the literature on economic development; that is, both were "vent for surplus" models of trade and growth rather than models based on growth through more efficient allocation of an existing stock of employed factors of production. Caves focuses narrowly on the linkages of the staple sector to other sectors, while urbanely noting in passing that there are "of course, the whole field of possible influences of the pattern of industry upon social and political development." He sensibly concludes that the staple model, at least in its simple form, "probably yields no normative conclusions" and that both vent-for-surplus models "received their respective laurels and brickbats as a source of guidance for policy on the basis of what the linkages have or have not done in a particular case."[9]

But he is very much of the Mackintosh cast of mind. As well as staple-induced growth, there will be "an underlying steady swell of neoclassical growth" such that "export-based growth may explain a large part of the *variation* in the aggregate rate of growth ... whether or not it explains a large part of the average level of that growth rate." Following Baldwin, he recognizes the possibility of staple production having unfavourable effects on the character of factor supplies and the resulting distribution of income and hence on the composition of final demand, but dismisses it as improbable: "The staple version includes no ... likely appearance of a maldistribution of income, especially if the rents accruing to natural resources (in the staples region) are allotted somewhat randomly among the erstwhile workers and capitalist elements of the population ... [A] happy partnership of immigrant labour and capital is further cemented by windfall gains to the fortunate finders of natural resources."[10] While Caves is basically correct with respect to the overall distribution of income, his facile comments on rents – in both this, and to a lesser extent, his second paper – deny him an important insight that others show can be derive from the liberal paradigm, and that has less happy implications for generating sustained growth (see below).

In the best – or worst – tradition of the new economic history, Robert Fogel having allegedly demonstrated the limited contribution of railroads to American economic growth, Chambers and Gordon set out to demonstrate that the opening of the Canadian West, or the wheat boom, has likewise made a limited contribution to Canadian economic growth. Had they succeeded, the staple approach would indeed be in disarray, but, in fact, they fail miserably. They ask the wrong, or at best distinctly second order, question, that is, what contribution did the export of wheat make to the growth of income *per capita* rather than what contribution did it make to the growth of aggregate national income. In so far as the staple theory has always been about understanding the successive opening up of the country, or increasing the stock of land, with resultant inflows of labour and capital, or, increases in *their* stocks, rather than about reallocating fixed endowments of factors of production, Chambers and Gordon, whatever they are doing, are hardly testing any known version of the staple thesis.[11]

To compound their problems, Chambers and Gordon appear not only to misspecify the model but handle the data badly. Both Bertram and Caves make new quantitative estimates which show wheat to have, in fact, made a major contribution to Canadian economic growth. Bertram confines himself narrowly to quantitative testing, but Caves shows that staple theory, depending upon the staple, does not necessarily yield easy growth. If, because of economies of scale in staples production, there are large capital requirements for staple enterprises, there will be "extraregional or foreign borrowing (with no incentive for local saving), absentee ownership and no contribution to the supply of local entrepreneurial talent or profit available for local reinvestment." On a closely related point, he notes that the drawing in of undiscovered resources vents a surplus and creates a rent, and that "where natural-resource rents accrue as profits to foreign entrepreneurs, the critical question for national welfare is the extent to which they are recaptured in taxation." Nevertheless, he makes the curious observation in a footnote that "The extent to which export-led growth possesses any special virtues in furthering sustainable growth remains to be demonstrated, but any that it possesses seems unlikely to derive from the creation of rents."[12]

In sum, the new economic history, which has been a central obsession of economic historians in recent years, to the extent it poses real questions has upheld the validity of the staples approach – though making little or no contribution to our theoretical understanding. The staple theory has survived the worse onslaughts of Americanization and for that reason alone must be seen as hardy and genuinely Canadian.

II

In the postwar period, and notably in the past two decades, a substantial literature has emerged on the structure of Canadian industry and on the closely related topic of foreign ownership. The concern of this literature is not with the staple theory *per se* – and therefore there will be no exhaustive review of it here – but it is necessary to enquire to what extent it sheds light on the viability of the staple theory, and to what extent the staple theory might shed some light on the topics of industrial structure and foreign ownership.

The historic tendency for staple production to take place under the aegis of foreign capital has persisted, indeed accelerated. In the first substantive study of foreign ownership in the postwar period, Hugh G.J. Aitken's *American Capital and Canadian Resources* (1961), that simple fact is the central theme. Unfortunately, it is obscured in most subsequent studies – in Safarian, the Watkins Report and the Gray Report – but it does figure prominently in Levitt.[13] The most straightforward explanation, which requires no stepping outside the liberal paradigm, is the high American demand for Canadian staples and the high capital-intensity of the new staples create an advantage for the typically large established American company over a potential Canadian company. Put differently, the staples approach enables us to "explain" the continuing and rising level of foreign ownership of staple production.

But this begs the question of why there is *so much* foreign owner-ship, not only in the staple sector but in the rest of the economy too, and particularly in manufacturing proper. Putting aside the tendency of Canadian economists to claim it does not really matter, and therefore presumably needs no explanation, those who wish to explain it ultimately fall back for the most part on a Schumpete-rian-like argument about the inadequacies of Canadian entrepre-neurship; this is true even of as perceptive a writer as Levitt. This, of course, is something less than a satisfactory answer, since it merely poses the question of the cause of the deficiency of Canadian entre-preneurship. As we shall see shortly, the first serious answer is of-fered by Naylor, but from a Marxist paradigm.[14]

The more conventional staples approach nevertheless contains some insights, having primarily to do with the tendency toward an excessive preoccupation with staple production that inheres in sta-ple production itself, eg., the sucking of domestic capital into the staple sector, notwithstanding the predominance of foreign capital, and the propensity of government to see staple production as a panacea for economic growth and neglect the working out of a proper industrial strategy. We are unlikely to be able to improve on Innis' cryptic formulation:

Energy has been directed toward the exploitation of staple products and the tendency has been cumulative ... Energy in the colony was drawn into the production of the staple commodity both directly and indirectly in the production facilities promoting production. Agriculture, industry, trans-portation, trade, finance, and governmental activities tend to become sub-ordinate to the production of the staple for a more highly specialized manufacturing community.[15]

Work on the structure of industry proper, notwithstanding many useful insights about the miniature replica effect, concerns itself *ad nauseum* with the Canadian tariff as *the* source of the prob-lem. This begs the question as to the "source" of the tariff and the answer tends, as before, quickly to degenerate into an appeal to the inadequacies of Canadian businessmen. With respect to the narrower mechanisms of the staple theory, Naylor reminds us of one that was once well-known in the literature, namely, that the National Policy, protectionist though it was, generated a flood of government revenue that greatly facilitated the building, and overbuilding, of infrastructure for staple production.[16]

The failure of a resource base developed to meet the exigencies of staple export to lead to an industrial complex – which is, after all, the heart of the matter – is ably described by a non-economist, Pierre L. Bourgault, in a study not for the Economic Council but the Science Council:

We are the world's largest producer of nickel, but we are net importers of stainless steel and manufactured nickel products ...; we are the world's second largest producer of aluminum, but we import it in its more sophisticated forms such as ... precision aluminum parts for use in aircraft; we are the world's largest exporters of pulp and paper, but we import much of our fine paper and virtually all of the highly sophisticated paper, such as backing for photographic film; we are one of the principle sources of platinum, but it is all exported for refining and processing and reimported in finished forms; we are large exporters of natural gas and petroleum, but we are net importers of petrochemicals; and although we are the world's foremost exporter of raw asbestos fibres, we are net importers of manufactured asbestos products.[17]

Neither orthodox studies of industrial structure nor a staple theory focussed microscopically on linkages seems quite to come to terms with this matter; we must either retreat to Innis or move forward to Naylor.

III

In the area of resource policy proper, two names stand out, Kierans and Nelles. A long-neglected theme in the economic analysis of staple production, but one that grows logically out of the liberal paradigm, is that intramarginal "land" commands its own reward, or economic rent. The relevant questions are: What is the size of the rents? Who gets them? What difference does their distribution make to sustained economic growth? Kierans' pioneering study on the metal-mining industry in Manitoba shows that the rents are large relative to the wage-bill, and that they disproportionately accrue to capital which is frequently foreign.[18] Clearly, the conventional focus on forward and backward linkages has obscured an important point, that is, that the prospects for sustained and more diversified development in the wake of non-renewable resource exploitation are decreased to the extent that rents, or "super profits," are appropriated by the resource-capitalists, and particularly if they are foreign capitalists.

Without respect to the nationality of capital, the rents, to the extent to which they are retained by the corporations, tend to remain locked into resource exploitation and eventually leave the region that had the resources. This is so because resource companies are generally not diversified outside the resource sector and are increasingly large multinationals prepared to exploit resources anywhere in the world. To the extent that the rents accrue, immediately or ultimately, to local shareholders as dividends or capital gains on shares, the staple-producing country benefits – specifically, that small portion of its population that owns most of the shares. To the extent governments in the staple-producing country appropriate the rents through taxation or public ownership, the country benefits – though the nature of the benefit depends on how governments spend the additional revenue and/or reduce other forms of taxation. Finally, regionally, or locally, the major consequence of losing the rents from non-renewable resources is the region's abandonment by capital once the resources are exhausted and all the rents extracted.[19]

The addition of an analysis of economic rent to orthodox staple theory has the important result of showing how staple production can create a "blockage" to diversified development, that is, by denying the potential, to create "underdevelopment." In effect, the liberal paradigm can be made to yield a version of the staple approach that explains phenomena strikingly similar to what is yielded by the Marxist paradigm in which the analogous mechanism is the outward drain of surplus.

Nelles' massive study of Ontario government policy in the new staple industries of forest products, mining and hydro electricity over almost a century is the most important descriptive work done within the context of the staple approach since Rich's monumental study of the Hudson's Bay Company.[20] He eschews economic theory, but his central concern with "the manufacturing condition" as Ontario's "little National Policy" is evidence of how staple production, at its best, leads to more of the same – in the sense of more value added within the resource sector – rather than causing a quantum leap into a diversified industrial economy under domestic control.

The Canadian North, as the new and last "frontier," is also attracting increasing attention from historians working basically around the theme of resource policy. The major writings of Zaslow and Rea are mostly valuable for their great detail.[21] Rea uses a simple staple model that focuses on linkages and ignores rent. Neither shows any real grasp of the economy of aboriginal peoples, and both fall prey – and Rea explicitly so – to the dual economy thesis, thereby missing the point that the non-renewable resource exploitation sets up mechanisms which create underdevelopment for native peoples. In the current context of the Berger Inquiry into the merits of a gas pipeline in the Mackenzie Valley, research sponsored by the Indian Brotherhood of the N.W.T demonstrates the destruction of the economy of native people in the "new" and last frontier, the Canadian North.[22]

I V

In the last decade, a mere handful of Marxist writers in Canada has suddenly been joined by a small army of younger scholars. At least from the perspective of the analytics of the staple approach, by far the most important contribution is Naylor's two-volume *History of Canadian Business* in the critical period from Confederation to World War I. Indeed, his work is, in my opinion, the most important historical writing on Canada since the early Innis and the early Creighton, and I am aware of what high praise that constitutes.

As we have already seen, liberal scholarship, in attempting to explain the dependent and structurally-underdeveloped nature of the Canadian economy has been able to do no better than appeal to the deficiencies of Canadian entrepreneurship. Naylor saves us from this theoretical quagmire by centring our attention on the nature of capital, and specifically on the distinction between merchant capital and industrial capital and the difficulty of transforming an economy dominated by the first into an economy dominated by the second. From a contemporary perspective, his concern is with "the overexpansion of resource industries relative to manufacturing, and the drainage of surplus income as service payments for foreign investment instead of its being used to generate new capital formation with Canada."[23]

The ties to the staple approach are obvious. Naylor's analysis centres on "two fundamental structural attributes of the Canadian

economy" between 1867 and 1914. The first is the legacy of its colonial status, both economic and political: it was a "staple-extracting
hinterland oriented toward serving metropolitan markets from
which, in turn, it received finished goods." Accordingly, Canada's
commercial and financial system, as well as its entrepreneurial
class, "grew up geared to the international movement of staples,
rather than to abetting secondary processing for domestic markets." Second, Canada "had only begun to make the difficult transition from a mercantile agrarian base to an industrial one," such
that "wealth was accumulated in commercial activities and ... commercial capital resisted the transformation into industrial capital
except under specific conditions in certain industries, in favour of
remaining invested in traditional staple-oriented activities.[24] The
necessary origins of Canada as a staple-producer are perpetuated
because of the nature of the capitalist class that emerges, and re-
emerge, out of the staple trades that spring into being to serve the
needs of the metropole.

Naylor, like Innis before him, provides a wealth of detail to support his very original contribution to Canadian historiography.
Suffice it here to note some of the more important specific mechanisms which Naylor cites as to how staple production leads to the
over-development of the staple industries and the underdevelopment of manufacturing. The capital requirements for infrastructure
to service the staple trades absorbed domestic as well as foreign capital and retarded industrial capital formation. Regionally, the Maritime Provinces were drained of surplus to finance Central Canada's
development objectives in the West, thereby retarding indigenous
industrial development, while Québécois industrial entrepreneurship was submerged under a wave of Anglophone-controlled
mergers.[25] The Canadian banking system, and Canadian financial
institutions in general, grew out of merchant capital involved in the
staple trades and took a form appropriate to facilitating the movement of staples from Canada to external markets rather than promoting secondary industries.[26] The National Policy was a policy of
industrialization-by-invitation and attracted foreign capital, and thus
foreign ownership under the aegis of the multinational corporation,
rather than encouraging domestic capital, which would have
strengthened industrial capital relative to merchant capital within
Canada and thereby facilitated a transformation out of a staples
structure. Railways were built to facilitate staple production and

only incidentally to create industrialization, and their operation favoured international trade over interregional trade. And so on.

For Naylor, the consequence was that by the end of his period, the Canadian economy was locked into "the staple trap."[27] His model, then, is a Marxist version of the Innisian version.

It might be thought that the Marxist paradigm necessarily yields a dependency version of the staple model, but this is apparently not certain. There are hints in the scholarly literature – not to mention vast amounts of diatribe in the sectarian literature – of a steady-progress version, in this case toward the creation of a viable national capitalist class that has come to rule Canada. Ryerson, writing pre-Naylor, emphasizes the slow but steady growth of industrial capital out of merchant capital in the nineteenth century.[28] MacDonald, in his critique of Naylor's earlier work, insists that "a close look at the evidence ... shows that mercantile and industrial capital were insep-arable," but he wrote without benefit of the much closer look of Naylor's two volumes and hence he, and those who rely on the *Canadian Historical Review* for their knowledge of Canadian economic history, risk being the victims of instant obsolescence.[29]

On this murky, but important, question mention must also be made of the work of Wallace Clement. In his study of *The Canadian Corporate Elite*, he understands that Canada is a staple economy and accepts Naylor's argument on the distinction between merchant and industrial capital and the tendency for the former to be Cana-dian and the latter foreign. Nevertheless, he concludes that "the Canadian economy remains controlled in large part by a set of families who have been in the past and still remain at the core of the Canadian economy," and that the split between the commercial and industrial capitalist classes "does not mean the total [Ca-nadian] bourgeoisie is not powerful – indeed, it may be more pow-erful because of the continental context."[30] On the basis of the evidence presented in *The Canadian Corporate Elite*, Clement's views are unconvincing. His subsequent study of *Continental Corporate Power*, however, is persuasive: the alliance between Canadian indige-nous mercantile-financial capital and American industrial capital is now seen as an unequal alliance that reduces Canada to a status of dependency.[31]

We can look forward to further controversy around Naylor's seminal argument and its extension by Clement, in the hope that it will illuminate whether there is one or two Marxist versions of the staple theory. For the moment, it seems to me that the dependency-version will, in any event, win hands down.

So much for the capitalists themselves; what of the nature of the state that emerges out of staple production? And what is the likelihood of it showing the way out of the staple trap? Now, to transcend staple production, that is, to escape subservience to the rising American empire, would surely have required a state prepared to go well beyond the limitations of the actual National Policy.[32] But the state itself is almost a by-product of the exigencies of staple production, an argument central to Innis' analysis and now to Naylor's.

For Innis, both the Act of Union and Confederation were essentially dictated by the need to raise capital, first for canals and then railways, to facilitate the movement of staples. For Naylor, Confederation and the National Policy reflects a state and a state-policy created by the merchant capitalist class in its own image. If anything of analytic substance remains to be said on this matter, it may be that more attention should be devoted to the process by which the Canadian state successively suppressed reemerging domestic capital within the staple sector itself, and within the manufacturing sector, in the interest of foreign capital.[33]

While none of the other new Marxist writers have matched Naylor in depth and breadth, some significant analytical gains have been made in fleshing out a Marxist version of the staple theory. The latter would require the recasting of the staple theory as a theory of class formation; a tentative first step can be outlined here.

If we are to begin at the beginning, we must enquire as to the fate of aboriginal peoples. How, in the most fundamental sense, do they fit into the staple thesis? Innis makes the essential point, at least implicitly, when he writes: "Fundamentally the civilization of North America is the civilization of Europe," and again "Canada has remained fundamentally a product of Europe."[34] Aboriginal ways of life, indeed aboriginal peoples themselves, were swept aside. Only in the fur trade era were aboriginal peoples functional to Euro-Canadians, and everywhere in the long-run the fur trade retreated in the face of settlement and was ultimately obliterated by it. Aboriginal people were made redundant.

This functional irrelevancy is dramatically demonstrated in the very terminology that is used to characterize Canada – and other like cases such as the United States, Australia and New Zealand.

Their aboriginal populations notwithstanding, they are called "new countries" or "empty lands" or "areas of recent settlement" or "undeveloped areas" – or simply "the frontier." Their histories can be written, and are written, as the story of successive waves of white settlers exploiting new frontiers and transplanting European institutions. The resistance of aboriginal people – and there has been resistance at every step – becomes in the history books little more than a lengthy footnote to the main story. The Riel uprising is crushed, Riel is hanged, and he casts his long shadow over subsequent history not because he was a native resistance leader but because he was a Catholic.

The analytical significance of this point can be appreciated if we imagine a very opposite situation, namely, that the aboriginal population had been much larger and had not been easily pushed to the margins of society, geographically and socially. Rather than being a "colony of settlement" Canada might have been a "colony of conquest" analogous to those of Asia and Africa. Or it might have been a "white settler colony" proper, like the Union of South Africa or Rhodesia. Or it might have been a mixed case such as abound in Central and South America. In any event, Canadian development would have been different and much more difficult. A pre-capitalist indigenous population that could not be ignored would be reduced to underdevelopment, and either slowly converted to the capitalist mode of production or contained by massive repression and discrimination. We would not have our very high *average* standard of living; though the European stock – if it had not yet been turfed out – might be doing very well. Methodologically, there would be no special case amenable to the liberal staple theory.

The aboriginal peoples were pushed aside, dispossessed of land, separated from the means of production and reduced to the status of an underclass or lumpenproletariat.[35] As settlers poured in from the Old World, a class of capitalists emerged in the staple region who created a state structure and a "national policy" in its own image. What remains? Depending on the staple, the creation of either of a class of commodity producers or a class of wage-earners. The distinction hinges on whether the staple activity is a trade or an industry. The great staple *trades* of cod, fur and wheat have been extensively researched, and wheat has been explicitly analyzed in Marxist terms in C.B. Macpherson's classic *Democracy in Alberta.*

Independent commodity producers are capitalists because they primarily use their own capital; they are not wage-earners and do not employ wage labour. The important question is not whether independent commodity production exists as a mode of production, but whether it is a dominant or subordinate mode. As a mode of production, it coexists with merchant capital and increases its sway. Hence, both in its own right but, more importantly, because it reinforces merchant capital, independent commodity production tends to retard the development of mature industrial capitalism.[36] In the case of the wheat economy, the prairie farmer was interested solely in costs of inputs to the wheat economy and hence disinterested in whether a viable industrial structure was created within Canada.

But timber and lumber were to some extent industries; the old staples created industrialization in their wake; and the new mineral staples are explicitly industries. Commodity producers are a declining class.[37] We must enquire as to the formation of the working class.

This is a critical matter neglected by Innis and thus far by Naylor. In spite of a considerable and growing literature on the history of labour, the analytical relationship between the evolution of the working class and the imperatives of staple production has yet to be definitively worked out – and this paper is not the place to attempt it.

The basic characteristics of the process were set out by Pentland some time ago. He argued that staples production, because of its seasonal nature and vulnerability to cyclical swings in prices and profits, was not conducive to the formation of a "capitalist labour market" in which the costs of labour were "socialized." It was not until the 1860s, when manufacturing growth, urbanization, railway construction and the emergence of a sizeable domestic market created an integrated economy, that the demand for labour became sufficiently large, geographically concentrated and seasonally balanced.[38] The raw material of the labour market came via the immigrant stream, and that was the case both for the unskilled and the skilled. But since many immigrants were "highly responsive to market incentives" and determined to be "farm proprietors rather than wage earners" measures were needed to ensure that they remained in the wage-labour pool. According to Pentland: "It was just such a rejection of wage employment that inspired Edward Gibbon Wakefield, in the interest of capitalist development, to demand new barriers to the ownership of land." Teeple has since argued that, in fact, a glut of landless labour existed in British North America by 1820, a situation he attributes not only to monopolizing land policies – a historically well-recognized phenomenon – but also, following Naylor to "the lack of industrial growth due to the presence of a mercantile ruling class."[39]

In general, Pentland, from our present perspective, veered more to a Ryersonian than Naylorian view of industrialization, so we need to be on our guard. And beyond the question of class structure lies the complex matter of the nature of the labour movement, and of not only its class consciousness but also its national consciousness. Canada's dependent trade unionism has been much discussed in the literature, and the rationale and consequences have been ably stated by Robert H. Babcock in particular.[40] He argues that the emergence of a continental labour market during the middle of the nineteenth century led American craft unions to undertake organizing drives in Canada in order to protect wages and working conditions in the United States from the effects of an inflow of cheap, non-union labour. The unprecedented inflow of American direct investment in Canada at the turn of the century gave greater impetus to Samuel Gompers of the American Federation of Labour to organize Canadian workers in order to protect the North American labour market. For Canadian workers whom the AFL unionized, this meant access to strike support and insurance benefits and improved wages and working conditions. But for the Canadian trade union movement as a whole, international craft unions also brought "structural characteristics and policy predilections that were products of the American environment," including short-term economic goals, apolitical unionism, and opposition to organizing unskilled workers. Accordingly, Babcock concludes that "the AFL operated as a divisive force when the Trades and Labour Congress was transformed from a body unifying Canadian unionists into an arm of the international crafts. In a country wracked if not wrecked by regionalism, the loss of a truly national labour institution was doubtless unfortunate.[41]

The full analytical relationship between dependent trade unionism and staple production needs to be pulled together from the literature. A critical aspect of this is the tendency of international unionism, directly in its own right and indirectly through its control of the New Democratic Party, to constrain Canadian nationalism and hence the potential for restructuring the Canadian economy away from its staple bias.[42]

Finally, in the process of doing all this, it would become apparent that staple production in Canada has not only generated economic growth – as emphasized by mainstream writers – but has also generated social disturbances (such as protest movements) and social rigidities (regional disparities and the social costs of regional underdevelopment).

V

There are clearly two liberal versions of the staple theory and one certainly, and perhaps two, Marxist versions. The continuing viability of the two dependent versions, one liberal and one Marxist and both owing much to Innis, augurs well for future work. In his one truly perceptive observation, MacDonald writes that Naylor has "synthesized, in an unprecedented way, radical and nationalist themes in Canadian economic thought" (265), but MacDonald errs in his grasp of the analytical, or methodological, respectability of that "thought" – as I hope this paper has demonstrated.

Finally, here are some suggestions as to the directions in which future research might go. There is always a need for serious theoretical work; specifically, Naylor's thesis might be re-examined in conjunction with Kay's masterful treatise,[43] where the dichotomy between merchant and industrial capital, and the consequences, in his case, for the nature of Third World underdevelopment, also figures so prominently. There can, of course, be no substitute for the detailed historical writing needed to expose the pervasive and peculiar impact of each particular staple; notwithstanding Innis' *Settlement and the Mining Frontier,* some of Aitken's writings, and now Nelles' very important contribution, the new staples, of mining and oil and gas, still await definitive analysis. As previously suggested, the impact of staple production on the working class, both in terms of its existence as a class and its consciousness of its existence, is in need of sustained analysis. Finally, the staple theory is so specifically Canadian in origin and development, and yet so apparently applicable to other new countries, as to make it highly probable that its application elsewhere in a comparative context would be beneficial to its continuing utility in Canadian studies.

NOTES

1 M.H. Watkins, "A Staple Theory of Economic Growth," *Canadian Journal of
   Economics and Political Science* 29 (1963) : 141–58; reprinted above.
2 I previously revisited the theory, albeit less explicitly, in "Resources and
   Underdevelopment" in Robert Laxer (ed.), *(Canada) Ltd: The Political
   Economy of Dependency* (Toronto, 1973); and "Economic Development in
   Canada" in Immanuel Wallerstein (ed.), *World Inequality: Origins and
   Perspectives on the World System* (Montreal, 1976). I define analytical interest
   in such a way as to exclude the writings of what might be called an institutional approach, having in mind the important, albeit different, writings of
   W.T. Easterbrook and Abraham Rotstein.
3 It is not my intention to classify people in a manner that may be unaccept-
   able to them. Whether or not availing oneself of the Marxist paradigm
   makes one a Marxist in any other sense is not relevant to scholarship. We
   now have it on the authority of Paul Samuelson that we all have something
   to gain from the use of Marxist analysis (see the most recent edition of
   Economics). One response to my 1963 paper by Innisians was that it emasculated Innis. Such people may object even more strenuously to the suggestion
   that Innis should now be translated explicitly into the Marxist paradigm.
   But there are only two paradigms, and translating into both is in order.
4 See Daniel Drache, "Rediscovering Canadian Political Economy," *Journal
   of Canadian Studies* 11 (August 1976): 3–18.
5 Gordon W. Bertram, "Economic Growth and Canadian Industry, 1870–
   1915: The Staples Model and the 'Take-Off' Hypothesis," *Canadian Journal
   of Economics and Political Science* (1963) 29: 162–84; and Richard E. Caves,
   "'Vent for Surplus' Models of Trade and Growth," in *Trade, Growth and the
   Balance of Payments: Essays in Honour of Gottfried Haberler* (Chicago, 1965).
   E.J. Chambers and D.F. Gordon, "Primary Products and Economic
   Growth: An Empirical Measurement," *Journal of Political Economy*
   74 (1966): 315–32. Among the responses to Chambers and Gordon are
   Bertram, "The Relevance of the Wheat Boom in Canadian Economic His-
   tory," *Canadian Journal of Economics* 6 (1973); Caves, "Export-Led Growth
   and the New Economic History," in Jagdish N. Bhagwati *et al*, eds., *Trade,
   Balance of Payments and Growth: Papers in International Economics in Honor of
   Charles P. Kindleberger* (Amsterdam, 1971); J.H. Dales, J.C. McManus and
   M.H. Watkins, "Primary Products and Economic Growth: A Comment,"
   Journal of Political Economy (1967); and Edward Vickery, "Exports and
   North American Economic Growth: 'Structuralist' and 'Staples' Models in
   Historical Perspectives," *Canadian Journal of Economics* 7 (1974).

6 Daniel Drache, "Harold Innis: A Canadian Nationalist," *Journal of Canadian Studies* 4 (May 1969): 7–12; and "Rediscovering."

7 So too did some prominent Canadian historians. The sub-title of Craig Brown and Ramsay Cook's *Canada, 1896–1921* is *A Nation Transformed*, thereby begging two questions. Certainly Innis and Creighton raised doubts as to the extent of nationhood from anything but a narrow juridical perspective, and Caves and Holton demonstrate that there was no discontinuity in this period that would justify the use of the word "transformed." See Richard E. Caves and Richard H. Holton, *The Canadian Economy: Prospects and Retrospects* (Cambridge, Mass., 1959). Yet Margaret Prang says that the sub-title of the book "could scarcely be more aptly chosen" (*Canadian Forum*, October 1974).

8 L.R. MacDonald, "Merchants against Industry: An Idea and its Origins," *Canadian Historical Review* (September 1975).

9 Caves, "'Vent for Surplus,'" 112–14.

10 "'Vent for Surplus,'" 102, 115; cf. R.E. Baldwin, "Patterns of Development in Newly Settled Regions, *Manchester School of Economics and Social Studies* (1956) which was central to the analysis of my 1963 paper, and also his "Export Technology and Development from a Subsistence Level," *Economic Journal* (1963).

11 Chambers and Gordon, "Primary Products." It all the more unfortunate that the Canadian edition of Samuelson's *Economics* (4th Canadian edition, 1975: 679) – though Canadianized by Anthony Scott, a specialist in resource economics – insists on taking Chambers and Gordon seriously.

12 Caves, "Export-Led Growth," 434, 436, 409.

13 A.E. Safarian, *Foreign Ownership of Canadian Industry* (Toronto, 1966); Canada, Privy Council, *Foreign Ownership and the Structure of Canadian Industry [the Watkins Report]* (Ottawa, 1968); Canada, *Foreign Direct Investment in Canada [the Gray Report]* (Ottawa, 1972); Kari Levitt, *Silent Surrender: The Multinational Corporation in Canada* (Toronto,1970).

14 R.T. Naylor, *The History of Canadian Business*, vols. 1 and 2 (Toronto: 1975).

15 H.A. Innis, *The Fur Trade in Canada: An Introduction to Canadian Economic History* (Toronto, 1930; 2nd ed. 1956), 385.

16 R.T. Naylor, *The History of Canadian Business 1867–1914*, 2 vols. (Toronto, 1975), 1: 56–7.

17 Pierre L. Bourgault, *Innovation and the Structure of Canadian Industry*, Science Council of Canada , Special Study No.23 (Ottawa, 1972).

18 Eric Kierans, *Report on Natural Resources Policy in Manitoba* (Manitoba, 1973).

19 Bourgault observes that Canada is becoming increasingly reliant on staple exports and that if we keep on this path "Before the children of today could reach middle age most of the resources would be gone, leaving Canada with a resource-based economy and no resources" (126).

20 H.V. Nelles, *The Politics of Development: Forest, Mines and Hydro-electric Power in Ontario,* 1849–1941 (Toronto, 1974); E.E. Rich, *Hudson's Bay Company,* 1670–1870, 2 vols. (London, 1958–1959).

21 Morris Zaslow, *The Opening of the Canadian North, 1870–1914* (Toronto, 1971); K.J. Rea, *The Political Economy of the Canadian North* (Toronto, 1968).

22 See Mel Watkins, ed., *Dene Nation: The Colony Within* (Toronto, 1977).

23 Naylor, *History,* 1: xix.

24 Naylor, *History,* 1: 3–4.

25 Naylor, *History,* 1: 15; see also Bruce Archibald, "Atlantic Regional Under-Development and Socialism" in Laurier LaPierre *et. al.* (eds.), *Essays on the Left* (Toronto, 1971).

26 Naylor, *History,* 1: 110, 67.

27 Naylor, *History,* 2: 283.

28 Stanley Ryerson, *Unequal Union* (Toronto, 1968).

29 MacDonald, "Merchants against Industry," 266 , which is a critique of R.T. Naylor, "The Rise and Fall of the Third Commercial Empire of the St. Lawrence" in Gary Teeple (ed.), *Capitalism and the National Question in Canada* (Toronto, 1972), 1–41. It is not at all clear what MacDonald intends us to believe about the nature of the Canadian capitalist class; he rejects Naylor's explanation without choosing to give us any indication of what he would put in its place. From what he does tell us, he seriously underestimates the extent of American control of the Canadian economy by 1914 (cf. Glen Williams, "Canadian Industrialization: We Ain't Growin' Nowhere," *This Magazine* (March-April 1975), and Tom Naylor "Commentary" on Simon Rosenblum, "Economic Nationalism and the English-Canadian Socialist Movement," *Our Generation,* 2 (Fall 1975): 20–1.) MacDonald also profoundly misunderstands the nature of the multinational corporation when he writes that "Possibly the origin of the branch plant should be sought not in industry but in trade: from a management standpoint it was the application to manufacturing of the organizational principles of a commercial branch of a trading company" (269). This flies in the face of virtually all known literature on the multinational corporation; see particularly the writings of Stephen Hymer, who made signal contributions successively to both the liberal and Marxist analysis of foreign ownership.

30 Wallace Clement, *The Canadian Corporate Elite: An Analysis of Economic Power* (Toronto, 1975), 150, 335.

31 Wallace Clement, *Continental Corporate Power: Economic Elite Linkages between Canada and the United States* (Toronto, 1977).

32 See my "The 'American System' and Canada's National Policy," *Bulletin of the Canadian Association of American Studies* (Winter 1967).

33 This point became very evident to me on reading Nelles' chapter of the nickel industry in *Politics of Development*; see my "Economic Development in Canada." On the subsidies to foreign capital in the period 1945–1957, and their apparent success in leading to a quantum leap in American ownership of the Canadian economy, see David Wolfe, "Political Culture, Economic Policy and the Growth of Foreign Involvement in Canada, 1945–1957" (M.A. Thesis, Carleton University, 1973).

34 Innis, *Fur Trade*, 2nd. ed., 383, 401.

35 For an elaboration on this and its relevance to the North today, see Watkins, "Dene Nation."

36 See *Monthly Review* (May 1976) for an exchange between Robert Sherry and James O'Connor on independent commodity production in early America.

37 This is a major theme of Leo A. Johnson, "The development of class in Canada in the twentieth century" in *Teeple (ed.) Capitalism*. On the nature of Canada's capitalist class and the general issues of Canadian dependency, however, Johnson's views are confused and unreliable. At best, there is an apparent tendency to agree with everyone. At worst, there is a willingness to endorse utterly useless sectarian scribbling; on the latter, see his effusive "Introduction" to Steve Moore and Debi Wells, *Imperialism and the National Question in Canada* (Toronto, 1975) and compare with the devastating critiques of the book by Ian Lumsden in *This Magazine* (Nov.-Dec. 1975) and Jack Warnock in *Canadian Dimension* (March, 1976).

38 H.C. Pentland, "The Development of a Capitalistic Labour Market in Canada," *Canadian Journal of Economics and Political Science* 25 (1959): 456–7. For a fuller statement see his *Labour and Capital in Canada, 1650–1860*, edited by Paul Phillips (Toronto: Lorimer, 1981), written in 1960 and published posthumously. Pentland deserves great credit for working within the Marxist paradigm when it was distinctly unusual to do so, and the tendency for his work to be ignored by the mainstream of Canadian economic historians – including myself in the 1963 article – tells us much about the limitations of orthodox economics as it impinges on economic history.

39 Gary Teeple, "Land, labour and capital in pre-Confederation Canada," in Teeple (ed.), *Capitalism*, 45.

50 The Staple Theory of Development

40 Robert H. Babcock, *Gompers in Canada: A Study in American Continentalism Before the First World War* (Toronto, 1974). See also Charles Lipton, *The Trade Union Movement in Canada 1827–1959* (Montreal, 1967); I.M. Abella, *Nationalism, Communism and Canadian Labour: The CIO, the Communist Party and the Canadian Congress of Labour 1935–1956* (Toronto, 1973); and the essays by Roger Howard and Jack Scott, R.B. Morris, and Lipton in Teeple (ed.), *Capitalism.*
41 Babcock, *Gompers,* 210–16.
42 James Laxer's "Introduction to the Political Economy of Canada," in R. Laxer, (ed.) *(Canada) Ltd.,* 37–40, is particularly suggestive.
43 Geoffrey Kay, *Development and Underdevelopment: A Marxist Analysis* (London, 1975).

3

The Dene Nation:
From Underdevelopment
to Development (1977)

The aboriginal people of the Mackenzie District, who call themselves the Dene (pronounced "Dennay"), today face the final onslaught of "progress" in the form of applications to build a natural
gas pipeline down the Mackenzie Valley through their homeland.
To their great credit, the Dene are struggling mightily against these
proposals. In the process, they are greatly strengthening their identity as a people and are once again asserting their rights as a nation.
They are telling the rest of the world, and southern Canadians in
particular, what colonialism has done to them and how they intend
to decolonize themselves.

The government of Canada established the Mackenzie Valley
Pipeline Inquiry under Justice Thomas R. Berger of the Supreme
Court of British Columbia (the Berger Inquiry) to consider the separate proposals of the applicants, Canadian Arctic Gas Pipelines Ltd
(Arctic Gas or CAGPL) and Foothills Pipe Lines Ltd, to build pipelines up the Mackenzie Valley. Arctic Gas proposed to bring both
Alaskan gas and Canadian gas – to the extent that the latter exists –
up the valley. Foothills proposes to bring only Canadian gas, but are
willing to transport Alaskan gas via the Fairbanks corridor (or

A revision of the Preface and "From Development to Underdevelopment,"
in Mel Watkins, ed., *Dene Nation: The Colony Within*, ix–xii, 84–99 (Toronto:
University of Toronto Press, 1977).

"Alcan") route. The two routes up the valley vary somewhat, but for
the Dene the differences are incidental. Either pipeline would pass
through the lands they have occupied and used since time immemorial. The land claim of the Dene is for these lands. It is with
respect to these lands that the Dene have gone to the courts to en-
deavour to file a caveat to stop further "development" that preju-
dices their claim.

Under these circumstances, the Dene have very properly made use
of the Berger Inquiry to further their cause. They have spoken elo-
quently to Judge Berger, both at hearings in their communities and
at the formal sittings of the Inquiry in Yellowknife. They have en-
listed the support of many non-Dene "experts" in a variety of fields
so as to translate their concerns into the language of the non-Dene.

In doing this, the Dene have gone beyond simply showing the adverse effects of a pipeline, serious though these would be. They
have gone beyond simply asserting their ownership of the land, real
though that is, or should be. Rather, they have come to the fundamental perception that their struggle is for the most universal of
human rights, the right to be a self-determining people. It is this
right which the Dene insist the federal government must recognize
as an integral part of aboriginal rights. The Dene recognize the extent to which they have become a colonized people and they have
begun to move down the long and difficult road to decolonize
themselves. In their striving for liberation, they have understandably found sustenance in the increasingly successful struggles of
colonized peoples elsewhere in the world.

The pipeline applicants, Arctic Gas and Foothills, assert in effect
that the proposed gas pipeline provides a new opportunity for
northern native people. The form that opportunity is said to take is
the increased potential for wage-employment. They point to the extent of present unemployment among native people as evidence of
the need for this opportunity, though they presumably overesti-
mate this to the same extent as they underestimate the number of
active hunters, fishers, and trappers. In any event, they have some
difficulty squaring their assertion with the extent of earlier job-
creating projects, notably in mining, but resolve the matter by insisting that the pipeline will constitute a break with the past. They
emphasize that the jobs created in the operations phase, but not of
course in the construction phase, will be permanent rather than
transitory – though, again, they beg the question of how this is

different from mining, as well as the question of how permanent is permanent. Finally, they appeal to the training program for northerners. They are right to do this, since it would appear to be the only novel feature of the pipeline relative to the other earlier projects, though it is certainly a moot point whether such a modest program can reasonably bear the weight of legitimizing the pipeline as a break with the past.

As well, the applicants assert their respect for native land claims, and urge both the native organizations and the government to settle them so that their projects can proceed. They appear to assert that a pipeline prior to a land settlement will not prejudice the claim, though they simultaneously pretend not to know what the claim is really about in the absence of specific details. They refuse to accept the Dene position that a pipeline can under no circumstances be started prior to a land settlement. They do not appear to have responded to the assertion that the Dene land claim is centrally about the political, and human, right to alternative development.

If we are to evaluate these assertions, and consider the probable impact of a pipeline, we need to know something about, first, the nature of past development and the present condition of native people, and second, the nature and extent of the land claim, or the nature of alternative development, both for their own sake and for the purpose of assessing prejudice to the claim.

At the same time, we can speak to the positive assertions of the Dene: that they own 450,000 square miles of land; that their title to the land should be recognized rather than extinguished; that their aboriginal and human rights transcend property rights to include political rights, namely, the right to self-determination as a nation; that their desire for economic independence can be met by creating alternative community-based economic development under their control; that further development, and particularly the proposed pipeline, threatens gravely to prejudice the land claim by eroding their aboriginal and human rights.

PAST AND PRESENT DEVELOPMENT

The first notion of which we should disabuse ourselves is that what the applicants have in mind for the North is novel from any historical perspective. Quite the contrary. The history of Canada, as written by the greatest of our historians, is as a succession of staple exports from successive geographic frontiers to serve the needs of more advanced industrial areas. The great export commodities have been fish, fur, square timber, lumber, wheat, pulp and paper, minerals, and oil and gas. The consequences for Canada have been profound. As Innis writes:

Concentration on the production of staples for export to more highly in-dustrialized areas in Europe and later in the United States had broad im-plications for the Canadian economic, political and social structure. Each staple in its turn left its stamp, and the shift to new staples invariably pro-duced periods of crises in which adjustments in the old structure were painfully made and a new pattern created in relation to a new staple.[1]

The methodology of this "staples approach" is directly helpful to us in considering the matter of "impact." The impact of the proposed pipeline is simply the "stamp" of the oil and gas industry on Canada in general and the North in particular. The North is experiencing "the shift to a new staple"; the result is a "period of crisis" and of "painful adjustments."

What is the impact of a staple? First, all of the staple trades have in common a bias towards serving the needs of more advanced met-ropolitan areas – once France, then Britain, and now the United States. This is clearly relevant when we are told, as in the present case, that the Dene interest must yield to the higher national inter-est. Not only is the hinterland interest being made subservient to the national interest, but by some sleight of hand the national in-terest is equated with the metropolitan interest.

Second, each staple leaves its particular stamp. Two great staple trades have dominated the North, the fur trade and now, increas-ingly, minerals (mining and petroleum, the economic characteristics of which are the same, that is, the highly capital-intensive exploita-tion of non-renewable resources). These two staples have had pro-foundly different economic impacts on aboriginal peoples.

But first we need to retreat for a moment and see how aboriginal peoples fit, in the most fundamental sense, into this approach to the story of Canadian development, past and present. Only in the fur trade era were aboriginal peoples functional to Euro-Canadians, and as the fur trade retreated in the face of settlement they were deemed irrelevant. It is that fate, which was visited upon other aboriginal peoples as the European frontier moved inexorably west and north, that now faces the Dene. Today aboriginal peoples are the majority in the NWT but, of course, that has been true initially in each of these successive frontiers.

There is an awful truth about the manner in which this country was "born" and has since been successively rejuvenated. We cannot change that history, but we can learn from it and resolve "never again." Put differently, the exigencies of staple production must make allowance in the North, for the first time, for the reality of aboriginal rights; unless that is done, nothing will really change.

Let us now look briefly at the specific and differing impacts of fur and minerals as staples. To begin, there is the theoretical question of the mechanisms by which production and trade of a particular staple leaves its stamp. It is clear from the quotation from Innis that these are pervasive, but at least with respect to the central economic mechanisms they can be broken down by focusing on the actual mode of staple production and the linkages to other sectors of the economy.

The mode of production can be understood for present purposes as the particular mix of factors of production – of land (that is, natural resources), labour, and capital – used to produce the staple within, at any moment of time, a given technological and institutional framework. The linkages are the spread effects from the staple sector to other sectors of the economy, and particularly the local economy, through the market mechanism. They can be conveniently classified as threefold: forward linkage, that is, further processing of the staple; backward linkage, that is, the production of inputs including capital goods for use in production of the staple; and final demand linkage, that is, the spending of the income received by the commodity producers or workers on consumer goods. In each case, the stronger the linkages, the greater the income generated in the local economy – or, in the language of the economist, the higher the multiplier.

The prosecution of the fur trade depended, at least initially in each region into which the trade expanded, on aboriginal fur gatherers. As such aboriginal peoples were commodity producers, not wage-earners, and the fur trade was literally a trade, or a commercial activity, not an industrial activity. Aboriginal producers became dependent to the extent that they became vulnerable to the exigencies of the trade, but they did not have to make two critical and traumatic adjustments that result from imposed industrialization. First, they did not have to become wage-earners, and second, which is really the opposite side of the coin, they did not have to yield ownership of the land. To put the matter differently, neither their labour-time nor their land became marketable commodities.

This point is of the first importance. For the student of economic history in general, no theme is so compelling as the process by which land-bound people – typically agrarian but sometimes nomadic – are turned, against their will, into industrial workers. In general, it has not been a voluntary process, the mere offering of another option as the applicants like to phrase it. Rather, the tendency has been for people to be pushed off the land or to have others sell it from beneath their feet. To turn land-bound people into landless wage-earners has typically involved coercion.

Now mineral production (including petroleum) is an industry not a trade, and it needs both rights to the use of land and people who will work for a wage. The Hudson's Bay Company, as a fur-trading company, did not need to own the land; indeed, it was in its interest to allow aboriginal ownership of land to continue, the better to trap on it, and to discourage white settlement. Only when settlement overrode the fur trade, or promised imminently to do so, as it did in the West, did the Bay see fit to transform itself into a real-estate company and to pretend, successfully as it turned out, that *it* owned aboriginal land and was entitled to compensation rather than the aboriginal peoples.

But for the mining and petroleum companies, no such ambiguity is tolerable. Ownership arrangements with respect to the land must be such that they have a clear right to take minerals from the sub-surface and to transport minerals over the surface. Hence, in the context of the present situation, they act on the assumption that it is not Dene land, but Crown land, and if that is not so now it should be made so by a land settlement that extinguishes aboriginal title; the land, then, either is or must become Crown land, and the companies know full well the propensity of the Crown to let them extract resources. Furthermore, since "land" is simply a commodity, should the Dene perchance own some land that is needed – either because title has not been resolved or because property rights have been vested with the Dene as part of a land settlement – the companies reply that they can buy it, and should the Dene be unwilling to sell, the companies say that they can, with the help of the Crown, expropriate it.[2]

This helps us to understand what a "land settlement" must necessarily mean to the industry, namely, extinguishing native title to the land or, as a minimum, limiting any recognition of aboriginal rights to property rights subject to expropriation, so as to remove an impediment to industrial activity.

The industry needs labour as well, but here we do not need to be cynical to see that Dene labour is hardly so essential as Dene land. Non-aboriginal labour is generally readily available from the South – and this is particularly so now given the extent of unemployment – and has the advantage that it is not "raw" labour but trained and disciplined labour. The record of the mining industry, or of the Imperial Oil refinery at Norman Wells, in this regard, namely, their failure over long periods of time to employ much native labour and, when they did, mostly in the most menial and casual occupations, is sufficient demonstration of how the economics of the matter works. True, the government now insists on the employment of native labour, and industry is generally compliant – in part because much of the training costs are paid by the government – but the motives involved are at best mixed. It is good public relations for both government and industry, and in general has more to do with politics than with economics. And there are incidental advantages. To the extent it works, it means less native use of the land, relative to what would otherwise be the case, and hence can be alleged to diminish the potency of a land claim based on land use (though not, of course, the possessory rights that flow from land occupancy since time immemorial). For the government, the whole scheme can to some extent be seen as a substitute for welfare. When all is said and done, what is involved for aboriginal peoples is a swap – a job in the wage economy for abandoning and yielding up the land. We need to have only the slightest knowledge of the value of the natural resources of the North to the companies to know what an unequal bargain that is for the Dene.

We can get some idea of that value by enquiring about the role of capital and the nature of its return, and a closely related matter, namely, who gets the return to land, or "economic rent." Up to a point, the matter is straightforward. Under the market system, the providers of capital receive dividends and interest. All we need add is that the owners of this capital may reside outside the region – as they clearly do in the cases of both the fur trade and mineral production in the North – and in that case no benefit therefrom accrues to the residents of the region.

But what if staple production yields profits above and beyond those necessary to service capital? This is not a hypothetical matter, but is rather to be expected in the nature of the case. The main reason is that staple production necessarily means exploitation of natural resources, or of "land," and since the latter is scarce, it is likely to command its own reward. The critical question then becomes who gets the reward, or who appropriates the rents. Logic suggests that the answer is the owner of the land. If, as is alleged in the North, the Crown owns the land, then it should get the rents, and that is a rationale for royalties and other forms of taxation of the resource industries. If the Crown fails to appropriate the rents – as it largely does in the North and as it apparently intends to continue doing in the future – they are transformed into "super-profits" and are appropriated by the owners of the capital or, in effect, the corporation itself for purposes of reinvestment. There is, however, no reason to expect that they will be reinvested within the staple-producing region which generated them, and every reason to expect that they will not be reinvested in the region in other activities that serve local priorities. What tends to happen, then, is that the return to capital and to land leaves the region; all that remains is the return to labour, and that only to the extent it is resident labour.

To cast the Dene simply as wage-earners, as the applicants do, is then not only to cast them in a role they may not want, but to deny them their role as the land-owners who should be entitled to appropriate the rents from projects which they choose to let proceed on their land. That denial is critical, for it means that the once-and-for-all rents generated within the region, from non-renewable resources that are in due course depleted, are ultimately reinvested at the behest of the corporation outside the region, rather than being reinvested within the region by the people themselves, in activities based on renewable resources that could survive after the non-renewable resources are exhausted.

In this respect, the oil industry is no different from the fur trade. The Hudson's Bay Company appropriated such enormous surpluses from the fur trade that it is now a major retailer, real estate developer, and shareholder in the oil and gas industry. Indeed, beyond that, the fortunes that originated in the fur trade went on to spawn yet greater fortunes in banking and railways. Of what benefit has this been to the northern aboriginal peoples who produced the fur?

When the resource is non-renewable, as it is for mining and oil and gas, the major legacy of failing to keep the surpluses in the region to seed other activities is the well-known Canadian phenomenon of the ghost town. As Northrop Frye observes in his "Images of Canada" television special on the CBC, "Canada is full of ghost towns: visible ruins unparalleled in Europe." The ghost town symbolizes everything that aboriginal peoples, as *the* long-term residents of the North, have to fear from the present mode of staple production; for by then who knows what cumulative damage will have been done to their land and its ability to support them?

There is also the matter of linkages of the staple sector to other sectors of the local economy. None of these linkages operate so as to create much economic activity in the North beyond the primary sector itself, and there is little reason to expect this to change. The primary product tends to be exported in a relatively unprocessed form, and there is a high propensity to import both capital goods and consumer goods. Rather, the linkages tend to generate economic activity in southern Canada, the US and elsewhere, thereby creating benefits outside the North. (This does *not* mean that there is necessarily a net benefit to southern Canadians. Whether or not there is depends as well on the effects of frontier development on primary product prices, and hence indirectly on the prices of other commodities embodying the primary product. If the price of the staple rises to make frontier production possible, this will lower the real incomes of those who, directly or indirectly, consume the staple. This phenomenon is clearly relevant with respect to high-cost northern oil and gas and very probably makes the net benefit to the great majority of southern Canadians negative.)

Predictably, the tactic of the businessmen and government of the staple-exporting region is to attempt to increase the linkages within the region. Whatever crumbs they achieve by this strategy are, of course, necessarily obtained by their having to opt wholeheartedly for continuing staple production. Hence, it is no surprise that local business interests in the North are solidly behind the pipeline, and that the territorial government conceives of aboriginal economic development as helping the Dene to get a piece of the action that will be generated in other sectors by the pipeline – in spite of the fact that the latter has about it something of the aura of asking the condemned man to take up rope manufacturing.

Nor can it be assumed that an existing local enterprise will necessarily reap any benefit at all from a resource boom; it may even be left worse off. In his testimony before the Berger Inquiry at the community hearing in Fort Resolution, Father Lou Menex gave no less than four examples for that community alone -in the fur business, river transportation, saw milling and commercial fishing – where existing native involvement was pushed aside by subsequent rounds of activity. Some of those awaiting the pipeline will experience not a linkage effect but a shrinkage effect.

It was noted at the beginning of this analytical discourse that staple production takes place within a framework of technology and institutions. These are not ordained from on high, but are human-made; nevertheless, for the staple-producing region they are largely imposed, being created and controlled by outside interests. This is very clear today in the mineral sector of the North, where the technology is highly capital-intensive and a small number of large companies are dominant. In so far as the technology is difficult to alter, the message for local people, and above all for the Dene as the permanent residents, is, again, not to be satisfied with merely being wage-earners in the mineral sector, but rather to focus on the rents which otherwise accrue to capital and are drained away. In so far as the corporations, as the dominant institutions, are difficult to alter, and the government is an alien institution subservient to corporate needs, the relevant message for the Dene is to create a new institutional framework within the North under the control of the Dene to which these entities must adapt.

Large-scale resource projects are said by their proponents to create "development." In fact, for native people what has resulted is properly characterized as "underdevelopment." The process of underdevelopment permits of a reasonably precise definition, namely, the "blockage of potential, sustained economic and social development geared to local human needs."[3] The primary mechanism by which local development is suppressed is by the outward drain of economic surplus from the region. The most significant loss from the failure to retain surplus is the destruction of local self-determination.

Let no one doubt that the outflow of income generated in the North is large. This is evident from an examination of the social accounts of the North by John Palmer of Indian and Northern Affairs for the period 1967 to 1970. In 1970, Gross National Product (GNP) per capita for all of Canada was $3,866, while Gross Domestic Product (GDP) per capita (conceptually virtually the same as Canadian GNP) for the NWT was much higher at $5,311. Now the high figure for the North is because GDP includes all income originating in the North, and hence includes non-resident earnings of both individuals and corporations, but that only demonstrates the extent to which wealth is in fact created in the North but drained out as wages and salaries to southerners and cash flow from northern businesses to southern interests. In 1970, of GDP for *both* the Yukon and Northwest Territories of $266.1 million, $80.4 million was not retained in the North, $32.2 million going out as wages and salaries and $48.2 million as business cash flow.[4]

Other comparisons are possible for the single year 1969. Per capita personal income (the income actually received by persons) was $2,915 for all Canadians, approximately $1,100 for Treaty Indians and Inuit of the NWT, and approximately $3,000 for other residents of the NWT. Total native personal income (with native defined, by those who collected the data, as Treaty Indians and Inuit) is estimated as $20.5 million in 1969 – though this is clearly too low because of an underestimate of the value of country food. In that same year, the gross return on capital (before tax) in the mining sector in the NWT was $37.4 million, of which only $4.6 million was retained in the North. Arvin Jelliss' rent estimates for the producing mines of the NWT show economic rents proper – after allowing for a 15 per cent return on capital, net of taxes and royalties – of $15.9 million in 1970 (and very much higher in 1973 and 1974).[5]

The ultimate hallmark of underdevelopment is marginality. Economically, it manifests itself as poverty, unemployment and welfare. (Rather than seeing welfare as "charity," we should appreciate its hidden dimensions. For the Dene, it avoids integration into the wage economy, and is therefore a form of resistance. For the dominant society, it is something it can afford, for there are not that many Dene, and the long-run effect of welfare, to the extent it demoralizes and degrades people, discourages concerted use of the land, and thus helps to dispossess the Dene of their land.) Socially, it manifests itself in alcoholism, family breakdown, and suicide. Politically, it manifests itself in feelings of hopelessness and apathy.

The Dene have so far been spared the fullness of that fate; they are, as the applicants like to say, in a state of transition. But the direction of history is clear. It has recently been succinctly summarized by the anthropologist, Peter Douglas Elias:

[aboriginal] socio-economic phenomena must be studied within the historic and contemporary framework of the development of industrial, class-capitalist Canada. With the passage of time, Canada tended to acquire the "typical" characteristics of class-capitalist society. The producers, in this case the native people of Canada, were separated from the means of production, embodied, essentially, in the land and the products of the land. The means of production became concentrated and monopolized in the hands of a single social class, and native became a class owning no possessions and, ultimately, having no exchangeable commodity other than labour. Even this "typical" model of capitalist development was surpassed by natives becoming a permanently underemployed class subsisting on social assistance ... An examination of the history of native and white contact reveals the processes that culminated in the total integration of native peoples into contemporary Canadian society as permanent members of the underclass.[6]

Hugh Brody tells us that the process is at work today with respect to the Inuit of the Eastern Arctic: "The most recent trends are pushing native people increasingly towards the lowest and least certain rung on the national class ladder: if separated from his own means of production and unable to have a sure relationship to the intruders' means of production, the [Inuit] – like many Canadian and American Indians before him – will be turned into a migrant worker, a casual labourer, and – as this lumpenproletarian condition develops – prostitute, petty thief and beggar. Abundant signs of this course of events are already visible."[7] It must be insisted upon that the purpose of northern native land claims is neither more nor less than to subvert this terrible historic process.

It is important to understand as well that this way of analysing the condition of native people is very different from those who insist, explicitly or implicitly, that the reality we are observing, particularly in the North, is a "dual economy."[8] According to this view, the North is a two-sector economy, consisting of a "modern" sector and a "traditional" sector, and these two sectors are substantially separate. The "modern" sector is seen as essentially an enclave, where "development" takes place, while the "traditional" sector is stagnant and full of problems, and is not experiencing the benefits of "development." The logic of this position is that the solution lies in moving people out of the "traditional" sector and into the "modern" sector. The transition, though painful, is necessary. At the end of the road – or in this case, at the end of the pipeline – what will be created is a one-sector "modern" economy with everybody experiencing the benefits of "development."

The thrust of my argument is very different. The concept of dual economy is not helpful in analysing the history of the Mackenzie District either in the era of the fur trade or in the recent, and present, era of mineral production. In the past, when the fur trade was dominant, the economy was a one-sector native economy with trapping commercialized. The Dene benefited, though at the long-run cost of dependency. The moral seems clear: had the fur trade been controlled by the Dene, rather than by the Hudson's Bay Company, tendencies to "mining" and consequent depletion could have been curtailed; surpluses could have been kept in the region to permit more diversified development around renewable resources, rather than being used to build edifices in Winnipeg and Toronto; and white trappers – who became an increasingly serious problem for the Dene in this century, as Father Fumoleau has shown – could have been excluded, assuming the political rights of the aboriginal majority were allowed to express themselves.[9]

Today, the economy is a two-sector economy with the mineral sector added to the pre-existing one-sector economy. But the two sectors are anything but separate. Rather, the operation of the "new" sector works, through a variety of mechanisms, to under develop the "old" sector. The economic surplus generated by the "new" sector is either used to generate further activity in the "new" sector or is drained out of the region; none even "trickles down" to the "old" sector. The white settlers attracted by the "new" sector impose alien institutions and pre-empt the power of aboriginal people; the aboriginal people experience degradation and anomie.

Again, there would seem to be a clear moral: *if* non-renewable resource exploitation is to continue, then instead of integrating the Dene into a one-sector economy – which they say they do not want and which does not appear to have worked elsewhere in Canada – what should be considered is creating a two-sector economy which has the real promise of being beneficial to the Dene. That is, instead of blithely assuming that a dual economy exists today but should be encouraged to wither away in the long run, we should see that what could be created is a two-sector economy where the two sectors would coexist harmoniously. That would require us to look carefully at the means by which the present mechanisms of underdevelopment could be turned into mechanisms of development.

The conclusion to this point is that staple production, by its inherent nature, brings into play powerful structural and determinative factors. The inference is that these structural tendencies can be broken only by new institutional arrangements that permit of genuine development.

THE LAND CLAIM

AND ALTERNATIVE DEVELOPMENT

The problem that some people may have in understanding the nature and extent of the land claim, is that both the word "land" and the word "claim" are somewhat misleading. To use the word "claim" is to imply that native people are claiming their homeland and rights; while the erosions of colonialism are real, we should at least say *reclaim*. But perhaps the best word is "declaration" (as in Dene Declaration), that is, the Dene are declaring their rights; my dictionary gives as the meaning of declare "make known, proclaim publicly"; that is, it is something the declarant already knows.

To the Euro-Canadian, the word "land" conjures up *property rights*, and property means something that is marketable and subject to expropriation. Clearly the word "land" means much more than that to the Dene and, specifically, in Euro-Canadian language, includes rights of control or *political* rights. The collective expression of political rights is what we would customarily call "self-determination." By "land claim," then, the Dene mean "a declaration of the right to self-determination"; thus, the Dene Declaration *is* the central statement of their claim.

Now, self-determination is a many-faceted phenomenon, with different dimensions reinforcing each other. Thus, significant economic independence, while it cannot in itself be sufficient, is nevertheless necessary for self-determination. Indeed, in so far as the Dene cannot achieve political independence – for they accept that they are part of Canada – the degree of economic independence needed may become that much more important.

What is here called "economic independence" is what the Dene call "alternative development." That term can be understood to mean an "alternative" to the "development" of the non-renewable resource sector, which, in fact, creates underdevelopment for native people. Along the lines suggested earlier, it could be seen as meaning a two-sector economy, that is, a non-renewable resource sector under external ownership but subject to Dene control, and a renewable resource sector under Dene ownership and control.

Take the renewable resource sector first. A strong, indeed compelling case can surely be made for exclusive Dene rights in this sector, not only to hunt, fish, and trap but with respect to the whole area of game management – indeed, of all renewable resource management including forests and water. While non-Dene northern residents and the bureaucracy of the territorial government might be expected to resist this logic, it could be acceptable to the developers and the federal government, for whom the main chance is non-renewable resources (with the single exception of hydro power). But there are hidden implications not only for the developers – as we shall see directly – but also for the Dene.

For the Dene, what is at issue is not only the *protection* of their traditional economy but the right, indeed the necessity, to *create* their own contemporary economy around renewable resources. Just as it is increasingly recognized that the genuine development of the Third World hinges on agrarian reform, on the modernization of agriculture to serve domestic needs, so the genuine development of the North hinges on the modernization of the renewable resources sector by the Dene to serve Dene needs. Productivity must be improved and, given the extent both of present underemployment and the rapid growth of the aboriginal population, the sector must be expanded so that more people can be gainfully engaged in it. It would appear that the Dene prefer involvement in the renewable resource sector to involvement, at least on a full-time basis, in the non-renewable resource sector, but a restructuring of the renewable resource sector must take place so that it becomes a clearly viable sector in material terms. Given the government's obsession with the non-renewable resource sector to the virtual exclusion of all other considerations, such restructuring is, to say the least, unlikely to take place except in the context of a land settlement and its subsequent implementation. In any event, it will hardly constitute Dene development unless it is done by the Dene themselves.

It would be a considerable advance to have the recognition of exclusive Dene rights to harvest and to manage renewable resources, but it would not be sufficient. There are two reasons why this is so, that is, there are at least two identifiable mechanisms of underdevelopment which impinge on the renewable resource sector from the non-renewable resource sector and which would have to be converted into mechanisms of development.

The first is that activity in the non-renewable resource sector does damage to the renewable resource base and thereby threatens the continuing viability of that sector. The Dene can only be effectively protected against this by having themselves the power to protect their land. Even the exclusive right to use the renewable resources will be of insufficient avail if the right is not protected. Hence, alternative development must include the right to control the non-renewable resource sector so as to limit environmental degradation and competing uses to an extent that is tolerable to the Dene.

The second mechanism of underdevelopment is the failure of economic surplus generated in the non-renewable resource sector to accrue to the benefit of the renewable resource sector. What is at issue here is not only the right of the landowner to appropriate the rent, but the loss of the potential to create Dene development when that does not happen. Put more concretely, to create a viable Dene renewable resource sector requires both capital goods and Dene with both "traditional" and "modern" skills. Both of these, in turn, require money. So long as the money is made available under the white man's control – whether it be so-called Indian economic development funds under government auspices, or whether it be the building and operating of schools that destroy all-round Dene skills – then Dene development is a contradiction in terms. Hence, the right to alternative development must include the right to tax the non-renewable resource sector, or impose royalties thereon, so as to fund the Dene economy, and the Dene institutions, which will permit of continuing Dene development.

This is not to pretend to make a judgment about exactly how much rent should go to the Dene, but some principles can be laid down. First, given the observed failure of the government to come anywhere near to appropriating fully economic rents in the North and the apparent intention to continue to operate that way for the indefinite future, there is a good deal of room for the Dene to appropriate rents at no cost to the great majority of southern Canadians, who are not shareholders in the oil and mining industries, but solely at the cost of reducing the super-profits of the corporations. Second, the Dene would have the right to forgo rent by vetoing projects, or short of that, compelling changes in them that would increase costs to the companies and hence lessen the rents available for appropriation. A specific variant on this – which has received the tentative blessing of the Science Council[10] – would be to discourage new town sites particularly for mines, and generally encourage the flying in and out of personnel from the south; this would presumably increase the costs to the companies, but would not necessarily increase the true social costs which include large costs for infrastructure, mostly borne not by the companies but rather by governments and individuals. Third, if rents accruing to the Dene are to be justified by some criteria based on need – that is, the Dene should get enough but not too much – then the criteria implicit in this analysis are simply what is necessary both to provide capital for community-based economic development – until it becomes viable and self-sustaining and has created full employment in the communities – and to permit the ongoing subsidization of Dene institutions. If schools are included in the latter because the Dene were to so wish, then it should be borne in mind that there is no necessary net cost to society since the schools are now funded by the government rather than by the Dene themselves. A final observation on this third principle is to remind ourselves that aboriginal peoples have a tradition of sharing; in spite of statements sometimes made to the contrary, there is no evidence the Dene are asking for a "king's ransom."

A major theme of this paper is that a concern with *economic* development compels us to concern ourselves with *political* control. In institutional terms this implies, in the context of a land settlement, both the right of the Dene to create their own institutions and the need to limit full political rights to long-term residents of the North; specifically, the logic of this argument, though focused on the economic, strongly supports a residency rule for participation in local and territorial elections, such as the ten-year residency rule proposed by the aboriginal organizations.

CONCLUSION

The most persistent argument used by developers, private and public, is that large-scale resource projects serve the "public interest." If the residents of the region where the project is to take place object, in the final analysis they are put down by appeal to the public interest. This is justified by saying that the "national interest" must override the "regional interest," with the reality for contemporary large-scale energy resource projects being that the relevant regional interest is the "aboriginal interest." The aboriginal interest – which is real -is then disposed of either by saying, in effect, that it must, regrettably, be overridden, or by asserting that in some long-run sense the two interests are really identical. Yet, virtually without exception, the massive energy projects underway or planned for Northern Canada serve outside needs – and by that I mean needs external to Canada. So the choice is not, in fact, simply between the national interest and the regional aboriginal interest. Typically, in this century, there is the overriding American, or continental, interest, and it cannot be simply assumed that what serves the American interest automatically serves the national interest. In terms of the applicants, Arctic Gas clearly serves, first and foremost, the American interest, since it wishes to transport natural gas from one part of the United States to another part of the United States – a kind of contemporary version of the Panama Canal. Foothills, properly viewed, serves the continental interest, since an alternative to its pipeline for some time at least – and which could have been done some time ago – is to eliminate exports of gas to the US; furthermore, were it to get the government nod then, like Arctic Gas, it would have to go to bed with the same US-controlled producing companies. Also, the Arctic Gas proposal, and now Foothill's Fairbanks corridor proposal, appear to hinge on a treaty with the US guaranteeing safe passage of American gas through Canada; the erosion of Canadian sovereignty implicit in such a treaty is reminiscent of the bygone era of the DEW-line in the North.

A significant dimension of the choice, then is choosing between the interests of non-Canadians and the interests of aboriginal people who are Canadians; it is of the essence of the nature of the nation-state that it should be biased in favour of its own citizenry.

It is not only the North, as the "new frontier," which is driven by the imperatives of staple production. So too, after close to four centuries, is Canada as a whole. We cannot forever grow by expanding into new geographic frontiers, for we are running out of places to go – and there is little merit in emulating the example of the US after its frontier closed around 1890, which finally landed it in Vietnam. The time may not be too far distant when some considerable restructuring of the Canadian economy, away from its staple-export-bias to meeting the needs of Canadians to a greater extent within itself, will be necessary. In any event, it is long overdue, and the need for a humane approach to further northern development is the best possible reason for beginning the task of restructuring now.

Many aboriginal people in this country are in their present impoverished position because of what has been done to them in the past. We can specify the mechanisms of underdevelopment by which the damage has been done. We can work out the means by which these mechanisms can be transformed into mechanisms of development. What excuse can there be for not doing it? Aboriginal peoples, right across Canada, self-evidently need control over their own economic development. That does not mean a stark choice between either "traditional" activity or wage-employment with non-aboriginal controlled enterprises. There is a third way, the way of alternative development.

The Dene assert that starting a pipeline prior to a land settlement would gravely prejudice that possibility. It is difficult to see how it could be otherwise. The companies ask: how can we avoid prejudice? The answer, which is understandably rejected by them, is that their very presence in the North before the Dene have reclaimed their historic rights, constitutes prejudice. They did not come with the consent of the Dene, so they should not be there. If they wish to be there, and to stay there, they must try to strike a bargain with the Dene. The role of the government is to let this happen, to give the Dene the space they need – the geographic space and the political space – knowing that what redounds to the benefit of its least prosperous citizens must ultimately redound to the prosperity of the democratic state.

NOTES

1 H.A. Innis, *Empire and Communications* (London 1948).
2 Rene Fumoleau documents how the Klondike gold rush led to the signing of Treaty 8 in 1899, and how Imperial Oil's discovery of oil near Fort Norman led to the signing of Treaty 11 in 1921 (*As Long as This Land Shall Last: A History of Treaty 8 and Treaty 11, 1870–1939* (Toronto, 1975)). It would be difficult to find clearer cases of government policy as a response to the needs of staple producers, and there is no reason for believing that the current land-claims process amounts to anything different.
3 Russ Rothney and Steve Watson, "A Brief Economic History of Northern Manitoba," (mimeo 1975), iii. They insist on the need to pay attention to

"restrictions on local social and economic development generated by institutional processes of surplus extraction in the region. These processes hinge upon specific relations between social-economic classes and between commercial metropoles and their economic hinterlands."

4 John Palmer, *Measurement of the Value of Economic Activity in the North* (Ottawa: Department of Indian Affairs and Northern Development 1974).

5 Arvin Jelliss, "The Loss of Economic Rents," in Mel Watkins, ed. *Dene Nation: The Colony Within* (Toronto: University of Toronto Press, 1977), 62–74.

6 Peter Douglas Elias, *Metropolis and Hinterland in Northern Manitoba* (Winnipeg 1975).

7 Hugh Brody, *The People's Land: Eskimos and Whites in the Eastern Arctic* (London, 1975), 229. On tendencies toward the emergence of a class structure along ethnic lines in the Western Arctic, see Peter Usher, "Geographers and Northern Development: Some Social and Political Considerations," *Alternatives* (Autumn 1974) and "The Class System, Metropolitan Dominance and Northern Development," a paper presented to the Canadian Association of Geographers, Vancouver, 1975.

8 K.J. Rea, *The Political Economy of the Canadian North* (Toronto, 1968) and *The Political Economy of Northern Development*, Science Council of Canada Background Study No.36 (Ottawa, 1976).

9 Fumoleau, *As Long as This Land Shall Last.*

10 Science Council of Canada, *Discussion Paper on Northern Development* (Ottawa 1975).

4

Canadian Capitalism
in Transition (1997)

Why are some countries rich, some countries poor, and others in
between? Why, even in the rich countries, are some years good,
with the economy booming, and other years bad, with the economy
stagnating or even falling back? These matters have concerned the
great political economists from Adam Smith in the eighteenth century to Karl Marx in the nineteenth to John Maynard Keynes and
Joseph Schumpeter in the twentieth.

As well, countries grow and suffer crises in different ways – not totally different, of course, but at least somewhat. In the best of circumstances, the result will be an indigenous political economy tradition
that grasps the nettle of that distinctiveness. Such has been the Canadian experience, from the old political economy earlier this century,
led by Harold Adams Innis and W.A. Mackintosh, to a new political
economy of recent years, with myriad contributors.[1]

Questions abound. Canada is a rich country, unambiguously so
by global standards (which does not mean that there are no poor
people in Canada, for there are many – indeed, indefensibly so,
given that overall level of affluence). How did it get that way?

Reprinted from Wallace Clement, ed., *Understanding Canada: Building on
the New Canadian Political Economy* (Montreal: McGill-Queen's University
Press, 1997), 19-42. Part of section I is omitted here.

Canada is noted for the abundance of natural resources, or staples, and its reliance on their export. Has that situation given a particular character or specificity, to the economy, while providing an important clue as to how growth has taken place, at least initially and perhaps even down to the present day? (How much does history count? How much does an economy's condition depend on where it was? In fact, economists who study economic growth do talk increasingly about "path dependency.") Staple exports have tended to set the pace for the economy, sometimes fast and sometimes slow. How have different staples left their distinctive stamp on Canadian society?

Canada is an industrialized country: its prime minister is allowed to attend the prestigious annual economic summit of the seven leading industrial nations of the world. But does the flip side of the staples cast of the Canadian economy give it the least-rounded industrial structure of the seven? (The now-defunct Science Council of Canada called the nation's industrial structure "truncated" and was abolished for such frank talk.)

Canadian political economists since Innis have been at pains to expose the branch-plant character of this pattern of dependent industrialization. The means of production in Canada are predominantly in private hands, but many of those hands are foreign. Canada is a capitalist country, and its capitalist, or business, class is dominant. But what is the nature of that class? Is it predominantly commercial or industrial, independent or dependent?

A striking feature of the half-century of economic history since the Depression and Second World War, both globally and in Canada, is the long boom of the 1950s and 1960s down into the 1970s and the generalized crisis thereafter. Political economists in general, and the Canadian practitioners in particular, have been much preoccupied with this phenomenon. There have for years been those (such as the Russian economist N.D. Kondratieff and Joseph Schumpeter) who saw such long waves, of some fifty to sixty years, going back to Britain's Industrial Revolution more than two centuries ago.[2] Mackintosh's post-Confederation economic history of Canada was premised on recurring booms and crises associated with the changing fortunes of staples exploitation[3] – what Innis graphically called "cyclonics." The question for the nineties: is the last crisis over, or has the next boom begun?

STAPLE THEORY OF ECONOMIC GROWTH

A persistent theme in the writings of the new political economists is that there are two variants of the staples thesis – a more optimistic version (going back to Mackintosh) of growth around a staples export base, culminating in a mature diversified economy, and a more pessimistic version (going back to Innis) of staples exploitation generating "rigidities" that reproduce economic vulnerability and dependence.[4] While it is possible to overstate the differences between Innis and Mackintosh (and lose the nuances in both), the point at issue is crucial: how mature has the Canadian economy become? Can it still sensibly be described as a staples economy?

In fact, these queries beg a prior question that must be frankly faced: to what extent does the emphasis on staples capture the totality of the Canadian growth experience since the beginning? The answer is that there has always been much by way of "local growth" that escaped the net, but staples such as fish and fur "dominated" the early economic history of Canada.[5] The economy of what is today Canada has been from its Euro-Canadian beginnings an integral part of a larger North Atlantic economy and has tended to grow and fluctuate with it;[6] the edge that has made the difference (good and bad) has been the varying fate of the staples trades and industries. Yesterday's "local growth" (home production for home markets) has become, in the modern era of free trade, export-dependent manufacturing and service industries (a point to be dealt with below). Comparatively, Canada has done better than staples-biased economies such as Argentina and Australia, in part because of an abundant endowment of hydro-electric potential and fossil fuels, plus the ability to shift from agricultural staples such as wheat to industrial staples such as minerals and newsprint.[7]

Still, a recent overview of Canadian political economy, after citing the apparent importance of manufacturing and tertiary activities, concludes:

This is not to say that the Canadian economy is now any less reliant on natural resource-based production to generate its wealth than it was in the past. Much of Canada's manufacturing base consists of processing resource-based commodities such as lumber, pulp and paper, and various mineral and oil-based products ... In all, resource and resource-based activities generate as

much as fifty cents out of every dollar produced in this country. This continued reliance of the Canadian economy on primary resources and resource-
based manufacturing puts it at odds with the situation in many other large
nation-states and has important consequences for the operation of the Canadian political economy.[8]

The new political economy is arguably a marriage of Innis and
Marx, of staples and class.[9] The staple bias affects the capitalist class
(as we see below); it also affects the rest of the class structure. A distinction must be made between the earlier staples – trades – and
the later ones – industries.[10] The direct producers in the staples
trades are not a working class, or proletariat proper, but independent commodity producers, varying from aboriginal bands in the
days of the fur trade to family farmers producing wheat. Conflict
takes place around the terms of the exchange of the staple for
trade-goods and interest paid on debts incurred by the direct producers; surplus is appropriated by capital via the mechanism of unequal exchange. The protest movements of western grain farmers
are ample evidence of these conflicts, from which flowed important
political and economic effects. In contrast, the staple industries,
such as mining and newsprint production, are industries proper,
with workers who are paid a wage over which they typically bargain
collectively through a union, with surplus value being appropriated
in the customary, Marx-described manner. From these conflicts
emerge important consequences for wage structures and hence for
living standards and for technological change; as an example, high
wages create a larger domestic market for consumer goods while
encouraging labour-saving innovation and (frequently) the import
of capital goods.
  It should not be forgotten, however, that whether the staple activity is a trade or an industry, capitalism makes the struggle of the
direct producers with capital unequal. Canadian capital has not
been able to formulate a full-fledged industrial strategy (see below); not surprisingly, neither Canadian farmers nor Canadian
workers, separately or together, have been able to assume that
task in its stead.[11] The project becomes truly daunting when allowance is made for the divisiveness of the intense regionalism
characteristic of the Canadian economy; that regionalism seems
to inhere in the strung-out, bi-national Canadian economy, but it

is further exacerbated by the uneven development associated with specialization in staples. The result has been, typically, to divide people, or popular forces, more than capital.

The distinction between staples trades and industries can be pushed one step further by examining the consequences for social or class formation of the particular mode of production associated with each staple. Like Innis, one would keep one's eye on the staple and its mode of production and the pervasive consequences; like Marx, one would systematically explore the relationships between the mode of production and class structure.[12] The American development economist Albert Hirschman calls this approach micro-Marxism.[13]

In the process one could, following Hirschman, judge the staples in terms of whether their impact for growth and development have been good or bad. Of course, what happens depends in some part on the environment, physical and political, within which the staple has its impact; fish created both the "aggressive commercialism" (Innis) of New England and the staple trap in which contemporary Newfoundland is mired now that the fish have disappeared (but from which it may be rescued by new staples; see below). As Ommer reminds us in her superb study of the historic Jersey-Gaspé cod fishery, the staple that leaves the colony underdeveloped can create development in the metropole; indeed, as in her case study, the two go together.[14] Still, some staples do seem mostly good from the perspective of the margin (such as wheat and the family farm and the egalitarian society and progressive politics that flows therefrom),[15] while others seem mostly bad (as with oil, which produces instant, unearned wealth and giant companies and right-wing politics and pollution).[16]

But assessment of goodness or badness also very much depends on where one is situated within the social formation. Consider the fate of aboriginal peoples. From this perspective it is arguable that only the fur trade has a claim to have treated them tolerably well; all subsequent staples, from wheat to hydro, have taken their home lands and rendered them dysfunctional. Some staples, like hydro megaprojects, may simply be genocidal and intolerable, but others might well be beneficial to aboriginal peoples if they occur within the context of a land-claims settlement that granted genuine self-governance and created a different institutional framework; the Berger Inquiry in the 1970s can be seen as exploring the possibility that even a giant gas pipeline might be acceptable to the Dene of the Mackenzie Valley under those circumstances.[17]

Consider also the consequences for women of the effects of different staples. In traditional historical writings, including that of the old political economy, women hardly existed, yet we know that aboriginal women played a key role in the fur trade and that the "family" of the "family farm," which grew the crops for consumption at home and abroad, self-evidently included women and their unpaid labour. As well, the single-industry resource communities that dot the Canadian hinterland (the pulp towns, the mining towns) provide limited opportunities for women to work at well-paying jobs.[18]

DEPENDENT INDUSTRIALIZATION

How does a staples economy come to be characterized by dependent industrialization? Begin with a general argument about early industrialization that has been made with respect to Britain and to continental Europe.[19] There are two paths to industrialization: one that emerges out of artisanal beginnings in the hands of new capitalists, and one based on the extension of pre-existing merchant capital into the new industrial sphere. The first is the strong path, which leads to a mature industrial structure; the second is a weak one, where industrial capital never comes fully to dominate financial capital.

Can this line of reasoning be applied to Canada? There are two problems in doing so. First, Canada's economy was dominated in its pre-industrial phase not simply by commerce and finance but specifically by trade in the staples. Second, Canada industrialized later, after capitalism had transformed itself from a competitive mode to a monopoly mode as a result of the rise of the large corporation, including its multinational variant.

Canada ends up on the weak path. Merchant-cum-financial capital remains dominant and tolerates, indeed invites in, foreign industrial capital to produce a weak path of dependent industrialization. Canadian financial capital may even be antagonistic towards indigenous industrial capital. But the critical point is the rise next door of the American industrial corporation; it is born multinational and, as the agent for foreign monopoly capital, creates barriers to entry for smaller, indigenous industrial firms.[20] Previously the technique of the more advanced United States had moved to Canada (or British North America) via the migration of individual American businessmen, who then become permanent residents, even founders of great Canadian families such as the Masseys; now it came in institutional corporate form. The result was to stifle indigenous Canadian development which, emulating the United States, had been proceeding, with a lag, along the strong path. Canada was shunned onto the weak path. The villain of the piece becomes American industrial capital, though Canadian capital can be seen as an accomplice.

The path of dependent industrialization was, for reasons we have seen, one of import substitution, of producing for the protected domestic market rather than taking on world markets in manufactures. While we may see that as second best, we risk missing the point that Canadian capital pioneered the import substitution industrialization model – it is in fact known elsewhere, particularly in Latin America, as the "Canadian model" – and that Canada has done remarkably well out of it in conjunction with the large domestic market associated with a succession of staple exports.[21]

The result is not an alliance within Canada between indigenous financial and industrial capital (creating, in Marxist terminology, finance capital) with industrial capitalists as the dominant, or hegemonic, fraction within the capitalist class. Rather, there is an alliance between Canadian financial capital and American industrial capital. Because of the size and power of the United States, the resulting alliance is (in Clement's felicitous phraseology) an "unequal alliance," with Canadian capital a junior partner. Within Canada, the hegemonic fraction remains financial capital.

This is almost, but not quite, the full story. Because Canada is a staple economy, we should distinguish within industrial capital between staple industries, or primary manufacturing, and secondary manufacturing proper. The former can be, and in fact are, more powerful than the latter. The hegemonic fraction is made up of financial capital and of staple capital, foreign and domestic, which is in alliance with American industrial capital. This "staples fraction," in fact, is disproportionately represented with the Business Council on National Issues (the highly influential organization that consists of the chief executive officers of the 150 largest private-sector corporations) and the structures of the state. As a consequence, the secondary manufacturing interest is weak in Canada, and it is difficult to develop an industrial strategy. Though Canada is industrialized, industry is in important respects immature and the country remains a staples economy – a pattern that has been called "advanced resource capitalism."[22]

Canadian capital has accepted a division of labour both sectorally and geographically. Historically, it has been able to dominate in commerce and finance, including infrastructure and real estate, but not in industry proper. In the staple sector the story is mixed, with the majority of resource industries under foreign control well into the postwar period. In those sectors where capital is able to dominate at home, it will have a base to try to become "world class" and operate abroad. This phenomenon exists in Canada, but the division of labour that constrains Canadian capital is its tendency to see only the American market, not the whole world as its oyster.

There is clearly a close, symbiotic relationship between the nature of the domestic business and the extent of foreign ownership of the economy; the weaker the former, the stronger the latter, and vice versa. (Canadian policy has been to let the foreigner in to undertake the tasks that Canadian business cannot do; Japan's policy has been not to let the foreigner in until Japanese business has demonstrated that it can compete.) And just as other class forces could not "get their act together" concerning the tariff, neither were they sufficiently strong and united to force Canadian capital to perform better than it did; in explaining the origins and persistence of foreign ownership in Canada, Gordon Laxer indicts the whole Canadian class structure![23]

Foreign ownership became an important political issue in Canada in the 1960s – under the leadership of the Liberal economic nationalist Walter Gordon – and the debates about it were central to the emergence of the new political economy.[24] Yet the ink had hardly dried on this literature when there was a considerable decrease after 1970 in foreign (mostly American) ownership and control of the Canadian economy relative to Canadian ownership and control. This outcome raises the possibility that the Canadian capitalist class is now – and perhaps long has been – more impressive than some of us have thought.[25]

Canadian ownership within the resource sector has increased (relatively) as domestic capital has been attracted by the large rents that can be appropriated. This development shows some maturing of Canadian capital, but towards becoming more efficient as rentier capital, rather than as industrial capital. Perhaps, as well, Canadian capital became more confident in its dealings with American, as the latter struggled to maintain its international hegemony vis-a-vis Japanese and European capital. While increasing Canadian control in the past quarter-century has mostly been relative to American, it has made Canada a base for continental rather than for global capital. And while dependence via foreign ownership decreased, dependence via trade increased, with the latter definitely rising under free trade and the former no longer falling (see below). In short, Canada did not transcend its staple-biased, semi-industrial status, nor its pervasive Americanization (and all that follows therefrom) in matters economic, political, social, cultural and military.

Research on Canadian class structure in a comparative context bears out these propositions. Canada's industrial and occupational composition – with fewer workers in manufacturing and a larger resource proletariat than the average industrialized country – bears the imprint of truncated development. But Canada has also incorporated distinctively American practices for the organization of capitalist production, deploying a disproportionate amount of labour power in control and surveillance of other workers, particularly in sectors traditionally dominated by American capital.[26]

An unexpected vindication of the political economy view of foreign ownership in particular and the Canadian economy in general is to be found in the so-called Porter Report, named after Professor Michael Porter of the Harvard Business School and co-funded by the Business Council on National Issues and the Mulroney government. The Canadian economy, we are told, has an abnormal bias to the export of unprocessed resources, a high and increasing reliance on the US market, a high level of foreign ownership, and a tendency among subsidiaries of foreign firms not to be efficient exporters. The report recommends policy directed towards transforming subsidiaries into more autonomous and efficient "home bases"[27] – but the exact opposite may be happening under free trade (see below).

BOOMS AND CRISES

An important problem facing social scientists and historians, and hence political economists, is the choice of the proper spatial and temporal units for study. On the spatial dimension, our (material-ist) argument relies on the reach of the commodity and the corpo-ration; the Canadian experience is therefore comprehensible only within a centre-margin, or imperial frame of reference.[28] With re-spect to the temporal dimension, social scientists tend to be almost obsessively present-minded and uninterested in history, while histo-rians tend to reify politics, even politicians, or rely on arbitrary peri-ods, such as centuries. Political economists need to take both economics and history seriously and define politics broadly.

There is merit in relying on long waves as the temporal unit for study.[29] Just as a fundamental characteristic of capitalism is that it has developed unevenly over space (centres and margins), another is that it has unfolded unevenly over time (booms and crises). As well as having shorter recessions and recoveries, the post-1945 ex-perience has lent new credibility to the view that longer cycles, or long waves, of boom and crisis, also seem to inhere in the evolution of industrial capitalism. In so far as each phase seems to encapsu-late a broad range of economic, political, and social phenomena that encompasses both institutions and technology, and to be com-mon to linked economies, it is highly useful as a discrete entity for the study of political economy.[30]

Take the most recent long wave (which may or may not be over as I write or as you read this). The global boom of the late 1940s, 1950s and 1960s has been called the Golden Years (Hobsbawm) and hailed as the greatest period of economic growth and prosper-ity in the history of capitalism. The boom was very strong in Can-ada, being comparable to the great wheat boom that lasted from the mid-1890s to the First World War. It was based on large-scale exports of resources to the United States, with inflows of American capital providing funds to expand staple sectors – including such new staples as oil and gas, iron ore, uranium and potash – and with markets secured by foreign ownership ties; its essence was neatly captured in the title of a book of that time, Hugh Aitken's *American Capital and Canadian Resources*.[31] Cheap energy, notably oil, fuelled the global boom; Canada, as a major consumer and exporter of en-ergy, stood to gain, whatever the price. Demographically, the "baby boom" and waves of immigration fed consumption and investment.

Both the staples bias of the economy and the pattern of depen-dent industrialization persisted, though altering in ways beneficial to Canadian economic growth at that time. With the decline of the British Empire, Canada moved wholly into the American empire at a time when the United States was the undisputed hegemonic power of the capitalist world. The close American embrace created clear benefits for Canada, while entrenching its staple status. It also caused some problems, notably in the military and automotive sectors, where imports systematically outran exports. US policy towards Canada, however, was largely benign; special-status arrangements such as the Defense Production Sharing Agreement (DPSA) of 1958 and the Auto Pact (1965) locked Canada into a pattern of dependent industrialization that was nevertheless significantly beneficial to Canada. The DPSA allowed Canada to cash in on the Pentagon spending, magnified by the Vietnam War, that played a key role in the American boom, while the Auto Pact permitted auto factories in Canada to achieve the economies of scale of the so-called Fordist production model of the postwar world.

Demand-led Keynesianism came to Canada but, notwithstanding its apparent potential to produce greater emphasis on the domestic market as the prime source of growth, did little to alter the staples bias of Canadian economic policy. But in Canada, as elsewhere, it did legitimize a much expanded welfare state (to provide a safety net and to maintain demand and hence employment) and underlay a new accord between capital and labour, in which workers were allowed increased rights to unionize and to share in productivity gains in return for abandoning any radical demands for widespread nationalization or workers' control.

Sometime around 1970 this greatest of booms petered out. Demand for Canadian staples slowed, and the birth rate fell, lessening the demographic push on demand. The United States lost the war in Vietnam and in 1971 had to devalue the dollar; it was no longer the hegemonic power in had been, having to give ground to Germany and Japan industrially and to the Organization of Petroleum Exporting Countries (OPEC) on the setting of the price of oil. The United States could no longer afford to be so benign, even to Canada; in the face of its troubles, Washington, as part of its broader policy of detente, first gave Canada more room to manoeuvre in the 1970s – leading to the modest economic nationalism of the Trudeau era – and then, with Reagan and the new Cold War, forced Canada to abandon such policies in the 1980s.[32] With the election of the Mulroney government in the mid-1980s, Canada was ready to "buy into" the US neo-conservative agenda of free trade and no economic nationalism.

The pressure from workers to increase both their wages and the social wage (the benefits of the welfare state) while companies tried to maintain their profit rates and the well-to-do their privileged position led to inflation that persisted even in recessionary times; the resulting "stagflation" broke the Keynesian compromise. The leap in globalization that resulted from the long boom increased the mobility of capital – both lessening the ability of any nation state to tax it and pushing up interest rates in order to prevent its flight. But labour remained mostly immobile and the state retained its ability to tax it. At the same time, workers in high-wage countries such as Canada were increasingly subjected to low-wage competition from abroad.

The good times for the many were over. Recessions became deeper and longer. Unemployment became persistent, and inflation was kept under control by the threat, and reality, of its increase. First, the private sector "downsized" – a process greatly facilitated by the burgeoning electronic technology; in the new post-Fordist world of flexible specialization, economies of scale were replaced by economies of scope, pyramidal structures tended to erode, and there was devastation in labour markets. Second, in the face of accumulating deficits and debt consequent on the poor performance of the private sector, the public sector shrank and began to dismantle the welfare state. From the 1980s into the 1990s, a new, right-wing consensus emerged, insisting that if the "fundamentals" were put right (in all senses of that term), the economy could again prosper.[33]

Less writing has been done of prior long waves in Canada, but enough is known to suggest their existence and the value of further study of them. Three prior long waves have been detected since Britain's Industrial Revolution: good years from the 1780s to circa 1815 and bad ones to circa 1850; a good phase from circa 1850 to the early 1870s and a bad one thereafter to the mid-1890s; and good years from the mid-1890s to the First World War and bad ones until the Second World War. For Canada, the second and third waves seem to have applied. The boom of the 1850s, associated with exports of lumber and wheat and the building of railways, marked the beginning of real industrialization in British North

America, while the Canadian economy slowed perceptibly in the 1870s and 1880s and unto the 1890s, awaiting settlement of the west and the surge of prairie wheat exports. With the turn of the century came the wheat boom and the Klondike Gold rush, floods of capital and people and railways galore, and a major surge in industrialization. The interwar years were troubled times, from the uncertainties of the 1920s to the Depression of the 1930s, as Canada made the difficult adjustment from the "old industrialism" of coal and iron, wheat and railways, to the "new industrialism" of oil and autos, hydro, newsprint and minerals.[34] And then the last long wave – and the question: is it over?

THE SITUATION TODAY

By the early 1980s, the Canadian economy seemed to have reached an impasse. Its staple bias and dependent, often inefficient industrial structure were impossible to ignore. Keynesian policy was passé. The Trudeau government toyed with post-Keynesian policies, not only of wage and price controls, but also of an activist energy policy and industrial strategy. Free market, neo-conservative policies had triumphed in Britain under Margaret Thatcher and in the United States under Ronald Reagan. With the election of the first Mulroney government in 1984 they came to Canada.

The core of right-wing policies in Canada was free trade, first the Canada-United States Free Trade Agreement of 1989 and then the North American Free Trade Agreement of 1993. Sold as an industrial strategy that would make Canadian manufacturing efficient, it may well be entrenching the staple status of the Canadian economy. The removal of barriers to trade permits each country to pursue more fully its comparative advantage. For Canada, already strong sectors (such as staples) grow further, while weak sectors (such as secondary manufacturing) shrink. Certainly the latter has happened, though a good part of that has to be attributed to the serious recession of the early 1990s and a misguided monetary policy that led to an overvalued Canadian dollar. Significantly, bilateral trade disputes between the United States and Canada, which were supposed to go away, have not. American interests still try to block rising resource imports from Canada. Predictably, the volume of two-way trade has taken a quantum leap upwards.

Cross-border investment flows have likewise increased; the two-decade decline in the level of foreign (American) ownership of the Canadian economy seems to have ended. American-based multinationals have tended to meld their previously separate Canadian production operations into a US-based North American division; head offices of subsidiaries have been shut down in Canada, and jobs lost. Overall, the Canadian economy has been further and decisively integrated into the American economy; the result has been an increased economic dependence of Canada on the United States that may result in greater political and cultural dependence.

In the face of its declining hegemony globally, the United States has moved to increase its hegemony continentally and how hemispherically; Canada is almost certainly more tightly tied than before. At the same time, greater continental economic integration has increased strains on the Canadian federation by increasing the potential for separate regions to "go it alone"; free trade has arguably advanced the case of Quebec separatism.

If staples remain critical for Canada's fate, we need to know the prospects for staples. Resource "megaprojects" – significantly, the word is a Canadianism – seem to be facing increasing objection from environmentalists and aboriginal peoples; James Bay II is a case in point. There has also been some concern that the best Canadian resources have been found and the Third World is the new frontier,[35] but recent years have seen discoveries of vast amounts of nickel-cobalt-copper in Labrador, of diamonds in the North West Territories, and of Hibernia-like oilfields off the west coast of Newfoundland.

The era of the Keynesian consensus – of the Keynesian welfare state (KWS for short; actually, the "w" does double duty, standing also for warfare) – is dead. What is taking its place? It is apparently being replaced, according to British writer Bob Jessop, by the Schumpeterian workfare state (SWS).[36] For Schumpeter, entrepreneurship and innovation were central to economic growth. They were the creative side of "creative destruction" that inhered in the process of capitalist development; "competitiveness," the buzz-word of our times, conjures up both the good (the drive for efficiency) and the bad ("downsizing" and low-wage competition). Keynesianism legitimized larger, positive government; Schumpeterianism delegitimized government. Keynesianism was consistent with assistance for the unemployed and the poor; Schumpeterianism wants to replace "welfare" with "workfare."

If that is indeed what is happening, the emerging arrangement is hardly a thing of beauty.[37] But that is not the crux of the matter. Rather: will it work? Is the world economy stable in the absence of a hegemon? Is the story of the mid-1990s the collapse of the Mexican peso, or the fact that the collapse was contained? Has the inflation that destroyed the KWS finally been brought under control?[38] If that has been done by permanently driving up unemployment, then how does the SWS deal with that? If income distribution becomes more unequal, will there be enough purchasing power to buy the cornucopia of goods? Will the SWS deliver enough of the goods to enough of the people to be viable long enough to constitute another long boom? (A question for the student reader: are your job prospects becoming more or less miserable?) Beyond all this, is it possible that the computer is an innovation on par with the printing press, with effects that will hardly be sorted out quickly? Is it also possible that the environmental consequences of past industrial growth have already begun to place limits on further economic growth?

As for Canada, the historian Donald Creighton wrote a long time ago of "the embarrassments peculiar to a staples-producing economy." The moral of this paper is that we have hardly seen the last of those. Still, we must not overstate our problems; as too many people in this world know, there are fates much worse than embarrassment.

NOTES

1 For a collection of Innis's writings, see Daniel Drache, ed., *Staples, Markets and Cultural Change: Selected Essays of Harold Innis* (Montreal: McGill-Queen's University Press, 1995). For Mackintosh, see in particular his "Economic Factors in Canadian History," *Canadian Historical Review* 4 (1923): 12–25, reprinted in M.H. Watkins and H.M. Grant, eds., *Canadian Economic History: Classic and Contemporary Approaches* (Ottawa: Carleton University Press, 1993); and *The Economic Background to Dominion-Provincial Relations*, Appendix III of the Royal Commission on Dominion-Provincial Relations, 1939; reprinted with an introduction by J.H. Dales, Toronto: McClelland and Stewart, 1964). For a bibliography on the new political economy, see Clement, ed., *Understanding Canada*.

2 The great Marxist historian Eric Hobsbawm has organized his brilliant new book on the twentieth century, *Age of Extremes: The Short Twentieth Century, 1914–1991* (London: Michael Joseph, 1994), around these waves. He writes: "[A] succession of 'long waves' of about half a century in length has formed the basic rhythm of the economic history of capitalism since the late eighteenth century" (268).

3 *Economic Background.*

4 See especially the voluminous writings of Daniel Drache on Innis, notably "Harold Innis and Canadian Capitalist Development," *Canadian Journal of Political and Social Theory* 6 (1982): 35–60 and, most recently, his "Introduction" to Drache, ed., *Staples.* See also Irene M. Spry, "Overhead Costs, Rigidities of Productive Capacity and the Price System," in William H. Melody, Liora Salter and Paul Heyer, eds., *Culture, Communication and Dependency: The Tradition of H.A. Innis* (Norwood, NJ: Ablex Polishing, 1981), 155–66.

5 See R. Cole Harris, "Preface," in R. Cole Harris, ed., *Historical Atlas of Canada, Vol. I: From the Beginning to 1800* (Toronto: University of Toronto Press, 1987).

6 This point has largely escaped Canada's historians who write as if Canada were a self-contained entity; perhaps the major moral of the staples approach – where Canada is necessarily a margin of an imperial centre – is that Canadian history cannot be usefully written that way.

7 C.V. Schedvin, "Staples and Regions of Pax Britannica," *Economic History Review* 43 (1990): 533–59.

8 Michael Howlett and M. Ramesh, *The Political Economy of Canada: An Introduction* (Toronto: McClelland and Stewart, 1992).

9 For an attempt to reduce Canadian political economy to Marx alone, see David McNally, "Staple Theory as Commodity Fetishism: Marx, Innis and Canadian Political Economy," *Studies in Political Economy* 6 (1981): 35–64, and "Technological Determinism and Canadian Political Economy: Further Contributions to a Debate," *Studies in Political Economy* 20 (1986): 161–70. The two articles fail to generate a single fresh insight about Canadian political economy. For a reply to McNally's first article, see Ian Parker, "Commodity Fetishism and 'Vulgar Marxism': On 'Rethinking Canadian Political Economy,'" *Studies in Political Economy* 10 (1983): 143–72.

10 This distinction is to be found in Innis; for its fuller articulation, see Paul Phillips, "Staples, Surplus and Exchange: The Commercial Industrial Question in the National Policy Period," in Duncan Cameron, ed., *Explorations in Canadian Economic History: Essays in Honour of Irene M. Spry* (Ottawa: University of Ottawa Press, 1985), 27–43.

11 For an analysis of such problems associated with the tariff in the earlier period, see Paul Craven and Tom Traves, "The Class Politics of the National Policy, 1872–1933," *Journal of Canadian Studies* (Autumn 1979) 14–38. In general, see Gordon Laxer, *Open for Business: The Roots of Foreign Ownership in Canada* (Toronto: Oxford University Press, 1989).

12 This is precisely what Wallace Clement has done in his studies in nickel mining and the fisheries. See his *Hardrock Mining: Industrial Relations and Technological Change at Inco* (Toronto: McClelland and Stewart, 1981) and *The Struggle to Organize: Resistance to Canada's Fishery* (Toronto: McClelland and Stewart, 1986).

13 Albert Hirschman, "A Generalized Linkage Approach to Development with Special Reference to Staple," *Economic Development and Culture Change* 25 (1977): 67–98.

14 Rosemary E. Ommer, *From Outpost to Outport: A Structural Analysis of the Jersey-Gaspé Cod Fishery, 1767–1886* (Montreal: McGill-Queen's University Press, 1991). Ommer contrasts the "success" of Iceland around fish with the relative "failure" of Newfoundland in "What's Wrong with Canadian Fish," *Journal of Canadian Studies* 20(3) (Fall 1985): 122–42.

15 See Mel Watkins, "Wheat as Staple," *Business History Review* 67 (1993): 280–87.

16 As I write in the Summer of 1995, there are stories in the press about how, with oil prices falling, the "oil-rich superpower" of Nigeria, "riddled with corruption," is "a nation committing suicide."

17 See in particular James B. Waldram, *As Long as the Rivers Run: Hydroelectric Development and Native Communities in Western Canada* (Winnipeg: University of Manitoba Press, 1988); Mel Watkins, "Dene Nation: From Underdevelopment to Development," in this volume; and T.R. Berger, *Northern Frontier, Northern Homeland: The Report of the Mackenzie Valley Pipeline Inquiry* (Ottawa, 1977; rev. ed. Toronto: Lorimer, 1988).

18 See Bonnie Fox, "Women's Role in Development," in Gordon Laxer, ed., *Perspectives on Canadian Economic Development* (Toronto: Oxford University Press, 1991), 333–52; Sylvia Van Kirk, *"Many Tender Ties": Women in Fur Trade Society, 1670–1870* (Winnipeg: Watson and Dwyer, 1980); and Meg Luxton, *More Than a Labour of Love: Three Generations of Women's Work in the Home* (Toronto: Women's Press, 1980).

19 Notably by the Marxist historian Maurice Dobb in *Studies in the Development of Capitalism*, rev. ed. (New York: International Publishers, 1964).

20 There are two writers on this matter, R.T. Naylor and Wallace Clement. While there are differences between them, together they are responsible for the Naylor-Clement thesis, which is the idea that launched the new

Canadian political economy. Their work is discussed in Mel Watkins, "The Staple Thesis Revisited," in this volume.

21 Glen Williams, *Not for Export: Toward a Political Economy of Canada's Arrested Industrialization.* 3rd ed. (Toronto: McClelland and Stewart, 1994).

22 The term is Drache's; see his "Staple-ization: A Theory of Canadian Capitalist Development," in Craig Heron, ed., *Imperialism, Nationalism and Canada* (Toronto: New Hogtown Press, 1977), 15–33.

23 Laxer, *Open for Business.*

24 See Canada, Privy Council Office, *Foreign Ownership and the Structure of Canadian Industry* (the Watkins Report), (Ottawa, 1968) prepared under the tutelage of Walter Gordon; and Kari Levitt, *Silent Surrender: The Multinational Corporation in Canada* (Toronto: Macmillan, 1970).

25 See Jorge Niosi, "The Canadian Bourgeoisie: Towards a Synthetical Approach," *Canadian Journal of Political and Social Theory* 7(3) (Fall 1983): 128–49.

26 This paragraph is a précis, mostly in the authors' words, of Don Black and John Myles, "Dependent Industrialization and the Canadian Class Structure: A Comparative Analysis of Canada, the United States and Sweden," *Canadian Review of Sociology and Anthropology* 23 (1986): 157–81; see also Wallace Clement and John Myles, *Relations of Ruling: Class and Gender in Postindustrial Societies* (Montreal: McGill-Queen's University Press, 1994), especially chap. 4.

27 Michael E. Porter and the Monitor Company, *Canada at the Crossroads: The Reality of a New Competitive Environment* (Ottawa, 1991).

28 The subtitle for Innis's *The Cod Fisheries* is *The History of an International Economy* (1954; rev. ed. Toronto: University of Toronto Press, 1978).

29 See David M. Gordon, Richard Edwards and Michael Reich, *Segmented Work, Divided Workers: The Historical Transformation of Labor in the United States* (Cambridge, England: Cambridge University Press, 1982).

30 This is what F.W. Burton had in mind when he wrote in 1934: "In Canada ... we must think if business fluctuations not simply as 'credit cycles,' that is, as rhythmic and purely monetary phenomena, but also as chapters in our national economic development" ("The Business Cycle and the Problem of Economic Development," in H.A. Innis and A.F.W. Plumptre, eds., *The Canadian Economy and Its Problems* (Toronto: University of Toronto Press, 1934), 143–58.

31 See also Melissa Clark-Jones, *A Staple State: Canadian Industrial Resources in Cold War* (Toronto: University of Toronto Press, 1987).

32 Stephen Clarkson, *Canada and the Reagan Challenge: Crisis in the Canadian-American Relationship* (Toronto: Lorimer, 1982; rev. ed., 1985).

33 There is a large literature on the postwar long wave. See in particular David Wolfe, "The rise and Demise of the Keynesian Era in Canada: Economic Policy, 1930–1982," in M.S. Cross and G.S. Kealey, eds., *Modern Canada, 1930–1980s* (Toronto: McClelland and Stewart, 1984), 46–80, and "The Crisis in Advanced Capitalism: An Introduction," *Studies in Political Economy* 11 (1983): 7–26; Robert M. Campbell, *Grand Illusions: The Politics of the Keynesian Experience in Canada, 1945–1975* (Peterborough, Ont: Broadview Press, 1987); Frank Strain and Hugh Grant, "The Social Structure of Accumulation in Canada, 1945–1988," *Journal of Canadian Studies* (Winter 1991–92), 75–93; Jane Jensen, "'Different' but not 'Exceptional': Canada's Permeable Fordism," *Canadian Review of Sociology and Anthropology* (1989) 69–94; Daniel Drache and Harry Glasbeek, *The Changing Workplace: Reshaping Canada's Industrial Relations System* (Toronto: Lorimer, 1992), especially chap. 2; and Stephen McBride, *Not Working: State, Unemployment and Neo-Conservativism in Canada* (Toronto: University of Toronto Press, 1992).

34 The terms are Innis's. For the post-Confederation period to the 1930s, see Mackintosh *Economic Background* and "Economic Factors;" for the longer period, see Maurice Lamontagne, *Business Cycles in Canada: The Postwar Experience and Policy Directions* (Toronto: Lorimer, 1984), particularly chap. 4. Burton ("Business Cycles," 153) writes: "The expansion of staple production and of transportation facilities has been rapid in good times; with a reversal of conditions, the distress of the staples industries has been severe."

35 See Paul Phillips, "New Staples and Megaprojects: Reaching the Limits to Sustainable Development," in Daniel Drache and Marc Gertler, eds., *The New Era of Global Competition: State Power and Market Power* (Montreal: McGill-Queen's University Press, 1991), 229–46.

36 Bob Jessop, "Towards a Schumpeterian Workfare State? Preliminary Remarks on a Post-Fordist Political Economy," *Studies in Political Economy* 40 (1993): 7–39.

37 In August 1995 the United Nations rated Canada the world's number 1 country – at a time when the unemployment rate hovered around 10 per cent and one of five Canadian children lived in poverty.

38 Inflation, and the "necessity" of fighting it, undermined the Keynesian attempt to "pump-prime" the French economy in the early 1980s and helped in the 1990s to push Sweden–with its highly developed KWS–into abandoning a central commitment to full employment; see Andrew Glyn, "Social Democracy and Full Employment," *New Left Review* 211 (1995): 33–55.

PART TWO

Trade and Investment

In Mel Watkins' interpretation of the staple thesis, the theme of economic and political dependency is brought to the fore. The economic dependency that arises out of a heavy reliance on raw material exports may, in the most immediate sense, involve a vulnerability to the whims of primary commodity markets, notorious for their price and demand volatility. In the longer term, it may involve the consequences of relying upon foreign capital, technology, and entrepreneurship and the barriers they impose to the creation of a more diversified, dynamic economy. The political ramifications range from the restrictions upon pursuing independent fiscal and monetary policy, with pressure to accommodate foreign firms and harmonize social policy, to more fundamental questions about national sovereignty. The five papers in this section outline the changing dimensions of Canada's historical dependency and the political options for pursuing economic nationalism.

The starting point for any such discussion is the "National Policy" of the late nineteenth century – the much heralded development strategy of railway construction, land settlement, and protective tariffs – designed to fend off American economic encroachment. Frequently held out as an example of an activist state engaged in "nation building," the first paper on the "American System" offers an important qualification. While Canada chose not to follow Britain's lead towards freer trade in favour of emulating American protectionist policy, it stopped short of introducing the educational and financial reforms undertaken by several European countries in order to foster a more highly skilled work force and a domestic entrepreneurship. There was, therefore, a viable third – more activist – option, designed to break the economic control of a colonial oligarchy and its predilection for "sound finance," that was not pursued.

The second paper – "New National Policy" – is a concise summary of the main arguments in the "Watkins Report." It begins with the observation that the dominant feature of the Canadian economy after World War II was the high percentage of foreign ownership. Partially a legacy of the old National Policy and the proclivity of high tariff walls to create "Canadian industries but not Canadian firms" (107), its current institutional expression is the multinational corporation. The capacity of international firms to move resources around the world tended to exacerbate the international division of labour and magnify the costs of dependency for the staple producer.

During the debates over free trade in the 1980s, it might have appeared that the central focus had shifted back to the tariff. The overview of "The Canada-US Free Trade Agreement," however, makes clear that trade agreements were not primarily about trade *per se* but about the free movement of international capital, unencumbered by traditional tools of government regulation. "Reflections on the Watkins Report" reiterates the central role of foreign investment and the multinational corporation in determining the direction of the Canadian economy since World War II and the political possibilities of a nationalist alternative.

The last paper in the section strikes out on a slightly different, but related, path. "The Car" may seem like an odd point of departure for a discussion of Canadian political economy, but the automobile has several iconic properties. First, it has long been symbolic of the deficiencies of the Canadian manufacturing sector, with its inability to produce a "Canadian-made" car. Second, it is an enigma in Canadian trade policy, with the Auto Pact resulting in the rationalization of North American automobile production within the context of "managed trade." Third, it has led to the development of a strong national trade union that has sought to play a role in shaping trade policy. The paper thus picks up on other central Innisian themes – the bias of technology and, more explicit in his latter work, the bias of communication – and offers the automobile as a contemporary illustration.

5

The "American System" and Canada's National Policy (1967)

> It must always be borne in mind that the economic model to which Canadians looked was the United States and there they had seen a great internal expansion facilitated by canals and railways and expressing itself in widening frontiers and growing towns and metropolitan centres.
>
> W.A. Mackintosh[1]

So much has been written about Canada's National Policy that would be entitled to be skeptical as to whether anything worthwhile remains to be said. This paper properly begins with an attempt at self-justification.

An examination of the literature suggests that it is not yet definitive. Much of it, as produced by Canadian political historians and economic historians suffers from parochialism. One can almost be convinced from some accounts that Sir John A. Macdonald invented the high protective tariff and consequently deserves to be either canonized or damned. It would be unfair and misleading, however, to say that American influence has been ignored; the opening quotation, which is not atypical, would itself undermine such an allegation.

Nevertheless, American influence on the National Policy has received insufficient attention, by both quantitative and qualitative criteria. Partly what is absent in the literature on the National Policy is simply sufficient emphasis on the United States to impress the

Reprinted, with minor revision, from the Canadian Association of American Studies, *Bulletin* 2(2): (Winter 1967) 26–42, which expressed indebted to Alan Bowker for research assistance and to Abraham Rotstein for helpful suggestions.

unwary reader with the importance of that dimension. Partly the
problem is that the United States has been seen much more in
terms of a threat to Canada, requiring a national policy as a Canadian response, than as providing an example to be emulated; the
issue, at this level, is a matter of proportion and perspective,
though the nature of the threat posed by the American corporation as the embodiment of entrepreneurial energy has not been
properly understood.[2]

Furthermore, certain "obvious" topics have, as far as I know,
been neglected. For example, what image did Canadians have of
the United States in the years when they were devising a national
policy that most writers concede drew heavily on American prece-
dent and practice? To what extent were Canadians *consciously* emulating the United States? How did the Canadian political parties
which, particularly on the issue of tariff, were usually at loggerheads, cope with the "facts" of the American experience? To what
extent were the "facts" correct? In particular, even if American national policies were accurately understood, were other ingredients
in the American growth process – such as the vitality of private entrepreneurship and the absence of constraints on banking – perceived as relevant to Canada?

There is a final difficulty. Even when reasonable allowance has
been made for the existence of the United States, it has rarely been
characterized – or so it seems to me – by a sufficiently clear-eyed
view of what America "really" has been – and is. The premises of
the liberal, bourgeois society, the institutions it destroyed and created, and the inherent power exercised by its example, have received little attention from Canadian historians with their suspicion
of "ideas" and of ideologies. As a result, the consequences for Canada of copying the American model, particularly in terms of opportunities foregone, have not been adequately appreciated. Were
there alternatives to the National Policy which would have worked
as well, or perhaps even better, to satisfy Canadian aspirations?

This paper, then, attempts, albeit cryptically, to speak to these
deficiencies. It does so in the rhetoric of the neglected art of
political economy.

The title of this paper suggests a universe comprised of two entities: the American System and the National Policy. Neither term is
unambiguous in its meaning, and an attempt at clarification is both
necessary and pedagogically useful.

The American System was an economic prescription advocated by Senator Henry Clay of Kentucky in the third quarter of the nineteenth century, which rejected what he referred to as the "colonial" or "foreign" system of free trade. The protective tariff was to be used to encourage American industrial development and urbanization which, in turn, would fostered a home market for domestic agriculture. Other policies that Clay supported, such as the use of public funds for internal improvements and role of the Bank of the United States to maintain a stable, national currency, were also identified with his American system although he "never joined these together into a nicely articulated whole." According to van Duesen "underlying all of these proposals was his aim of building up the wealth and power of the Republic, of shaping for the United States a grand destiny that would be carved out in proud independence from old Europe. The system in its broader aspects was a concept that had little room for fear of a strong central government, but rather regarding it as an agency to be used for promoting the public welfare. It was the dream of a nationalist."[3]

Canada's National Policy, in a literal sense, began, of course, as the high protective tariff of Sir John A. Macdonald in 1879, and for some it continues to mean simply that. But historians, particularly economic historians, have been using the term for some time to include as well transportation policy, and immigration and settlement policy. Of late, the tendency has been to broaden yet further. As R. Craig Brown observes, "the spirit of the National Policy went much deeper than railways, immigrants, and tariffs. Beneath these external manifestations was the will to build and maintain a separate Canadian nation on the North American continent."[4] The "nationalism of the national policy" has been made explicit, and so too its similarity to the American System.[5]

The major policy instruments of both the American System and the National Policy were the protective tariff, national support for transcontinental railways, an open-door immigration policy, and a land policy designed to encourage settlement and build railways. In so far as American policy consistently preceded Canadian policy, there is a *prima facie* case that Canada imitated and did not innovate. The extent of the imitation, and its appropriateness – and particularly the latter – are, however, important issues which merit systematic examination.

The so-called "Tariff of Abominations," which marked the first peak of the protective tide in the United States, preceded Macdonald's famous 1878 amendment to the Budget by half a century. In the debate on that amendment, and subsequent debates on the tariff, both advocates and opponents were indeed conscious of the fact that Canada was copying the prime ingredient of the American system. Conservatives attributed the successes of the American economy to the tariff, while Liberals charged "servile imitation" and maintained that, in consequence, Canada would suffer from such alleged American afflictions as more serious crises, "over-stimulation of manufactures" with consequent increases in the number of unemployed and of "tramps," and the corruption of political life. The "American fact" could be disputed – though those who did were to languish in the Opposition – but it could not be ignored. At the same time, Canadian protectionists could, and did, cite other examples, particularly Bismark's Germany. In 1859, Galt defended his tariff of "incidental protection" with the claim that he was rejecting the American system in favour of "the European system." By 1878, the drift of the world economy toward protection was clearer – a drift, however, substantially based on appeal to American secular prosperity – and it was possible for Macdonald to use not only the stock argument that Britain had adopted free trade only after establishing its preeminence through protection, but that, within his lifetime, Britain would abandon free trade.

Canadian resort to protection is hardly surprising. Indeed, given the appeal of the tariff to countries wishing to industrialize and the limited number of instruments available to nineteenth-century governments for promoting industrialization, what needs to be emphasized is the slowness with which Canada moved to protection. The half-century lag behind the United States is symptomatic of backwardness, in terms both of economic and political aspirations, and of tolerance of state action. Having finally cast the die in 1879, however, Canada, with the zeal of the late convert, made of the tariff more than it deserved. As proof of "fiscal autonomy," it became "proof" of independence within the Empire. A device adopted in the midst of depression to restore prosperity by preventing American manufacturers from dumping in Canada – "The sweepings of the manufactories of Buffalo were sold in our markets to crush our people" (Macdonald) – became an instrument that was expected to create self-sustained economic growth. By linking the tariff with the building of railways, it came to be seen as foolproof; if the tariff provided protection, it would enhance manufacturing, increase freight for the railways and eliminate railway deficits, while if the tariff earned revenue, customs duties could be used to meet any deficits incurred by the railway as domestic manufacturing suffered in the face of imports. It is only slight exaggeration to say that the tariff became a substitute for the non-existent flag, and the result was to give it the character of the sacred. Inflation of its economic worth lessened the likelihood of a broad view being taken of national economic planning, while the inflation of its political worth sharpened the materialistic hue that was anyway characteristic of nationalism in "the age of Darwinism and industrialism."[6] Having belatedly followed the United States in the adoption of the protective tariff, it was to become much more an article of faith for Canadians than it ever did for Americans.

The American spirit of public improvements, as manifested in canals and railways, imprinted itself on the Canadian consciousness. In the area of railway promotion, American example was followed most slavishly. The Grand Trunk fiasco had given British railroading a bad reputation. American transcontinentals were not only the obvious model, but the only clearly relevant one. The threat of the American railway – to Canadian carriers generally and control of the Northwest in particular – left little room for response other than to fight fire with fire. As with the tariff, however, the fire got out of control. When, in 1880, Macdonald stated in the House "although the plan of the American Government in railroad building is precisely the same as our own, still, wherever ours varies in practice to that of the American System, it is on the side of greater liberality," he displayed the patriotism and the purse that were eventually to turn Canadian railway policy into a frenzy of overbuilding.

Canadian homestead regulations, as set out in Dominion Order in Council of 1871, borrowed heavily from the American Homestead Act of 1862. The latter, however, had drawn inspiration from Simcoe's land policy in Upper Canada. Furthermore, both American and Canadian land policy drew jointly on Australian and New Zealand experiments. Not only was there "Canadian content," the policy was effective in doing what mattered: preventing speculation and encouraging settlement. The direct promotion of immigration through the activities of agents abroad was effective, at least as

measured by the numbers who came when the economic opportunities existed – while it had the incidental benefit of creating an
embryonic trade commissioner service which was, in turn, an embryonic diplomatic corps.

   The separate consideration of each policy instrument has its limitations. It is necessary to see the policies, for each country, as a set,
or package, which constituted an overall "plan," and to consider
both the effectiveness with which the separate policies interacted to
create a national economy and polity, and why the boundaries of
the set were drawn the way they were.

   It was the intent of the proponents of both the American System
and the Canadian National Policy to facilitate economic growth
and enhance nationalist sentiment. Modern economists define economic growth simply as rising income per capita, but at least in
nineteenth century North America, it is more properly seen as rising *aggregate* income, expanding population and spatial extension,
which might then be expected to bring in their train improvements
in the standard of living through economies of scale and spreading
of social overhead costs. In a context of highly-elastic supply curves of
labour and capital via immigration and foreign borrowing, and of a
continuing potential for growth through the borrowing and adaptation of European, particularly British, technology – and of American technology for Canada – the national policies of both the
United States and Canada were appropriate for creating extensive
economic growth. At the same time, however, some aspects of policy, such as the height of the tariff, may have created a tendency toward the lowering of per capita income.[7] Also, the policies more
clearly facilitated extensive growth than initiated it, while acting so
as to worsen the boom-and-bust character of the North American
economy. In Canada, aggregate growth rates were slow for two decades after the tariff of 1879, and recovered only in response to
favourable conditions in world markets; thereafter, the levels of immigration and capital inflow are characteristic of a boom that
tended to get out of hand and to overshoot in the years immediately prior to World War I.

   Expanded interregional trade was regarded by both Americans
and Canadians as a critical dimension of economic growth with
favourable political overtones. Exploiting the complementarities of
regions was the nineteenth century version of "balanced growth."
Though reflecting in part simply a prevailing faith in economies of

scale, the emphasis on interregional trade was critical both because of its appeal to all sections of the country and because it provided the missing link between the vested power of agriculture, as the old environment, and the emerging power of industry, as the new environment. Significantly, both Clay and Macdonald in their advocacy of industrialization, placed a high priority on the need to create a home market for agriculture. So strong was the desire to "balance" growth regionally that we find, in the Confederation Debates, that speakers extol the virtues of sectional complementarity in the United States, notwithstanding the Civil War and its vivid demonstration of the dominance of an industrialized region over an agricultural region. The distorting prism through which the United States was viewed is nowhere more evident, particularly when one recalls that, throughout the Debates, the Civil War was constantly being cited as evidence of the need for a strong central government, and of the power of the industrial North which was the threat to the British North American colonies which compelled Confederation.

The national policies of both countries had political as well as economic goals. An economic historian speaks with less confidence of political matters, but it could hardly be disputed that, without respect to cause, American nationalism was potent stuff at least by the middle of the nineteenth century. Indeed, American economic policy to create extensive growth, that is, of an expansionary variety, seems to be more a symptom of preexisting nationalism than an instrument to create nationalism, though the spatial extension of the economy necessarily brought with it the spatial extension of the polity and heightened feelings of nationalism. In Canada, on the other hand, the National Policy, as evidenced in embryonic form by the tariffs of 1858 and 1859, preceded the creation of the polity and became, as suggested earlier, a flag around which to rally. The need for national policies became a rationalization for Confederation and for centralizing power relative to the provinces – and relative to the United States. After Confederation, a protective tariff designed to increase interregional trade worked also to exacerbate strife between regions specialized in export industries advocating free trade and regions specialized in import-competing industries advocating higher tariffs. Nevertheless, the set of national policies gave substance to the polity as a spatial entity and, directly and indirectly, enhanced Canadian nationalism. If Canadian nationalism had – and has – its quantitative and qualitative limitations, the fault lies less with the national policies that were pursued than with the failure to conceive of national planning in broader terms.

If not explicitly, then implicitly, any national "plan" includes a monetary policy. The American System as conceived by Clay included a major role for the Bank of the United States to maintain monetary stability. In fact, under the tidal wave of Jacksonian democracy, the Bank was swept away and with it much of the potential for central control of currency and banking in the interest of stability. The result, however, was not runaway inflation, but an increase in the supply of credit which increased the rate of economic growth.[8] The capacity of the American system to generate economic growth was increased by amputating its predilection for "sound" banking. In British North America, however, the banking system was based on Hamiltonian principles, modelled on the First Bank of the United States, and so remained. The American System was adopted as Canada's National Policy on the basis of what it had been in rhetoric rather than what it had turned into in practice. The plaudits which the Canadian banking system has received for its stability are not inconsistent with a view that its operation has not necessarily been in the best interests of rapid economic growth.[9]

The transformation of the American banking system not only increased the supply of credit, but unleashed within the banking sector the very entrepreneurial forces which had played a critical role in engineering the transformation.[10] To alter the structure of finance capitalism is to have pervasive consequences going well beyond the direct effects – which were presumably favourable – on the rate of economic growth. The "festival of *laissez-faire*" that gripped the banking sector diffused generally, or was, at least, symptomatic of a broader transformation of the American economy.[11] The money centre shifted from Chestnut Street to Wall Street and political control over the economy shifted from established interests to "new men." The lingering power of colonial oligarchies was ended in the North; even in the South the cotton aristocracy was riddled by *nouveaux riches*. What was involved was that basic transformation of American society – that decisive flowering of the liberal bourgeois fragment – that passes under the rubric of Jacksonian democracy.[12]

Analogously, the failure of the Canadian banking system to transform reflected the absence of societal transformation and the continuing grip of colonial oligarchies. In contrast to the

American "pattern of transformation," Canada remained in a "pattern of persistence."[13] Canada copied the forms of the American System, but a vital part of the substance was not imported and did not emerge spontaneously.

The Canadian rejection of the "excesses" of Jacksonian democracy is well known, but the implications for the political economy of Canadian development have not received sufficient attention. The simplicity of Canadian economic and political development prior to the National Policy had permitted an elite to hold power, and an American-style national policy was successfully imported without substantially lessening the grip of the elite. Rapid economic growth took place in spite of the absence of political and social transformation because of favourable terms of trade for Canadian staple exports and the willingness of American corporations to extend the American technological frontier into Canada. Private entrepreneurship in Canada remained deficient and, Canadian historiography notwithstanding, the deficiency was not made up by public entrepreneurship. The absence of private entrepreneurship created a vacuum to be filled by government, and the nature of political control that underlay the strengthened government was not to prove conducive to the growth of indigenous private entrepreneurship. It is highly significant that the market opportunities defined by the tariff – and the tariff does nothing more than define market opportunities – were, from the beginning, exploited by American entrepreneurs. The branch plant economy of today can be detected in embryonic form by the 1880s. The deficiencies of Canadian private entrepreneurship were offset not by Canadian public entrepreneurship but by American private entrepreneurship, and the long-run consequences for the Canadian economy and polity have been considerable. The Canadian elite failed to appreciate the extent to which the new technology was more than the railway. It built the railways and ran the banks but did little else. Its limitations are evident in the fact that, with firm control of the polity, it let control of the economy slip into American hands to the point where the polity became eroded. It failed to appreciate American manifest destiny operating via the penetrative powers of the price system. Canadian national policy remained firmly in the hands of a closely-knit elite committed to use the state to create economic development, but not at the risk of weakening elite control. High tariffs and lavish railway subsidies expressed the limits of political action.

In the United States, the operation of the American System undermined the central authority espoused by Clay, but the desired
development of the economy and polity not only took place in
spite of this but because of this. In Canada, central authority was
maintained but the conventional view that this increased the potential for government action should be placed against the view
that the continuation of elite control reduced the likelihood of
government action. The reputation of the federal government for
decisive action in the nineteenth century rests on its response to
the American "threat," but a state that intervenes in economic affairs only when threatened externally has a limited vision of the
role of government.

The Canadian emulation of the American liberal, bourgeois society has been biased toward the elitist. The obvious opportunity
foregone has been to be more American. The point is known to
every Canadian, and a significant number have, over the years,
chosen that option by emigrating. Paradoxically, Canadian economic historians have lately moved to the view that the stifling
character of Canadian life might have been avoided by a choice of
free trade rather than protection in the nineteenth century. While
to take this argument literally would exaggerate the role of the tariff, it is a valid line of reasoning if the tariff is used as shorthand
for the pervasive protective mentality characteristic of elite control. But to see the alternatives as simply a choice between free
trade and protection is to fall into the same trap as did the Canadian political parties in the post-Confederation period and to dis-
play too limited a perspective.

The choice between free trade and protection was, in effect, a
choice between the "British system" and the "American system" –
and was so seen at the time – and it is hardly surprising that the
American system was chosen on the grounds of relevance. But was
there perhaps a third possibility, the "European system"? Canadian
tariff exponents cited European examples – presumably thereby
obscuring the charge of slavish imitation of the American system –
but the depth of their understanding of European developments
appears slight.

At least from present perspective, the major lessons of the economic history of Continental Europe are: the more active role of
national governments that in either Britain or the United States,
with state action being greater the more backward the economy;

the important role played by the investment bank, which added entrepreneurial and management functions to the traditional banking functions; and the importance of technical education, particularly in Germany which industrialized more rapidly than any other Continental country.[14] Canada might have learned from those lessons. The Canadian economy was more backward than the American and the need for state action therefore greater. The European-style investment bank would have circumvented the choice between the stability of British banking and the intolerable freedom of American banking. The Canadian suspicion of American mass education and preference for the elitist British system – and, in Quebec, the appeal of theology and law – reduced both the quantity and quality of education with consequent neglect of science and technology relative to the United States, Britain and Continental Europe. A serious commitment to education would have equipped Canadians to deal more adequately with the new technologies, and would have prevented the charge that can be made even now that the Canadian elite prefers to turn on the immigration tap when the labour market is tight rather than make a genuine attempt to improve the skill-level of the Canadian labour force.[15]

The major theme that evolves from this paper is that the conventional statement that the Canadian government has played an active role in promoting economic development obscures more than it enlightens. In fact, a government under elite control tends to neglect activities that might threaten that control and, in the Canadian case, to be self-satisfied if it does more than its American counterpart. Arguably, the Canadian government, rather than being praised by historians for what it has done, should be chastised for what it has failed to do.

NOTES

1 W.A. Mackintosh, *The Economic Background of Dominion-Provincial Relations* (1939; Toronto, Carleton Library, 1964).
2 H.G.J. Aitken, "Defensive Expansionism: The State and Economic Growth in Canada" in Aitken (ed.), *The State and Economic Growth* (New York, 1959).
3 C.G. Van Deusen, *The Jacksonian Era 1828–1824* (New York, 1959).

4 R. Craig Brown, *Canada's National Policy 1883–1900* (Princeton, Princeton University Press, 1964).

5 R. Craig Brown, "The Nationalism of the National Policy," in Peter Russell (ed.), *Nationalism in Canada* (Toronto: University of Toronto Press, 1966).

6 Brown, "The Nationalism of the National Policy."

7 J.H. Dales, "The Cost of Protectionism with High International Mobility of Factors", *Canadian Journal of Economics and Political Science* (1964); and "Protection, Immigration and Canadian Nationalism," in Russell (ed.) *Nationalism in Canada*.

8 A.H. Conrad, "Income Growth and Structural Change," in S.E. Harris (ed.), *American Economic History* (New York, 1961).

9 Bray Hammond, *Banks and Politics in America* (Princeton: Princeton University Press, 1957).

10 Hammond, *Banks and Politics.*

11 Hammond, *Banks and Politics*; W.T. Easterbrook, "Long Period Comparative Study: Some Historical Cases," *Journal of Economic History* (1957).

12 Louis Hartz, *The Founding of New Societies* (New York, 1964).

13 Easterbrook, "Long Period."

14 A. Gerschenkron, *Economic Backwardness in Historical Perspective* (Cambridge, Mass., 1962).

15 John Porter, *The Vertical Mosaic* (Toronto, 1965).

6

A New National Policy (1968)

The old National Policy served Canada in its day, as an instrument of nation-building and a means of facilitating economic growth. The challenges have changed and a new National Policy is required. The nation has been built, but its sovereignty must be protected and its independence maintained. A diversified economy has been created, but its efficiency must be improved and its capacity for autonomous growth increased.

The "Watkins Report"[1]

National Policy could mean simply the policy of a national government. But in Canada, National Policy means the Canadian system of protective tariffs as enunciated by Sir John A. Macdonald in 1878. Both historians and economic historians have, over time, tended to broaden the term to encompass the set of policies pursued by the Canadian government in the late nineteenth and early twentieth centuries in the interests of promoting economic development – tariffs, railway subsidies and all-Canadian transcontinentals, cheap land, and an open door to immigrants.[2] But few would deny that the tariff was central to the strategy of promoting Canadian industrialization; certainly it has been the prime issue in the debate over economic nationalism, or economic independence, that reached an early peak in the campaign of 1878 and has gone on ever since.

Among academics, a serious difference of opinion persists to the present day about the efficacy of the National Policy. Historians seem to be virtually unanimous in their view that the tariff was an invaluable instrument of nation-building and that economic

Reprinted, with minor revision, from "A New National Policy" in Trevor Lloyd and Jack McLeod (ed.), *Agenda 1970: Proposals for a Creative Politics* (Toronto: University of Toronto Press, 1968).

nationalism was necessary to political independence and the creation of a national economy. Economists, on the other hand, have tended to imply at least that the National Policy, by lowering the standard of living, weakened the material base on which political independence must stand and on which continuing economic growth must be based.[3] Economic historians, including this writer, have not been fully identified with either camp. Their most articulate spokesman on the tariff has vehemently attacked it for its evil effects on the quality of Canadian life while nevertheless providing a rationale for it by arguing that if fulfilled its mercantilist (but misguided) goal of creating a larger population and aggregate income in Canada.[4]

There would be general agreement, however, that the National Policy, in terms of its relevance, is now a thing of the past. While there is still immigration to Canada, the great population-absorbing frontiers are closed. The railway is now the old technology and its potential for nation-building exhausted – though it may have untapped potential for urban and inter-urban passenger transport. The protective tariff clearly lingers on and is far from irrelevant to the contemporary economy and polity. Nevertheless, it is a remnant from the past in the important sense that the Canadian government has been consistently committed to multilateral tariff reduction since the Second World War as part of a broader commitment to multilateralism. Differences of opinion among Canadians seem largely to be with respect to the rate at which the tariff should be abolished, and the manner – unilaterally, bilaterally, multilaterally, or selectively by sector. The vanguard of the abolitionists has been the economists, while Ottawa has preferred to let other countries set the pace toward multilateral free trade and has been intrigued by selective arrangements, such as that with the automobile industry.

There are, then, no longer any hot advocates of tariff protection. In so far as tariffs are its content, economic nationalism is hardly a viable creed. But history does not stand still and so it is that the central issue of economic independence today, pro and con, is foreign ownership.

Now foreign direct investment – foreign investment that carries with it ownership and control – is not a new phenomenon in Canada. Indeed, its roots were firmly planted in the period of the old National Policy. The Canadian tariff segregated the Canadian market and induced industrialization behind its wall to serve that market. Foreign firms, previously exporting to Canada, now found it necessary to shift production to Canada. Specifically, Macdonald's protective tariff induced a spurt in branch plants, particularly American-controlled subsidiaries, in Canada. The call implicit in the tariff to bring forth entrepreneurship to meet new opportunities in the Canadian market fell frequently on foreign ears. In sum, the tariff created Canadian industry, but not necessarily Canadian entrepreneurship, and hence not necessarily industry under Canadian ownership and control.

The full implications of this point have largely escaped attention by Canadian academics. Historian, including economic historians, have not addressed themselves in a serious way to the question of why the tariff created Canadian industries but not Canadian firms. Some credit for the existence of these industries must clearly be given to the expansive drive of American corporations; as they spread nationally in the late nineteenth century, some spill-over across the northern border was presumably inevitable. But to some extent those corporations flowed into a vacuum resulting from an entrepreneurial failure in Canada, a deficiency existing in spite of the St. Lawrence merchants who had emerged around the fur trade and who have been so much praised by Canadian historians.[5] Economists, in Canada and elsewhere, have judged the tariff in terms of its effects on economic efficiency and have had little of a convincing nature to say about its effects on economic growth. In particular, there has been a curious reluctance to recognize that national economic development – within the capitalist framework – requires domestic entrepreneurs, or a native bourgeoisie, to lead the process of growth.[6] While economic historians have generally been somewhat more realistic, Canadian economic historians have learned so much by focusing on the commodity – the so-called staple approach associated in particular with the writings of Harold Innis[7] – that other approaches, particularly the entrepreneurial, have never been pushed far enough to be credible alternatives.[8]

It is true that one of the most honoured themes of Canadian historiography, including economic history, has been that the state has played an important role in promoting and shaping Canadian economic development, that, as it were, the national government has played the leading role.[9] In this historical scenario, the deficiencies of private entrepreneurship have been compensated for by public entrepreneurship. But the point has clearly been exaggerated, as the extent of the actual reliance on foreign entrepreneurship attests. It would be more accurate to argue that a national government allied with the private elite was committed to use the state to create economic development, but not at the risk of weakening elite control; high tariffs and lavish railway subsidies expressed the limits of political action, while, significantly, education, particularly business schools, and freer banking – which might have facilitated the rise of new domestic entrepreneurs – were neglected. It can be argued that the Canadian government, rather than being praised for what it has done, should be chastised for what it has failed to do. More public entrepreneurship, in its own right and to stimulate private entrepreneurship, was needed to fill the vacuum which was created by the deficiencies of private entrepreneurship and which was filled by foreign, particularly American, entrepreneurship.[10]

The economist's critique of the tariff, and the old National Policy, needs to be re-examined in these terms. The problem with the tariff was not that it was too much, but rather that it was too little. Instead of creating a Canadian bourgeoisie capable of leading Canadian growth it tended to create only an emasculated bourgeoisie satisfied to manage a branch-plant economy.[11] The tariff, as it were, created "infant industries," but not "infant firms."[12] And foreign firms, once attracted in by the tariff, had a vested interest in its perpetuation, while their very presence inhibited the emergence of Canadian firms.

To the extent that one is willing to accept the view presented here – that a successful national policy, including tariff policy, should have created Canadian entrepreneurship capable of dominating the Canadian economy – then the prime task of the old National Policy is yet to be completed. The burden of this paper is that this should be seen as the central task of a new National Policy, and that other aspects of policy, including tariff policy, should be framed in this light.

THE COSTS OF AN EMASCULATED BOURGEOISIE

Let us now put foreign ownership at the centre of the stage. We must begin by recognizing that foreign ownership of Canadian economic activity is not simply a phenomenon induced by the Canadian tariff. This is true in two important senses. On the one hand, there is the straightforward fact of foreign ownership of much of

Canada's resource industries.[13] These industries, being export-oriented, do not owe their existence or their ownership to the Canadian tariff. Rather, they exist because of Canadian endowments and
foreign demand, and tend to fall under foreign control as a means
to ensure access to the foreign market, that is, the owner of the
firm is typically the buyer of its output.

The consequences of this, in terms of the thesis being argued,
are very significant. Resource industries are, after all, the source of
the staple exports which remain, down to the present day, the leading sectors and pace-setters in Canadian economic growth.[14] Such
is the role of foreign trade, particularly in the early stages of economic growth, in virtually all countries, that it can be argued that to
permit widespread foreign ownership of export industries is seriously to inhibit the creation of a domestic entrepreneurial class
and thereby to reduce significantly the possibility of autonomous
national development.[15] Admittedly, the case for domestic ownership of export industries is one of degree, for there is no gainsaying
that foreign ownership facilitates access to foreign markets, though
at the loss of marketing flexibility in the long run. But at least
in some cases, domestic ownership is likely to prove feasible – provided the attempt is made – and the major benefit, usually neglected by economists, of facilitating domestic entrepreneurship
would thereby be reaped. The present high level of foreign ownership of Canadian resources strongly suggests that Canadian policy,
both at the federal and provincial levels, has been insufficiently directed toward this goal.

The second important reason why it is wrong to attribute foreign
ownership in Canada simply to the Canadian tariff is that it ignores
the very significant institutional innovations that rare represented
by the evolution of the modern and above all the American, corporation.[16] At the same time as the railway was creating a new
potential for Canadian industrialization, it was also creating the
American giant corporation capable of exploiting the national
market shaped by the railroads. The proximity of Canada and the
tendency of American businessmen to regard Canada as not a foreign country facilitated the spread of the American corporation
across the Canadian border. The innovation of the corporation organized along functional lines in the late nineteenth century was
followed successively in the twentieth century by the innovation of
the multidivisional corporation organized along product lines and

the multinational corporation as an integrated entity producing in a number of countries. The latter has grown enormously since 1945, and most close students of this phenomenon are predicting continuing expansion.

To recognize these facts is to realize that no set of feasible Canadian policies could – or should – have tried to stop the entry of American corporations into Canada. The point is again one of degree. It is likely that the tariff acted to increase the extent of American ownership of Canadian manufacturing, but it is difficult to see how the absence of the tariff would have eliminated it. Rather, it would seem, along lines previously argued, that the basic determinants, from the Canadian side, were the deficiency of Canadian entrepreneurship and the failure to use public policy to encourage Canadian entrepreneurship and discourage foreign ownership.

It is, then, the combination of the Canadian tariff, Canadian resource endowments relative to American resource needs, and the entrepreneurial drive of the American corporation relative to Canadian entrepreneurial deficiencies which account for the present place of foreign, and particularly American, ownership in the Canadian economy. The extent of foreign ownership and control is too well known to require detailed presentation in this paper.[17] Suffice it to say that foreign corporations in 1963 owned more than half of Canadian manufacturing industries and almost two-thirds of mining and smelting and petroleum and natural gas, and that ownership was predominantly American. Not surprisingly, the opening sentence of the Watkins Report reads "The extent of foreign control of Canadian industry is unique among the industrialized nations of the world."

In the language of the economists, foreign direct investment creates both benefits and costs for host countries such as Canada.[18] While economic benefits resulting from our easier access to foreign technology, capital, entrepreneurship, and markets are difficult to measure with precision, it is clear that they are positive and have made a substantial contribution to Canada's present high standard of living.[19]

But there inheres in the process of reaping potential benefits from foreign ownership a variety of costs. One of these, much emphasized by the Watkins Report, is a simple failure to get as large benefits as possible because of inappropriate industrial policy in Canada. In particular, benefits are emasculated by the absence of sufficient competition in Canada to keep costs and prices down. There is a large literature by Canadian economists lending support to the view that this phenomenon is primarily attributable to the combination of a high tariff and a weak anti-combines policy. The possibility that the costs inheres in foreign investment in so far as the American industrial structure is imported into Canada, with a consequent proliferation of firms of less than optimal size, is less frequently admitted. But the basic fact underlying these arguments that is almost never made explicit is the deficiency, quantitative and qualitative, of indigenous Canadian firms. Foreign firms are not compelled to be efficient by the presence of efficient Canadian firms, and barriers to entry from foreign firms are low because of the absence of established and viable Canadian firms. Rather, foreign firms occupy markets and create higher barriers to entry for domestic firms, thereby inhibiting Canadian entrepreneurship. In this sense, the major "cost" of foreign ownership is not the emasculation of benefits *per se* but the emasculation of the Canadian bourgeoisie.[20]

It seems almost redundant to add that political consequences inhere in this economic nexus. At the first level of analysis – again providing a basic theme for the Watkins Report and drawing particularly on the thinking of Stephen Hymer and Abraham Rotstein – foreign investment implies control by large foreign-based corporations with a consequent tendency for the locus of decision-making to be outside the host country and to be more susceptibly to the policy of the home government than the host government.[21] Key decisions relevant to Canadians are made by Americans in board rooms in New York and conference rooms in Washington. But the basic fact is Canadian complicity in this arrangement consequent on the nature of a Canadian elite dominated by its emasculated business class. The Canadian bourgeoisie is fit only to live in a concessionary economy and the Canadian economy has explicitly taken on the character. Faced with the American interest equalization tax and American balance-of-payments controls on direct investment, Canada has sought "special status" at the cost of further diminishing its credibility as an independent country and further increasing its vulnerability to American retaliation – meaning chiefly American indifference to Canadian pleading – in the event of any Canadian initiative deemed unfriendly by Washington.

What kinds of economic policy have been proposed, particularly by Canadian economists, and, up to a point, practised, in the midst of these events? What may we already have by way of a new national policy? Essentially two things: monetary-fiscal policy and industrial policy. The former implies, following Keynes, the manipulation of the money supply and government spending and taxation in pursuit of the goal of full employment without inflation. While the Canadian government apparently committed itself to Keynesianism in the White Paper of 1945, its willingness to translate rhetoric into practice was slow and uneven. The major (perhaps only) contribution of the Carter Report of the Royal Commission on Taxation in 1967 may be simply that Keynes' General Theory, albeit as refined and emasculated by (liberal) neo-Keynesians, has now been translated into the Canadian vernacular. Unfortunately, the major contribution of the Economic Council of Canada in specifying the trade-off between the level of unemployment and the rate of price increase in Canada has been to show that the relevant variable is the performance of the American economy.[22] So far as pretensions to an independent monetary policy are concerned, Canada has been described as the 13th Federal Reserve District; and such are the constraints on fiscal policy that an increase in taxes to control inflation in Canada, as in the supplementary budget in the fall of 1967, is likely to leave Canadian prices unchanged, since the latter depend on the American price level, while at the same time increasing unemployment in Canada.[23] Monetary-fiscal policies remain important weapons to facilitate Canadian growth along the American growth path, but a neo-Keynesian National Policy – "let the price system work and lean against cyclical winds" – must not be confused with policies designed to create, or even maintain, Canadian independence vis-a-vis the American system. More bluntly, the capacity of the Canadian government to create jobs and keep inflation under control is negligible.

Canadians, aided and abetted by the Economic Council, have discovered a productivity gap between Canada and the United States – that is, that Canadians are on the average poorer than Americans – and have rationalized a set of industrial policies intended to rationalize Canadian industry in terms of its structure and performance: more and better education, particularly in management and vocational skills; more research and development; and effective anti-combines policy; and, above all, tariff reduction.

Industrial policy, so conceived, has serious limitations, both of omission and of commission. Notably absent is any policy toward foreign ownership other than the open door. Even when we are faced with the hard fact that Canadian industry is a miniature replica of American industry, it is steadfastly insisted that this results from the Canadian tariff and would disappear were the latter removed. The Economic Council has gone so far as to list seven factors which cause limited specialization within Canadian manufacturing without managing to stumble across foreign ownership.[24] Errors of commission, while less blatant, are nevertheless real. There is a failure to recognize that the neglect of R&D and of education are predictable symptoms of an emasculated bourgeoisie. There is a failure to see that a more vigorous Canadian anti-combines policy might inhibit the emergence of stronger Canadian firms able to challenge effectively the American-based giants and that, in any event, to move Canadian policy closer to American policy is not to guarantee real competition (the latter hardly being the most conspicuous feature of American capitalism).

Above all, there is a failure to recognize the limitations of tariff reduction as a policy weapon – for at least five reasons. First, in so far as the Canadian tariff has increased the population-sustaining capacity of the Canadian economy, the elimination of the tariff might reduce that capacity. To force emigration in the name of efficiency was widely practised by industrializing Europe in the nineteenth century but is curiously archaic as a twentieth-century policy. Second, to argue that lowering the Canadian tariff would increase competition in Canada via import competition is to ignore the extent to which the importers would be affiliates of Canadian firms whose pricing decisions are not predictable from assumptions of atomistic competition. Third, the tariff is an instrument of government policy and as such has virtue – that is, no government faced with a number of goals unthinkingly abandons a policy instrument. Economists advocating free trade, free capital movements, and, following Carter, a neutral tax system may be (unintentionally) weakening the capacity of the federal government, already hamstrung by the constitution, to pursue certain national objectives.[25] Fourth, while tariff reduction would provide some incentive to rationalize Canadian industry – indeed, in some cases at the risk of otherwise perishing – it does not in itself provide the means, be it capital, entrepreneurship, or planning, necessary for rationalization.

Finally, while the tariff facilitates rationalization, given the existing extent of foreign ownership, it must do so within multinational corporations and in a manner appropriate to their mode of operation. When foreign-based firms rationalize their Canadian operations, the decisions will be made in head offices outside Canada, and a pattern of specialization is likely to be adopted that will require more parent company control for the indefinite future. This point provides an answer to those people who sense that free trade must have political costs, but have difficulty specifying the channels of political influence. If fewer decisions are made in Canada by Canadians, that is a political cost – and this could very easily happen under free trade unless there is a strong national government.

There is undoubtedly a case for rationalizing the Canadian tariff structure, but only as part of a broader national policy. In general, the set of monetary-fiscal policy and industrial policy now widely supported in Canada have not interfered with, but rather have probably facilitated, the recent drift toward continentalism.

Although free traders have had too easy a time in this country recently, it is nevertheless true that a new national policy must centre on foreign ownership rather than the tariff; the beginning, but hopefully not the ending, would be to implement the proposals of the Watkins Report – if not its letter, at least its spirit. There is a need to increase the economic benefits from foreign ownership – by rationalizing the structure of Canadian industry, by proper taxation, by Canadian participation in ownership (including minority shares). There is a need to decrease political costs by setting up Canadian legal and administrative machinery to countervail the intrusion of United States law and practice with respect to trade with certain communist countries, anti-trust procedure, and balance-of-payments guidelines and controls imposed on direct-investment firms. Above all, however, the burden of this paper is that things must be done to promote domestic entrepreneurship, private and public, the creation of the Canada Development Corporation being an obvious first step.

To come to terms with foreign ownership would cause Canadians to view other policy objectives and instruments in a more realistic light. The present obsession with increasing Canadian productivity might be exploited, but "rationalization" should be recognized for what it should be – that is, "economic planning" – and the existence of alternative modes of rationalization recognized. There is no need for Canadian industrial policy to operate solely within rules imposed by the multinational (American) corporations. If the object of the exercise is to rationalize Canadian industry under Canadian control – and the economic and political arguments for the latter are strewn throughout this paper – then rationalization causing each Canadian firm to specialize vis-a-vis it American parent, thereby locking the Canadian industrial structure into the American industrial structure, must be spurned in the interest of promoting mergers within Canada which would create Canadian-based giants capable of surviving in a world of American-based giants.[26]

Other instruments of policy would also fall into perspective. Further special exemptions from United States monetary and commercial policies should be seen as part of a policy of economic planning rather than as a chapter in the theology of economic liberalism. And anti-combines policy should be revised in such a way as not to inhibit Canadian firms from growing to challenge American firms, at home and abroad.

Just as the old National Policy had extra-economic implications in terms of nation-building, so would a new National Policy of the sort being sketched here. The failure to limit American extraterritoriality via the medium of the American subsidiary constrains the exercise of an independent foreign policy in Canada and thereby limits an essential component of modern nationhood. Canada will be in most anomalous position should Ottawa succeed in diplomatic recognition of China while our major corporations which happen to be American-controlled face formidable obstacles from Washington in trading with China; it would be intolerable to have a major Canadian initiative in the direction of co-existence diminished in this fashion.

It would be dangerous to pretend that the problem of national unity could be solved in Canada by coming to terms with foreign ownership, but there is good reason to believe that unity would be fostered, not hindered, by so doing. It is inherent in the nature of foreign power to divide and rule and American corporations are not able to escape from this compulsion. Regions within Canada are understandably concerned to get their fair share of foreign-controlled industry and hence to compete among themselves to the extent of their laissez-faire policies. Only a national policy is feasible, and to make common cause against foreign encroachments can be a satisfying component of nationalism. Nor is it unrealistic to argue that Quebec, as it enters a more advanced stage of capitalism, would find Canada a more attractive country to which to belong if Canadian capitalists could be taken seriously. For the new generation of French-Canadian technocrats and capitalists, it would seem important to have Canadian institutions, private as well as public, in which they can not only speak their own language but pursue their own industrial ambitions.

It has become customary to view the political dimension of policies toward foreign ownership as meaning that independence would create costs in terms of lowering the standard of living. But the dichotomy between political independence and economic benefits may be false – at least in the long run. The extent of foreign ownership of Canadian economic activity has meant the creation of a branch-plant economy in Canada. A branch plant is not where the action is, in terms of new products, technologies, and ideas; and neither is a branch-plant economy. Insufficient attention has been devoted to the inherent limitations, in terms of potential for economic growth in a world of constant innovation, of a branch-plant economy. A distinction is sometimes made by economists concerned with the poor countries between economic growth (rising per capita income within an existing institutional shell absorbing foreign technology but not generating its own) and economic development (the institutional transformation of the economy as a precondition for autonomous and sustained growth). Considerations of this type have led Kari Levitt to label Canada as the richest underdeveloped country in the world. Development would consist of substituting a native bourgeoisie for a foreign-dominated bourgeoisie.

But the most important political dimension of a new National Policy would be the simple need to assume the burden of the old National Policy of "defensive expansion" vis-a-vis the United States.[27] As the American industrial system has evolved into the military-industrial complex, the threat to survival, both personal and national, has crossed new thresholds. "Defence" must mean what is says, rather than be an antiseptic word for complicity. "Expansion" must mean not rising standards of living at any political price, but rather the nurturing and sustaining of Canadian institutions and values that may bend but not necessarily break in the face of America's erratic swings from remaking the world in its own image to withdrawing into the isolation of fortress America and leaving the rest of the world to go it alone. The latter possibility is rapidly becoming a probability and Canada may shortly have to assume the burden of its own destiny by default.

REALITIES

It has not been the intention of this paper to insist that a new National Policy should ignore all matters that do not relate to foreign investment. It is right to care about poverty, housing, and pollution. But the term National Policy had already been appropriated to describe economic independence and it seemed legitimate to build on that tradition.

Nor has it been intended to exaggerate the efficacy of a new National Policy. It is central to this paper that multi-national corporations do run the "free world" and that talk about the independent power of the technocrats is more a future possibility (not necessarily desirable) than a present reality. To know where the power lies is to know that it will be difficult to do much about it. Nevertheless, it seemed better to search for possibilities rooted in our history rather than play at being blind men or engage in flights of fancy.

Nor, finally, has it been intended to come down too crudely on the side of Canadian capitalism. It is necessary, however, to "tell it like it is." Canadian reformers have been hung up too long by refusing to recognize that their dislike of the Canadian establishment (to use their euphemism) only plays into the hand of the American establishment. A capitalist is also a citizen and liberals who argue that a capitalist is merely a capitalist are vulgar Marxists unwilling to face the reality of nationalism. Canada is committed to the capitalist path of development, and, in the final analysis, Canadians should prefer home-brewed capitalists over alien capitalists. If Canada is to be a capitalist country – and the prospects for change in this respect are hardly part of the agenda for 1970 – then a case can be made for a Canadian bourgeoisie whose competence and initiative are of a high order.

To argue for a policy of Canadian independence is not to neglect the urgency of social reform for Canada. The tasks of redistributing income, alleviating poverty, disposing of the benefits of the new technology in a more democratic way – none of these are precluded by focussing on economic independence. Indeed, it is difficult to see how Canadians can humanize the operations of an economy over which they have lost control. What does it mean to

argue that Canadian social reformers should forget about economic independence so as to focus more clearly on the welfare
state[28] when Ottawa appears to lack the simple capacity independently to create jobs and control inflation?

And to suggest that Canadian nationalism is a good in itself is not
to praise nationalism but rather to insist on the need for protection
from American fall-out:

[A] strong Canadian nationalism capable of reversing the absorption of
this country in the United States is an essential first step towards the emergence of the kind of Canada that could possibly make some small contribution to the realization of the anti-nationalist ideal [of the establishment
of the federal republic of mankind]. Canadian sovereignty is not being
eroded by the republic of mankind; it is being eroded by the American
Empire. A Canadian elite which permits increasing integration of this
country with the United States, whether or not it does so under the cover
of well meaning cosmopolitan slogans, will be serving not the interests of
humanity, but those of the most powerful and possibly the most dangerous
nationalism in the world. The point of Canadian nationalism is not to preserve a sovereign Canadian nation state for ever and ever no matter what,
but to preserve it so long as the only unit capable of absorbing it is a larger
and more terrible nationalism.[29]

NOTES

1 Canada, Privy Council Office, *Foreign Ownership and the Structure of Canadian Industry: Report of the Task Force on the Structure of Canadian Industry*
   (Ottawa, 1968), 415 (known popularly as the Watkins Report). It will
   quickly become evident to the reader that this paper is primarily about foreign ownership. Given my association with the Watkins Report, it must be
   emphasized that the views expressed in this paper are mine. I do not speak
   for the government of Canada or for any other members of the Task Force
   which prepared the Report, though my own views have benefitted greatly
   form my association with the latter.
2 A key article in this respect is V.C. Fowke, "The National Policy – Old and
   New," *Canadian Journal of Economics and Political Science* 18 (1952): 271–86;
   reprinted in W.T. Easterbrook and M.H. Watkins, *Approaches to Canadian
   Economic History* (Toronto: Carleton Library, 1967).

3 I have previously dealt with this difference in interpretation in "Economic
   Nationalism," *Canadian Journal of Economics and Political Science* 32 (1966):
   388–92, in the process of reviewing an excellent documentation of the historian's position presented in Robert Craig Brown, *Canada's National Policy, 1883–1900: A Study in Canadian-American Relations* (Princeton, 1964).
   The boldest statement of the economist's position is Harry G. Johnson,
   The Canadian Quandary (Toronto, 1963).

4 John H. Dales, *The Protective Tariff in Canada's Development* (Toronto, 1966).

5 See in particular, D.G. Creighton, *The Empire of the St. Lawrence* (Toronto,
   1956).

6 Two possible reasons for this bias of economists in general are, first, the
   mechanistic, non-institutional nature of neo-classical economics, and, second, the Marxist overtones of recognizing the critical role of capitalists in
   capitalist developments.

7 See in particular his *The Fur Trade in Canada* (Toronto, 1930) and *The Cod
   Fisheries* (Toronto, 1940).

8 The leading exponent of entrepreneurial history in Canada has been W.T.
   Easterbrook. See, for example, his "Long Period Comparative Study:
   Some Historical Cases," *Journal of Economic History* 17 (1957): 571–95.

9 For the best development of this theme, see H.G.J. Aitken, "Defensive Ex-
   pansion: The State and Economic Growth in Canada" in Aitken, ed., *The
   State and Economic Growth* (New York, 1959), reprinted in Easterbrook and
   Watkins (ed.), *Approaches.*

10 For a fuller development of this argument, though seriously deficient of
    hard research, see my "The 'American System' and Canada's National
    Policy," in this volume.

11 This theme is brilliantly argued, albeit without new historical research, in
    Kari Levitt, *The New Mercantilism: The Case of Canada* (mimeo, 1968). A sim-
    ilar argument, in terms of barriers to entry of Canadian firms consequent
    on the entry of foreign firms, is implicit in Kenneth Wyman, *Non-Resident
    Control and the Structure of Canadian Industry: Case Studies* (mimeo, 1967).

12 This point is implicit in a discussion for restrictions on foreign owners,
    rather than a high tariff, to induce Canadian entrepreneurship by
    Stephen Hymer, "Direct Foreign Investment and the National Economic
    Interest" in Peter Russell, ed., *Nationalism in Canada* (Toronto, 1966).

13 For a comprehensive treatment of this phenomenon, see H.G.J. Aitken,
    American Capital and Canadian Resources (Cambridge, Mass., 1961).

14 For a fuller development of this argument, see R.E. Caves and R.H.
    Holton, *The Canadian Economy* (Cambridge, Mass., 1959), part I; see also

my "A Staple Theory of Economic Growth," *Canadian Journal of Economics and Political Science* 29 (1963): 141–58, reprinted in Easterbrook and Watkins (eds), *Approaches.*

15 From an analytical perspective, we need a "theory" of economic growth which effectively weds the Ricardian theory of comparative advantage with the Marxian theory of the leading role of the bourgeoisie. Given the demonstrated efficacy of the staple theory in explaining Canadian historical development, an important topic awaiting serious research is the effect of different staples in facilitating, or inhibiting, Canadian entrepreneurship.

16 See Alfred D. Chandler, Jr., *Strategy and Structure: Chapters in the History of the American Industrial Enterprise* (Cambridge, Mass., 1962).

17 For the most recent detailed statistics, see Dominion Bureau of Statistics, *The Canadian Balance of International Payments 1963, 1964 and 1965 and International Investment Position* (Ottawa, 1967); for a summary of the present position based on DBS data, see Watkins Report, 5–13.

18 The cost-benefit approach pervades the Watkins Report.

19 For a heroic attempt to quantify benefits, see R.G. Penner, "The Benefits of Foreign Investment in Canada, 1950–56," *Canadian Journal of Economics and Political Science* 32 (1966): 172–83; see also various sections of the Watkins Report.

20 The essence of the situation is embodied in the Canadian-American Committee, where Canadian executives of American-controlled firms and their American "counterparts" preach to themselves – and to others silly enough to listen – the of emasculation. It lies beyond the confines of the paper to explain why Canadian union leaders also participate in this farce.

21 Hymer, "Direct Foreign Investment"; Rotstein, "The 20th Century Prospect: Nationalism in a Technological Society," in Russell, ed., *Nationalism in Canada.*

22 Economic Council of Canada, *Third Annual Review: Prices, Productivity and Employment* (Ottawa, 1967), and the Council staff study, "Price Stability and High Employment. The Options for Canadian Economic Policy: And Econometric Study," by R.G. Bodkin, E.P. Bond, G.L. Reuber, and T.R. Robinson.

23 This is a non-sentence summary of a half-hour CBC TV interview of Professor Mundell of the University of Chicago at the time of the supplementary budget.

24 *Fourth Annual Review: The Canadian Economy from the 1960s to the 1970s* (Ottawa, 1967), 155–6.

25 For a critique of the Carter Commission (Royal Commission on Taxation) *Report* in these terms, see Stephen H. Hymer and Melville H. Watkins "The Radical Centre – Carter Reconsidered," *Canadian Forum* (June 1968).

26 It might then develop that American extraterritoriality via American anti-trust law, by inhibiting American-owned subsidiaries in Canada from participating in such rationalization programs, will have to be recognized for the serious problem that it is.

27 Aitken, "Defensive Expansionism."

28 This is the favourite gambit of Carleton University economists in letters to Ottawa newspapers.

29 Gad Horowitz, "Trudeau vs Trudeauism," *Canadian Forum* (May 1968).

7

The US-Canada
Free Trade Agreement (1988)

In October 1987, the US and Canadian governments announced that they had successfully negotiated a comprehensive bilateral free trade agreement. The full details of the accord were made public in December. On January 2, 1988, President Reagan and Prime Minister Mulroney signed the agreement. If approved by the US Congress and the Canadian Parliament, it will come into effect on January 1, 1989. The Canadian Left, plus some centrist forces, have resolved, however, to prevent this from happening.[1]

The agreement is sweeping in its scope, going well beyond what has been conventionally involved in the creation of a free trade area. Of course, tariffs between the two countries will disappear, phased out over a ten-year period. These have been eroding steadily since the Second World War through the GATT (General Agreement on Tariffs and Trade), but the process will be accelerated. Canada, which presently has the higher remaining tariffs, faces the larger adjustment, a burden which will fall on its workers.

THE PERILS OF PROTECTIONISM

In recent years, however, tensions in US–Canada relations have been associated not with the tariff but with non-tariff barriers.

Reprinted from *Monthly Review* (September 1988): 34-42.

Much of the impetus for this agreement on the Canadian side came from a desire to deal with those issues. Specifically, as Reaganomics generated a massive US trade deficit – with corresponding trade surpluses by major trading partners like Canada – protectionist pressures grew in the United States. Americans were tempted to blame their rising propensity to import on the alleged unfair trading practices of other nations, and to cast the net widely in defining an unfair trade practice. Regional development policies, special unemployment insurance payments to seasonally unemployed fishermen in the Atlantic Provinces, lower stumpage charges on lumber in British Columbia than in the Pacific Northwest: all have been cited by Americans as unfair Canadian trade practices instead of, as the Canadian government insists, legitimate policies lying within its purview.

The US response to these perceived inequities was to impose countervailing tariffs or anti-dumping duties in specific cases, to the detriment of Canadian exports and jobs. Many Canadians feared that the United States would adopt still more punitive protectionist measures across-the-board; given Canada's extraordinary reliance on exports to the United States (which constitute about 80 percent of the total), its vulnerability was evident.

The reaction of the Canadian government was to try to cut a deal which would somehow exempt Canada from the general US trend toward protectionism. The strategy was based on the view that US protectionism was such a serious threat that it required an extraordinary response by Canada, and that concessions could be wrung out of the United States at a cost tolerable to Canada.

The resulting agreement sets up a binational dispute resolution mechanism that is empowered to judge whether either party *applies* its trade law unfairly. Hence, US law remains in place, and can even be extended. Canadian critics have properly insisted that this mechanism fails to speak to the main problem – the continued existence of US protectionist law and policy.

Nor does the agreement contain a subsidy code which would define certain (Canadian) government policies as legitimate and therefore not subject to (US) counteraction. Rather, it sets up a period of five years, which can be extended to seven, during which both parties will try to negotiate such a code; failure to do so can constitute grounds for abrogation of the entire agreement by either party on six months notice. This provision would seem to invite disaster for Canada. The pressure will be on Canada, the smaller country, to align its policies with the United States; should it fail to do so, it will risk the prohibitive costs of disrupting the new patterns of trade and investment which will have been created through the agreement.

Incredibly, the deal includes no automatic exemption for Canada from generalized US protectionism. It happens that this prospect has significantly lessened, as the overvalued US dollar has fallen decisively and the Crash of 1987 has made members of the US Congress fearful of the charge that protectionism will bring down the global house of cards. But that only means that Canada, which made major concessions to get this deal, did so to evade what has turned out to be a low-risk threat.

CANADIAN CONCESSIONS

The list of what Canada gave up is lengthy.

To an extent unprecedented in existing trading arrangements, this agreement opens up the service sector: financial institutions, insurance, advertising, data processing, management services, and the like. The Reagan administration pushed for this concession, believing that comparative advantage in this sector lies with US companies. The Mulroney government acquiesced, though what little research has been done on the consequences for Canada indicates that the impact will be adverse.[2]

To have free trade in services, companies must be able to move as they wish and must never be treated differently because they are foreign. These conditions are known as the right of establishment and the right of national treatment, and they are enshrined in this agreement.

To round out this guarantee of corporate mobility – this charter of rights for business – Canada agrees to cease monitoring all but the biggest of US takeovers of Canadian firms and not to impose domestic content provisions on the Canadian operations of US companies. Likewise, Canadian companies get more secure rights to operate in the United States, but that may well work to the disadvantage of Canadian workers as their employers flee to the right-to-work, weakly unionized southern states.

Opposition to this so-called trade agreement, then, should be seen as opposition to the rights of capital to roam freely throughout the continent while less mobile labour remains rooted in national communities. It should not surprise anyone that capital on both sides of the Canadian-US border supports this agreement, while organized labour on both sides (notably the AFL-CIO and the Canadian Labour Congress) opposes it; within Canada, steelworkers who are part of an international (ie. US) union and autoworkers who are now in an independent Canadian union both oppose it. Defeat of the agreement would therefore be a major victory for progressive forces, particularly in Canada where the opposition between capital and labour – and labour's allies in the churches, the women's movement, poor people's groups, environmentalists, the peace movement, the cultural community, aboriginal people's organizations, and so forth – is evident for all to see.[3]

The breadth of this opposition reflects the pervasive reach of the agreement. It gives the United States virtually unlimited access to Canada's more abundant energy resources, thus promising to push up the energy prices paid by Canadians in the future and, by increasing the rate of resource exploitation, to add to environmental degradation and intrusions on northern lands occupied by aboriginal people.

The agreement claims to exempt cultural industries, but the Canadian cultural community has not been convinced; Canadian writers, film-makers, actors, and musicians overwhelmingly oppose it. One reason is that they are not fooled by the false promise of improved access to the US market. They know that the issue for Canadian culture, faced with the onslaught of the US cultural industries, has always been access by Canadians to the Canadian market. Another reason is because of a bizarre clause in the agreement that says that if either party (read Canada) initiates new policies with respect to the cultural industries, the other party (read the United States) "may take measures of equivalent commercial effect" – and can apparently do so anywhere it wants!

The service sector, which is being opened up to heightened US competition, also includes public-sector activities like health care. The Mulroney government insisted throughout the negotiations that social programs were not on the table, but the fine print of the agreement lists, as services covered, "health care facilities management services." The definition of "health care facilities" includes every kind of hospital, public health clinic, and so on. "Management services" mean what it says: managing or running these. Canada relies much more on the public sector than does the United States for the delivery of health care – and in the process does so more cheaply and in a more egalitarian way. This agreement is an open invitation to the US private sector to come to Canada and lobby for the privatization of health care.

Canadians also have a tradition of greater reliance than Americans on public enterprise, or what in Canada are called Crown corporations. Hidden away near the end of this agreement is a clause titled "Monopolies," which talks about the rights of the other party to the agreement when one party "designates a monopoly." Translated into Canadian English, that means "creating a Crown corporation." This agreement actually binds Canada to consult with the United States in that event and "to minimize or eliminate any nullification or impairment of benefits" to US companies.

That sets Canadians to wondering: If this deal had been in effect in the past, would private US insurance companies have been able to block Medicare? Would Denticare be possible in the future? The Canadian Left has valid complaints against the Canadian capitalist state, including the tendency of too many Crown corporations to behave like their private-sector counterparts, but exposing Canadians to the tender mercies of the private sector is hardly the solution.

Both the health care issue and the monopolies clause also show that there are concrete connections linking free trade and privatization with attacks on the welfare state. The free-trade agreement is the means by which the neo-conservative corporate agenda, which has already so ravaged the United States, will come to clobber Canada.

There exists between Canada and the United States one sectoral trade agreement that has worked well for Canada in terms of jobs, the Auto Pact covering trade in the automotive sector. It has led to greatly increased specialization and trade in that sector. Since it includes domestic content provisions – which constitute employment safeguards for Canadians – it is an example of managed trade, or of effective industrial policy, rather than market-driven free trade. It is the specific contribution of this free-trade agreement to erode the safeguards for Canada in the Auto Pact *and* to tie the hands of government in such a way as to ensure that no other industrial sector will ever be allowed to have an arrangement of that nature.

The sum of this and other concessions – on tariffs, on investment controls, on energy – will tightly constrain the ability of future governments in Canada to pursue an industrial strategy. Yet a look around the world today strongly suggests that the most successful economies are those where such policies are pursued; even the United States, despite its rhetoric to the contrary, does so under the aegis of the Pentagon, albeit to its long-run detriment. This agreement is supposed to give Canadian firms preferred access to the large US market. It is uncertain that the agreement actually does that: but even if it did, it denies them the supporting government policy that would be needed to succeed in exploiting that opportunity.[4]

ECONOMIC CONSEQUENCES FOR CANADA

The Mulroney government is, nevertheless, trying to sell free trade with the United States as the means to create economic growth and jobs in Canada. A look at the present pattern of Canadian trade with the United States suggests a very different outcome, with jobs more likely to be destroyed than created as a result of the agreement.

The characteristic feature of the Canadian economy, in comparison with other advanced industrialized economies, is its heavy, indeed excessive, reliance on exports of resources, mostly to the United States and often in surprisingly unprocessed form. Those exports create a very large trade surplus, which is then offset by trade deficits everywhere else – in agriculture, manufacturing, and services.

Free trade is likely to intensify existing patterns of trade. A country finds that its already strong sectors are best able to withstand the stiffer winds of competition and take advantage of market opportunities, while its already weak sectors are pushed to the wall and decline yet further. Existing trade surpluses grow; so do existing trade deficits.

If free trade enables Canada to expand at all, it will exacerbate the resource-bias of the economy. This trend will be bad news for workers, since resource-production employs few people per unit of output. It is in the manufacturing and, above all, service sectors where there are jobs, but these sectors are where Canada is likely to end up relying more on imports.[5]

POLITICAL RESPONSE

The politics of the free trade issue – the constellation of political parties and provincial governments pro and con – make the

outcome of the intense debate that is going on inside Canada
hard to call. Public opinion is essentially split down the middle;
polls tend to show that a slight majority favours the agreement,
but that opponents feel more strongly about the issue.

The Conservative federal government, with a large majority in
Parliament, supports the deal, but both opposition parties – the
Liberals (a centrist party, the traditional governing party in Canada) and the New Democratic Party (the social democratic labour
party) – oppose the agreement and say they will work to obstruct its
legislative implementation and will tear it up if given the chance.
Polls for some time have been showing the electorate to be about
equally divided among these three parties. An election does not
have to be called until September 1989; the free trade agreement
could by then have come into effect, and some wonder if the opposition parties' commitment to abrogate it would be honoured, particularly by a Liberal government, given the customary willingness
of such governments in the past to heed the advice of big business.

Of the ten provinces, two oppose (the largest, Ontario, and the
smallest, Prince Edward Island); one is in limbo (Manitoba, whose
NDP government, which opposed the deal, was replaced in May
1988 by a minority Conservative government); and seven support.
(Of the two territorial governments in the North, that of the Yukon
Territory, of NDP persuasion, opposes.) There is no pretending that
this lineup is other than bad news for the opponents of the deal.
The breakdown is perilously close a confrontation between popu-
lous and (relatively) prosperous Ontario – presently the main bene-
factor of the country's uneven development, with most of the
manufacturing jobs and head offices – and the rest of the country,
reliant on resources and resentful of Ontario's advantage. The regional passions aroused play into the hands of the free traders.

Quebec, long grouped with Ontario as part of Central Canada,
has lined up with the resource hinterlands, with decisive consequences for the alignment of forces within the federal state. Many
Francophone Québecois (almost half in the referendum of 1980)
have wanted sovereignty for Quebec, with an economic association
with the rest of Canada along the lines of a free-trade area. Proponents of this arrangement – notably Jacques Parizeau, the independentist leader of the opposition party, the Parti Québecois – also
saw it as a step toward a North American free trade area between
Canada and the United States as facilitating the emergence of a

sovereign Quebec. Meanwhile, the Liberal pro-federalist Premier of Quebec, Robert Bourassa, also supports free trade, conjuring up visions of vast resource sales to the United States: hydroelectric power from James Bay today, perhaps water tomorrow.

Resource-dependent provinces, such as Alberta, have tended to resent federal initiatives as intrusions on provincial rights, but the free trade agreement turns out to be the federal initiative that they like – even though it claims to bind the provinces and override their rights. When the chips come down, right-wing governments (like the Conservative government of Alberta) are prepared to yield up rights to the "market" which they will not yield to interventionist national governments. They have been prepared to defend the agreement as insurance against any centrist or left-leaning national government being able to do anything in the future. This stance is stunning evidence that even in Canada – that paradigm of a federal state where it is often alleged that all that matters in its politics is federal/provincial conflict – ideology matters, and class matters.

The free trade debate has the virtue that it has put class politics, and hence socialism, more firmly on the agenda of Canadian politics. That makes it essential, however, that the free trade agreement should be definitively defeated. Otherwise, the Canadian Left risks trying to build socialism in a country denied its own future.

NOTES

1 For an earlier commentary on the debate within Canada about US-Canada free trade, see Sadequal Islam, "Free Trade and Protection: the US-Canada Case," *Monthly Review* (November 1987).

2 See Marjorie Griffin Cohen, *Free Trade and the Future of Women's Work: Manufacturing and Service Industries* (Toronto: Garamond Press, 1987).

3 The big business lobby for the agreement is described in Duncan Cameron, "The Dealers: Who's Behind Free Trade," *This Magazine* (February 1988). The Marxist case for protection as the alternative to the corporate agenda for free trade is cogently argued in Michael A. Lebowitz, "Trade and Class: Labour Strategies in a World of Strong Capital," *Studies in Political Economy* (September 1988).

4 Stephen Clarkson of the University of Toronto, a leading critic of the trade deal, foresaw that outcome in 1982: "The price for admission to the American market would be the economic policies needed to put Canadian in-

dustry in a position to compete there" (*Canada and the Reagan Challenge*
(Toronto: James Lorimer and Company, 1982), 137).

5 This analysis draws on the theorizing of the so-called staples school
of Canadian political economy, which has grown out of the writings of
Harold Innis. It is consistent with the findings of a confidential study
of the impact of the free trade deal on the Canadian economy by the economics department of one of Canada's biggest banks (the Bank of Nova
Scotia). Done to help its credit managers decide who should and should
not get loans, its conclusion is stark: "Beyond resources, all other major
sectors are net losers."

8

The Waffle and
the National Question (1990)

The Waffle Manifesto was entitled "For An Independent Socialist
Canada." Its opening sentence reads: "Our aim as democratic socialists is to build an independent socialist Canada." The very essence of
our position, of our politics, was the linking of independence and socialism, of the national question and the class question. John Bullen,
in his splendid history of the Waffle, shows how that linkage was, in
his words, the Waffle's "principal political tenet."

In 1965 George Grant had written in *Lament for a Nation* that
socialism could not be the salvation of Canada because Canadian
socialist leaders "had no understanding of the dependence of socialism and nationalism in the Canadian setting." We were resolved
to change that.

We said that independence could only be achieved through
socialism because the Canadian business class, and the political
parties which represented Canadian business, could not be relied
upon. "There is not now an independent Canadian capitalism and
any lingering pretension on the part of Canadian businessmen
to independence lacks credibility." With the passing of Walter
Gordon, there are no longer even such lingering pretensions.

We said an independent socialist Canada could be achieved
through the NDP as the party of working Canadians. Yet on the

Reprinted from *Studies in Political Economy* (1990) 32: 173-76.

132

national question and on the role of the trade union movement we truly waffled in the Manifesto. Under the influence of staff representatives from international unions and of Ed Broadbent, the only elected politician involved in the Waffle in its early days (who abandoned us at the insistence of David Lewis), we called for more democracy in the labour movement and for workers' control, but we made no mention of the importance of an independent Canadian union movement.

In the era of the American war in Vietnam and of the New Left as a global phenomenon, we translated anti-war and anti-corporate sentiment into Canadian nationalism, and we even tried to do it within a parliamentary party. We threatened the mainstream of moderate Canadian nationalism and brought about the creation of the Committee for an Independent Canada. For a brief and heady period, there were teach-ins across Canada in which an independent Canada was assumed, and the debate was about whether it should be a capitalist Canada or a socialist Canada.

The 1970s are now seen as a nationalist interlude between, on the one side, the era of special status for Canada within the American empire of the 1950s and 1960s, otherwise known as the great sell-out, and on the other side, the Reagan-Mulroney era of the 1980s, with Canada (to paraphrase Stephen Clarkson) as exemplary client state. It was a decade brought to us by Pierre Elliott Trudeau of all people; fervid anti-nationalist though he was, he knew his priorities and was willing to tolerate a little Canadian nationalism the better to defeat Quebec nationalism. It was, incredibly, even brought to us by Richard Nixon who decided that a beleaguered America could not afford to treat us–as he saw it–so benignly and would grant us no further special status. Thus with Watergate about to burst, Nixon came to Ottawa in 1972 and unilaterally declared us independent!

Lest we forget, these were the years of the Canada Development Corporation, of the Foreign Investment Review Agency (FIRA) and Petro-Canada, and of the Third Option to lessen Canadian dependence on the US, culminating, post-Waffle, in the National Energy Program. The Waffle contributed to the nationalist environment within which these things happened but, wanting more, much more, we were not impressed at the time and, I suspect, have been disappointed, though not all that surprised, that much of it did not last.

Relative to domestic ownership, foreign and American ownership in Canada fell in the 1970s and continued to do so into the
1980s; though it remains so high that Canada's right to be in the
Guinness Book of Records as the ultimate comprador nation has
hardly been put at risk. It should be conceded that none of us on
the nationalist side anticipated this decline. And if, after the event,
we have been slow to hail it, it is because we are not sure, given the
context in which it happened, that it actually mattered.

There were those who insisted that it proved that the Canadian
business class, and the Canadian economy, were now more mature.
The problem with that interpretation, however, was that trade dependency on the US grew at the same time, since the Third Option
had miserably failed. We soon discovered that the new macho business class really just wanted protection against possible American
protectionism. In the face of that threat it was Canadian workers
and their unions which went nationalist, while Canadian business
turned totally continentalist and dragged the whole country into
free trade with the U.S. The Canadian business class, having opposed any policies that would have reduced our vulnerability and
dependency, now argued that the only way to deal with them was to
increase them. Ironically, it turns out that Canadian business had
simply become mature enough to insist wholeheartedly on continentalism, and to have the cohesion and the clout to get its way.

The key change, the true big reversal, was in the labour movement which moved away from international union dominance
toward national unions, creating thereby a stronger base for the articulation of a nationalism that is, by its nature, left nationalism. If
we waffled at the outset, we quickly made up for lost time; a Waffle
Labour Caucus argued for Canadian unions, while Wafflers worked
with the militantly nationalist Confederation of Canadian Unions in
the Texpack and Artistic Woodworkers strikes. Indeed, having
moved, we did so to the point that it became our undoing, for it was
the international union leadership, in alliance with the Lewis family
party establishment, that led the purge. By the time the Canadian labour movement itself became Canadian, which it unambiguously
did with the breakaway of the Canadian Autoworkers in the 1980s,
the Waffle was history.

The 1980s has otherwise been a thoroughly miserable decade,
of American truculence and bluster under Reagan and of Canadian retreat, first under Trudeau and then yet more so under

Mulroney. The Free Trade Agreement was the culmination of this Canadian slide into colonial status.

What did we learn about Canadian political economy from the Great Free Trade Debate, and from the federal election that became a veritable referendum on the issue, that may be germane to our assessment of the Waffle? We saw, as already implied, a stridently continentalist business class which was wholly and depressingly consistent with the Waffle's best analysis and worst fears. We likewise saw a unified, nationalist labour movement, to whose existence, I like to think, the Waffle had modestly contributed.

We saw a bumbling NDP leadership that, hard though it was to believe, could not grasp the nationalist nettle of free trade as firmly as corporate lawyer John Turner and the Liberal party. In Abe Rotstein's memorable phrase, the NDP, unable to get anywhere in Quebec, demonstrated its inability to deal with the nationalist question in either official language. Such apparently is the continuing cost to the NDP of our expulsion.

Perhaps our leaving deprived the NDP of the continuing stimulus it needed to relate to Canadian, and Quebec, nationalism. We cannot rewrite history, not even our own slight role, but if our staying would have made the NDP more genuinely nationalist, I can almost be persuaded that we should have tried harder to stay.

But the Free Trade debate also witnessed the creation of the Pro-Canada Network by broad range of popular sector groups, and of a host of local coalitions against free trade. This represented a most impressive social movement. We old Wafflers should all be happy if future historians see the Waffle as an embryonic version thereof.

Thus, although we lost on free trade, we saw remarkable evidence of a strong, left nationalist sentiment as recently as one year ago. Let us, by all means, emphasize the Waffle's contribution to that legacy. Tell me: who on the left has a stronger claim?

9

Foreign Ownership
and Canadian Nationalism:
Reflections on
the Watkins Report (1994)

When asked the profound and perennial question – "Does Canadian nationalism exist? – the challenge is to find a new way to answer it in this post-modern world of post-nation states. My answer consists of a case study – a case in which I was personally involved. In 1968, I helped to author a report on foreign ownership, titled *Foreign Ownership and the Structure of Canadian Industry*. Done for the Government of Canada, it came to be known, albeit by default, as the Watkins Report.[1] I cannot assume some quarter-century later that anyone but the most specialized of Canadian historians knows of what I speak. Foreign ownership was an important public issue in Canada in those bygone days. To anticipate my major point: it no longer is in the literal sense – except for Mel Hurtig's National Party which attracted a minuscule vote in the last federal election – but it ought to be.

For while the phrase may mostly have disappeared from Canadian political discourse, the phenomenon has hardly disappeared from the Canadian political economy. Canada's right to be ensconced in the *Guinness Book of Records* as having the highest level of any (otherwise) advanced industrial economy is as firm today as

First presented on a panel addressing "Does Canadian Nationalism Exist?" at the International Congress of Mexican Association of Canadian Studies, Mexico City, April 1994.

it was in 1968.[2] While the level fell in the 1970s and into the 1980s – probably reflecting a decline in US hegemony that created more space for marginal capital such as Canada's – the most recent data shows it rising again since the implementation of the Free Trade Agreement (FTA). Are not critics of free trade right on this point: today's FTAs are merely prosaic names for Charters of Rights and Freedoms for the Corporations, permitting them to locate their production facilities where they please while selling freely everywhere? Some commentators have actually taken to calling them "free production agreements."

Indeed, *the* reality that lay behind foreign ownership from the outset in the late nineteenth century was the giant multinational corporation and it has not exactly withered away. Existing companies, from Olympia & York to IBM, get themselves in trouble and lose power though the former has recently resurfaced in Mexico. But new ones as regularly merge; as Rogers takes over Maclean-Hunter in Canada, and Viacom, Blockbuster and Paramount marry in the US – which, predictably, spills over into Canada – there is talk that the world's media may shortly be dominated by four or five monster firms. "The conglomerates," says Manhattan publisher Andre Schiffrin, "are wiping out the small firms and the small countries at the same time."

Globally, transnational capital seems to be very much in the saddle. In the 1980s, foreign direct investment throughout the world increased at three times world trade and four times world output. The down side of that coin is that the world economy is in something of a mess with unemployment rampant. It is always possible there is some connection, and that one really ought to worry about how to regulate corporate capital in the public interest. Which was, of course, always what the issue of foreign ownership was really all about; it was the reason, the rationale, for the response called economic nationalism.

Those days of yore were the days of Walter Gordon, and of anti-war protest, and of the general ferment of the New Left. Gordon, as Minister of Finance in the Pearson Liberal Government had lost on the budget of 1963 when he had to withdraw a proposed tax on foreign takeovers of Canadian corporations. He subsequently left Cabinet, and by late 1966 planned to resign partly for health reasons. He was persuaded to stay because of polls showing continuing public concern about foreign ownership and a fear by the Liberals that the New Democratic Party would capitalize on this. But Gordon was never a politician like the others. He was in politics not because he like power *per se* but because he had an agenda, of the things he believed in. He insisted, as the price of his presence in the government, that a task force be appointed to write an official White Paper on foreign ownership.

There were eight of us named thereto, chosen by Ministers for (it being Canada) regional and linguistic balance. There was hardly any other sort of balance. All economists, though at least some of us tried to practice political economy. All men; Kari Levitt was shortly to publish *Silent Surrender,* a more powerful critique of foreign capital in Canada and its Canadian allies than the Task Force was able to muster.[3]

Our work was overseen by a committee of Cabinet and a more or less matching committee of deputy ministers. The Cabinet Ministers included Mitchell Sharp, an opponent of Mr. Gordon's economic nationalism, and a formidable one as Minister of Finance. Twenty years later, in the great debate of 1988, Mr. Sharp opposed the FTA, but this tells us less about him than about the changing times; the world has shifted right and made Mr. Sharp look like a progressive.[4] There was also Jean Marchand, still the senior of the three wise men (Marchand, Trudeau and Gerard Pelletier) from Quebec. Gordon saw him as his friend and ally, but Marchand, having got Quebec representation on the Task Force expressed no further interest. His project was the very different one of Quebec and Canada. A young John Turner was on the Cabinet Committee too. Gordon saw him as far to the right and did not live long enough to see even him, as leader of the Liberal party in its brief moment of glory, oppose free trade in 1988.

The committee of deputies included Simon Reisman of later infamy as chief negotiator of that FTA. He kept insisting that I was not working for a Minister but for the Government and recommending that I take as long as I wanted. The message was: do this right and you'll have a great future. It tells us much about the nature of the Ottawa mandarins and how correct George Grant was as to their continentalist role.[5]

The Task Force Report was downgraded from a White Paper and called the Watkins Report because, with Mr. Gordon now finally leaving parliamentary politics, no one else would take the credit; it was not an auspicious beginning. In Mr. Sharp's telling comment:

"the report was only the expression of the personal views of a group of professors and had no bearing on government policy."[6]

The report was infused with the economist's bland and technocratic language of benefits and costs. The novelty consisted of admitting of the possibility of costs and not simply of the certainty of benefits – of the economic costs of a branch plant economy and the political costs of extraterritoriality. Both still haunt Canada. The former is now obscured by more intense global rationalization which tends to eliminate the worst inefficiencies consequent on the "miniature replica effect" without altering the basic dependence and vulnerability. For the latter, it is even the same specific issue, of whether American-controlled subsidiaries in Canada are allowed to trade with Cuba. The root issue was, and is, the room for manoeuvre of national governments vis-a-vis international capital. The Report's message was that, while political space was limited it was did exist, and that governments should use it, rather than lose it by themselves giving it away.

Much was made, then and now, of the comparison between the behaviour of foreign and domestically-owned firms and the discovery that sometimes the Canadian-owned variant performs less well than the subsidiary. This misses the larger point of who is in charge, of the possibility that the very dominance of foreign capital in the Canadian political economy sets the tone and pace. A study of the ill-fated National Energy Program quotes a Canadian government official: "We underestimated the affinities – intellectual, ideological and commercial – between foreign companies and Canadian companies, particularly the ideological factors." Said another official: "It [the Canadian business community] regarded itself as an international business community allied with US investors. It regarded anything attacking the US business community as an attack on themselves."[7]

On the narrower economic criteria, one is never quite sure whether what is being proven is that foreign capital is good or it is not as bad as domestic capital. Perhaps the proper comparison is of subsidiaries with their parents, particularly with respect to R&D and the range of job-generating head office activities; in these respects, there is no doubt that the subsidiary is a second-class firm.

The Task Force had to confront the insistence of orthodox economics that the inefficiency of the Canadian manufacturing sector was the result not of foreign ownership but of the tariff. We took the sensible view that while the tariff protected inefficient industry, that inefficiency was inherent in a branch plant economy. We rejected the view that free trade was the panacea. What remained of Canadian manufacturing would necessarily be efficient, but no one knew how much would remain. By late 1991, near the end of the third year of the FTA, a senior vice-president of a large Canadian bank observed, "Many of those who supported the [FTA] believed that if would cause Canadian firms to pull up their socks and do whatever was needed to compete in the North American market. What perhaps was overlooked is that many Canadian companies, whether foreign or domestically owned, might adjust to the [FTA], not by standing and fighting, but by cutting and running across the border."[8]

As the free trade debate came to dominate politics from the mid-1980s, the need to worry about how much foreign ownership would stay, compromised the clarity of the message about the need for regulation of foreign capital and helps to explain why foreign ownership is not an issue in and of itself. In fact, since in the implementation of the FTA in January 1989 there have been Canadian companies taken over by foreign-based competitors and then closed down.[9] At the same time, Canadian operations of American firms are being consolidated into North American divisions to the further detriment of Canadian activities, and foreign nationals appear to be filling more of the dwindling number of top executive jobs in Canada. Mr. Gordon used to argue that foreign companies ought to be required to sell a minority share in their subsidiaries to local interests to make the latter more accountable, and the Task Force endorsed that, but the government ignored the advise. Some companies, like Campbell Soup and General Electric, already did so but in the 1990s they bought out the minority shareholders in order to tighten control.[10]

The Chief Executive Officers of a number of American subsidiaries met earlier this year in Toronto to deplore their loss of autonomy. They put free trade first as the cause of their problems, but I would bet that all of them voted for free trade in 1988.[11] "Canadians have a good standard of living," writes MIT economist Lester Throw, "but they can never have the best. The best jobs ... are back at headquarters and that is somewhere else."[12]

Economic nationalism was not a high priority for Mr. Trudeau, though he was willing to throw an occasional bone to the English

Canadian nationalist the better (in his mind) to keep them onside in his project to contain Quebec nationalism. Besides, in the global detente of the 1970s there was a bit more room for autonomy by countries like Canada at the margin of empire. The Task Force Report was followed in due course by the Gray Report[13], impressive in the detail of its diagnosis and its prescription, and bearing the name of an actual Cabinet Minister, Herb Gray; by the creation of the Foreign Investment Review Agency and the Canada Development Corporation when Mr. Trudeau was pushed into a minority government position in the early 1970s and had to rely on the NDP for support; and in Mr. Trudeau's second coming in the 1980s, by the National Energy Program and its provisions for Canadianizing the oil and gas industry. Briefly, it looked like the Task Force Report had a legacy.

It was not to be. Stephen Clarkson documents the fullness of the retreat by the Trudeau government in the face of Reaganomics that became a rout with the Mulroney government.[14] FIRA did little; renamed Investment Canada it now shills for foreign investment. The Canadian government bought wholly into the neo-conservative "competitiveness" model where the object of the exercise is to create a climate conducive to foreign capital. Traditional economic nationalism has been stood on its head.

Regulation of foreign direct investment never had the support of Canadian business, which has a long history of subservience to imperial and particularly American business. The creation of the Business Council of National Issues in the 1970s, with the big branch plants all there, silenced any lingering nationalist voices among Canadian big business. As well, rapidly increasing Canadian direct investment in the US gave Canadian capital an increasing interest in continentalism. Foreign ownership polices had the support of Canadian labour and other social movements but they were too weak to get their way.

From a nationalist perspective, the whole story is clearly a bit of a downer. This year being the centenary of the birth of Harold Innis, we should recall that he saw the fate of the intellectual as having insight into much and power over nothing. These times are not the end of history and the issue of foreign ownership, of the power of transnational capital to escape national control, lives on. Orthodox economics remains of slight help, but there is a heady revival of Canadian political economy focussed precisely on the issue of foreign ownership;[15] as well, there has emerged outside Canada – and inside, notably in the writings of Robert Cox – an International Political Economy that insists on the importance of the transnational corporation as an actor. These two schools are brought together very effectively in Barbara Jenkins' recent *The Paradox of Continental Production: National Investment Policies in North America.*

There is, too, the fascinating spectacle of the 1991 report on the Canadian economy by Michael Porter of the Harvard Business School that is remarkably similar to a political economist's description: the abnormal bias toward the export of unprocessed resources, the high and increasing reliance on the US market and, above all for present purposes, the high level of foreign ownership and the tendency of subsidiaries not to be world-class performers.[16] Porter insists that Canadian policy should be directed toward transforming foreign subsidiaries into more autonomous and efficient "home bases." Predictably, in a report done for the Business Council on National Issues and the Mulroney government, the manner in which this should be made to happen has a neo-conservative cast with an excess of predictable but dubious "competitiveness" policies, but the grasp of the nature of the Canadian economy is sound and permits of other solutions that might once upon a time have been labelled nationalist.

If foreign ownership is seen as a relevant issue for Canada from the ivory towers of both MIT and Harvard, perhaps it will even come again to be so seen in Canada. For the moment, it is strikingly absent from the thinking of the new Liberal government: having accepted NAFTA there is not a hint of economic nationalism in its agenda. It is even backing away from a firm stand on cultural nationalism, specifically the issue of Canadian ownership of book publishing, the only area of nationalist concern where the Mulroney government maintained the semblance of a policy. But there is the nagging question of why unemployment is so high in Canada, particularly relative to the US even as the economy is linked ever more closely to the American. Could it be that there are structural deficiencies, including that inefficient and withering branch plant economy?

The market mentality reigns supreme and is highly corrosive of any sentiment of economic nationalism. Still, there are limits. Fifty years ago, Karl Polanyi wrote that the idea of a "self-regulating market" is "stark utopia."[17] Some regulation of capital, some constraints on its "freedom" in order to limit chaos, is in the interest even of capital. To abandon control of capital is to abandon politics, and to abandon politics is to risk a dystopia. The American commentator James Fallows wrote recently: "It is precisely the internationalization of the economy that makes national strategies more important. Because not everything moves across borders as easily as currency-futures do, governments may need to pay more attention to the welfare of 'Japan' and 'France' and 'Canada' than most people realize."[18] My colleague Abraham Rotstein, writing in the Polanyi tradition, saw Canadian economic nationalism back in the 1960s as an understandable response to the impact of transnational capital.[19] The only amendment that is in order in the new era of the NAFTA – albeit a most important one for present purposes – is that those who wish to tame the multinational corporation need to operate continentally as well as nationally.

Within Canada, Canadian Studies has served the useful function of a refuge from the orthodox disciplines and their persistent tendency to denigrate nationalism. It has aided intellectually in what Innis once described as the need for "taking persistent action at strategic points against American imperialism in all its attractive guises."[20] It might be hoped that an interest in Mexico in matters Canadian – which is being matched by a fresh interest in Mexican matters in Canada – will increase the awareness by scholars in both countries of our shared dependency and will lead to fresh perspectives on "North America," even to reflections on a new "continentalism" that transcends the present state-corporate version.

NOTES

1 Canada, Privy Council Office, *Foreign Ownership and the Structure of Canadian Industry: Report of the Task Force on the Structure of Canadian Industry* (Ottawa, 1968).
2 "According to deputy treasury secretary Roger Altman, Canada has the distinction of having more of its assets owned by foreigners than any other member of the G-7 industrial nations. Altman was attacking Japan for keeping out foreigners ... The foreign-owned share of total domestic assets in Japan is below 1%, he said. That compares with 9% in Germany and 26% in Canada" (*Financial Post*, 12 March 1994).
3 Kari Levitt, *Silent Surrender: The Multinational Corporation in Canada* (1970).
4 See his memoirs *Which Reminds Me ...* (1993)

5 See George Grant, *Lament for a Nation* (1965).

6 Cited in Walter Gordon, *A Political Memoir* (1977).

7 Barbara Jenkins, "Reexamining the 'obsolescing bargain': a study of Canada's National Energy Program," *International Organization* (Winter 1986).

8 David Crane, *Toronto Star* (November 26, 1991).

9 Comments by Alan Nymark of Investment Canada at the University of Toronto, March 1994.

10 See David Crane, *The Next Canadian Century: Building a Competitive Economy* (1992).

11 "Head office flexes its might: Branch plants losing clout," *Globe & Mail* (18 January 1994).

12 Lester Thurow, *Head to Head: The Coming Economic Battle Among Japan, Europe and America* (1993).

13 Canada, *Foreign Direct Investment in Canada* (1972).

14 Stephen Clarkson, *Canada and the Reagan Challenge: Crisis in the Canadian-American Relationship* (1982).

15 To mention only the highlights, Levitt's book was followed by the formulation of the so-called Naylor-Clement thesis showing how the Canadian business class had willingly formed an unequal alliance with the American business class, and later by Gordon Laxer who implicated the broader Canadian civil society in the takeover. See Wallace Clement, *Continental Corporate Power: Economic Elite Linkages between Canada and the United States* (Toronto: McClelland and Stewart, 1977); R.T. Naylor, *The History of Canadian Business, 1867–1914*, 2 vols., (Toronto: McClelland and Stewart, 1975); and Gordon Laxer, *Open for Business: The Roots of Foreign Ownership in Canada* (Toronto: Oxford University Press, 1989).

16 Michael E. Porter and the Monitor Company, *Canada at the Crossroads: The Reality of a New Competitive Environment* (1991).

17 Karl Polanyi, *The Great Transformation* (1944).

18 James Fallows, *New York Review of Books* (March 1, 1990).

19 Abraham Rotstein, *The Precarious Homestead: Essays on Economics, Technology and Nationalism* (1973).

20 Harold Innis, *Changing Concepts of Time* (1952), 20.

10

The Car and
Canadian Political Economy:
An Innisian Perspective (1994)

It has been said of Britain that it is more likely to have a biography of a minor poet than of a major politician. It could be said of Canada that it is more likely to have a history of almost anything than of an industry, even a major industry. We have more labour history than history of industries where labour works; indeed, what industrial history we have is frequently written by labour historians who have first to establish the credentials of the protagonist. Canadian working people, notwithstanding the pervasive influence of American unionism until very recently, evidently make more history than do Canadian business people. We also have industrial history written as incidental to tariff history, perhaps reflecting that Canadians, arguably, have been more innovative with respect to tariffs than with respect to industry. Now that the US-Canada Free Trade Agreement (FTA), the North American Free Trade Agreement (NAFTA), and the World Trade Organization (WTO), tightly tied Canada's hands with respect to tariff-making, this way of writing industrial history (for whatever industry remains) will presumably disappear.

It should come as no surprise, then, that we do not have a comprehensive history of the Canadian automobile industry. In

---

This paper is based on a paper presented at a conference on "Cars and Continentalism" held at University College, University of Toronto, May 1994.

Michael Bliss' history of Canadian business, we are told, "The literature on the coming of the automobile to Canada is thoroughly inadequate" (though the auto industry has long been the largest secondary manufacturing industry in Canada), and "Nothing of importance has been written on the McLaughlins and General Motors of Canada" (though the latter has long been Canada's largest company).[1] Bliss thinks it is unnecessary to tell us why, and it has not deterred him from writing a huge book, but it is, of course, a side effect of foreign ownership. Earlier this year, the *Economist* headlined an editorial "The day of the national car is over"; for Canada, it was over before it began. Headquarters have always been somewhere else, at least for the real decisions.

This paper attempts to transcend these inherent limitations by appeal to the insights of the late Harold Innis who profoundly understood that Canada was a margin and wrote serious history in spite of that. Transportation was a major theme in Innis' historical writing, beginning with his doctoral thesis on the Canadian Pacific Railway.[2] The Conclusion begins, "The history of the Canadian Pacific Railway is primarily the spread of western civilization over the northern half of the North American continent"; for the history of the automotive industry in Canada, one could simply amend that to read "the spread of American civilization." In contrast to the conventional view of myself and others, John Watson writes, in his superb thesis on Innis, "By 1929, Innis had worked out a coherent sketch of Canadian economic development which revolved not so much around staples as around transportation systems."[3] Similarly, Graeme Patterson cites Innis's *Empire and Communications* to show that "it was waterways [transportation], not pulp and paper [the staple, as is usually alleged], that directly led to the late work."[4] J.B. Brebner, commenting on *Empire and Communications* in a 1950 letter to Innis, thought "your terminus is probably 'Power and Communications,' including transportation." While there is no evidence that Innis was moving in this direction, "Empire and Transportation" would not be a bad title for an Innisian study of the car.[5]

I

Innis was concerned with how particular activities had such pervasive impacts that society seemed virtually to be organized around them. Automobiles themselves were too contemporary to merit more than passing reference from Innis as historian, but he would perhaps have appreciated the considerable literature, scholarly and popular, that sees the automobile as hegemonic in much of the twentieth century. With respect to the labour process, the prevailing mode of regulation of much of this century is labelled "Fordism," incorporating, and hence transcending, both such potent "isms" as Taylorism and Keynesianism. Ford itself is still the third largest industrial concern in the world, being outranked by General Motors (which is first) and by Exxon, which supplies the gas for the cars, in second place. Womack and his collaborators call their book on the automobile *The Machine that Changed the World*, and argue that it did so not just once – with Henry Ford and Alfred Sloan, whose genius was in segmenting the vehicle market – but a second time, with Eiji Toyoda and Taiichi Ohno at Toyota after World War II.[6] For John Kenneth Galbraith, the great dissident economist and the successor to Thorstein Veblen who Innis so much admired, the automobile is arguably the dominant object of "the affluent society" and the auto industry the archetype of "the new industrial state."[7] In each of the three great markets of the world – North America, Europe and East Asia (centred on Japan) – purchases of cars and trucks account for about 15 per cent of personal consumption, while a recent report of the US-based Natural Resources Defense Council calculates total car-associated costs, which it calls the "price of mobility," as 25 per cent of GNP.[8]

A powerful technology like the car creates a support system that adds to its momentum. Alexander Wilson, in his superb book *The Culture of Nature*, writes with respect to the US: "The highways encouraged car acquisition and use, the cars in turn consumed more gas, and the tax on the gas ensured the construction of more highways. The interstate highways, completed in the mid-1980s, amounted to a massive government subsidy to the auto industry and its many dependents, including tourism."[9] Car purchases were central to the boom of the 1920s and then the 1950s and 1960s, while in down times like the 1930s road construction was a favoured anti-cyclical instrument. Paving, and repaving, roads remains a customary pre-election activity down to the present manic activity here in Ontario in preparation for the provincial election.

In the Canadian context, and in deference to the staples approach, the automobile industry is as important to the economy of southern Ontario (Canada's Michigan) as any commodity is to any province. Likewise, since the auto industry is the leading example of what Quebec has not got its fair share of within Canada, Ontarians fear, or ought to, that if Quebec separates the auto industry will be up for grabs. Significantly too, provincial New Democrats have long lived off the promise to bring auto insurance under public ownership and have done so in Manitoba, Saskatchewan and British Columbia. In 1948, the Ontario CCF promised to do so in its first term. Years later Robin Sears, a senior official of the Ontario NDP, admitted that European socialists ridiculed him for the NDP's gung-ho approach to public auto insurance, mocking that the party was certainly not going after the commanding heights of the economy. Sears defended it by saying they did not understand the importance of the automobile in North American's independent lifestyle.[10] He had a point; it is a sign of the extraordinary caution of the NDP government that was finally elected in Ontario in 1990 that it reneged on this commitment.

A creative concern of Innis – that provides the key to the impact of the car on the political economy of Canada – was with respect to regionalism. In 1931 he wrote, "The extension of the American empire, the decline of its natural resources, and the emergence of metropolitan areas, supported capitalist expansion in Canada and reinforced the trend to regionalism ... The pull to the north and south has tended to become stronger in contrast to the pull east and west."[11] The automobile is critical to the powerful nexus of continental economic integration and Canadian political disintegration on which Innis was so prescient. In the Foreword to the aptly titled book on the Canadian auto industry, *Driving Continentally*, Murray Smith makes the straightforward present-day point that "The automotive sector is the bellwether of North American economic integration under NAFTA;" indeed, it is already the most continentally-integrated of any sector.[12]

The writer since Innis who is most concerned with the symbiotic relationship between continentalism and regionalism is Garth Stevenson; it is not coincidental that he has also written extensively on transportation. "Canada's history and its national identity, more than those of any other political community in the world, have been associated with the development of transportation and communications." He adds with respect to the present times: "Canada's most important mode of transportation is highway transportation."[13] In sharp contrast to the east-west bias of the railway and the pervasive presence of the federal government, the pull of highways was north-south and the relevant government that of each province. Canada's first modern, limited-access highway, the Queen Elizabeth Way (QEW), built in the 1930s, ran from Toronto to Fort Erie, meaning Buffalo. (The inaugural flight of TransCanada Airlines in 1937 was from Vancouver to Seattle.) In contrast with most other modes of transportation and communication, "the provinces own and maintain the highways, which by a curious legal fiction are assumed to end and begin at each provincial boundary."[14] The paved TransCanada Highway was not authorized until 1949; Quebec stayed out under Duplessis because of opposition to federal grants with strings attached, and it was not completed until 1962, well after the transcontinental connection by air (1939), pipeline (1958) and TV microwave (1958). Though roads like Dundas Street were originally built for military reasons, to secure a line of communications away from the American border that would not be vulnerable to American attack,[15] the long-run consequences have been of the continentalist cast.

Innis' concerns and concepts remain highly relevant to the contemporary world and contemporary scholarship. He was a political economist, and then and now that means that institutions (such as the state, corporations and trade unions) matter as well as the market; they are not, as orthodox economists imply with respect to the first and third, merely inertial. He most certainly believed that the temporal, historical dimension was relevant. The old political economy with its emphasis on staples and transportation laid the basis for the new political economy of the post-1960s with its emphasis on dependent industrialization and matters of class and gender.

The Canadian auto industry is, in the words of James Laxer, "the classic case of branch plant industrialism;"[16] indeed, it is a highly successful example thereof, yielding both the benefits of high-wage jobs and the costs of a truncated structure. The recent Porter Report, bearing the imprimatur of both the Business Council on National Issues and the then Conservative Government of Canada, spells out the latter:

General Motors of Canada is Canada's largest exporter [Ford is second and Chrysler third], but strategy development and most home based activities such as design and engineering are carried out in the United States. Supporting industries to the Canadian transportation cluster, such as batteries ... and tires ... are also heavily foreign-owned and foreign home-based. Although the automotive assembly industry contributes greatly to the Canadian economy, the lack of home bases in Canada means that Canada reaps fewer direct and indirect advantages from the presence of those industries than would otherwise be the case. The lack of Canadian home bases also creates vulnerability as trade becomes more open.[17]

Studies done by the government itself show that in the auto industry "virtually no research and development is done in Canada," while in the parts industry Canadian-owned firms that accounted for just 17 per cent of shipments performed 46 per cent of the research.[18]

Canada is the only member of the G-7 not to have developed an indigenous car (something that even lesser economies like Sweden and South Korea have done), yet Canada is a member of the G-7. It has an imported, dependent auto industry, but a quantitatively large one that is finally efficient relative at least to the US parent country. The latter owes much to the Auto Pact, but its very success may have (falsely) encouraged a move to free trade that may be gravely threatening to both Canada's industrial future and its political future. A manufacturing sector has emerged with difficulty around the staples sectors of the Canadian economy in some part through conscious state policy of an interventionist kind; there is a distinct risk that free trade will undermine manufacturing and result in a reversion to a more staples-biased economy. Ontario's leading export to an industrially stagnant Britain is white beans, while two mainstream writers have recently reminded us that "Although Mexico is a newly industrialized country, it sells a higher percentage of fully manufactured goods to Canada (69 per cent) than Canada exports to it (24 per cent).[19] There is, following Innis, much to be learned about Canada from the careful contemplation of the car, including the failure of Canada to produce one.

II

Let us reflect briefly on what historical record there is of the industry in Canada. When Henry Ford developed his mass-production methods, the US quickly vaulted past France into first place among the world's automobile producers and stayed there until Japan passed it the 1980s.[20] The sixth Ford built was sold in Canada.

When the Canadian tariff on carriages was extended to cars, US automakers established assembly operations in Canada.[21] The initiative for the transplants came from Canadian carriage makers, Gordon MacGregor in the case of Ford and R.S. McLaughlin for General Motors. They were not bought out and taken over or persuaded to become comprador, they made the advance. (In the search for a name for the new Toronto NBA franchise, Toronto Compradors was somehow overlooked.) The key was patents, access to technology and technique, and what began as licensing and joint ventures did not progress along a learning curve to independent Canadian operations but regressed to wholly-owned, branch-plant, subsidiaries.[22]

British imperial preference arrangements gave Canadian-based companies an advantage over American-based companies and enabled the former to reap economies of scale by extending effective protection for the export trade.[23] In the interstices of empire, manoeuvring within the North Atlantic Triangle, Canada was that privileged part of the American empire where manufacturers, regardless of nationality, had special access to the markets of the British Empire. Where the British Empire market (albeit excluding Britain itself which warranted its own American operations) was insufficient, Ford allocated the Latin American market to its Canadian subsidiary; as well, Ford subsidiaries in the further reaches of the British Empire, like South Africa and British Malaysia, were owned and controlled through the Canadian subsidiary. By 1913, Ford's Walkerville factory turned out more cars than any plant in the British Empire, including England. Forty per cent of the cars were exported, two to three times as many as did Ford US.[24]

So it was that by 1920, with the further boost to the industry from producing for the world's first mechanized war, Canada was second in the world to the US as a vehicle producer simply by assembling American cars. But Canada, as an affluent, sparsely-settled North American society, was also second in the world (again, to the US) in per capita car ownership and, in spite of its small population, third in ownership (with Britain second) in absolute terms.[25] This should dispose of the simplistic argument, frequently encountered in the popular literature, that Canada failed to develop an indigenous industry because the Canadian market was too small; Canada remains second in per capita ownership but has slipped to sixth or seventh place among vehicle producers. The reality was that no Canadian car could survive in the face of branch-plant competition from Ford, GM, Chrysler, Studebaker and others; Canadian manufacturers tried to cater to the high-priced luxury market but could not hold even this niche. CCM (which sold that sixth Ford) made the Russell, a fairly popular choice until 1916 when it disappeared with the merger between CCM's Russell Motor Car Company and Willy-Overland Sales. By 1926, the only car made in Canada that was not also made in the US had the dubious distinction of being the only Canadian-made car propelled by steam; output of the Brooks Steamer was one car a day.

From an early date, therefore, the Canadian industry was a miniature replica of the American. It boasted many of the same models and American cars made in Canada conformed strongly to American standards (though heavy-duty shock absorbers were developed in Canada for use on the bad roads in the West). There was some effort to restyle models for the Canadian market, but the differences were superficial. The Buick was first marketed in Canada as the "McLaughlin," but in advertisements "McLaughlin" kept shrinking and "Buick" growing until only "Buick" remained. There are after all, scale economies, in this case spillovers, in advertising as well. In 1906, advertisements appeared in *Canadian Motor* for "Canadian-made Oldsmobiles"; the pitch was for jobs.[26]

The Canadian model of dependent industrialization reached its zenith in 1929. It had inherent limitations. With the historic exception of Ford, the Canadian industry was biased towards assembly rather than comprehensive parts production (the Canadian tariff on most parts was lower than on completed cars). Moreover, foreign ownership in cars led to foreign ownership in associated industries; "Firestone Tire and Rubber, B.F. Goodrich and Company, Goodyear Tire and Rubber, Seiberling, and US Rubber all followed the big three automakers into Canada."[27] As a result, jobs were fewer and were excessively of the semi-skilled or unskilled variety, while the head offices of the Canadian subsidiaries were more like regional offices for the Canadian operations with managers having limited, if any, input on key parent-company decisions.[28] In spite of its ability to export, the multiplication of models that may already have been excessive in terms of efficiency even for the large American market (that certainly became the case later with the built-in obsolescence of frequent model changes), meant considerably higher prices for Canadian than Americans for virtually identical cars.[29]

This fed popular resentment against the tariff despite the fact that even at its peak in the mid-1920s, the Canadian tariff of 35 per cent was "quite moderate" by international standards, below the US and France at 45 per cent, and virtually the same as the 33 1/3 per cent of traditionally low-tariff Britain.[30] By 1926 anti-tariff sentiment, particularly in western Canada, had built to the point that the Mackenzie King government cut the tariff to 20 per cent, making it one of the lowest in the world. It simultaneously, however, bowed to rising nationalist sentiment that wanted more made-in-Canada commodities, and brought in tough Canadian-content rules; companies that produced or purchased 50 per cent of the value of their finished automobiles within Canada would get a 25 per cent drawback on all duties paid on imported parts and materials.[31] This was a clever combination of managed trade, rather than free trade in the literal sense, that culminated in the later Auto Pact. The automakers were fiercely opposed and threatened shutdowns, but the Canadian location still gave preferred access to imperial markets. King further placated their concerns by repealing the excise tax on cars that met Canadian content regulations, thereby increasing effective protection while permitting a further cut in prices.

Traves offers insight on the power, or surprising lack thereof, of foreign capital: "The principal auto manufacturers were isolated from the major centres of political power. In Canada, the auto industry developed on reinvested profits, not bank loans or stock flotations, and politically powerful financiers, brokers and bankers had no significant political stake in its fortunes."[32] Naylor and Clement argue that Canadian industry is weakened by the dominance of Canadian financial capital but it is even weaker when it fails to forge any substantial links. King held the car manufacturers "in very low regard"; in his diary in 1923 he described them as "the hardest looking lot of manufacturers' promoters I have seen, a genuinely brute force gang from Ford's and other concerns."[33] While imports increased dramatically, prices fell, parts makers did not suffer and, by 1928, all of the Canadian car makers had qualified for duty drawbacks. During the first two years of the Depression, four of the leading American exporters during the 1920s – Nash, Hudson, Graham-Paige and Packard – established assembly operations in Canada. Traves concludes: "The 'Canadianization' program begun in 1926 thus achieved a significant success within just a few years of its adoption."[34] It is an instructive story of how popular pressure and government innovation triumphed over big business to the benefit of Canadian consumers and workers.

In the 1930s, as production sagged badly, Canadian plants turned out only between 4 and 5 per cent of cars and trucks produced in North America.[35] Trade agreements of 1932 gave Britain duty-free access to the Canadian automobile market, a provision that was to facilitate rising imports into Canada in the postwar years. The Canada-US Trade Agreement of 1936 reduced the tariff on cars to 27.5 per cent but increased Canadian- (or Empire-) content to 60 per cent. Studebaker, Hudson and Packard, the low-volume producers, ceased production and reverted to exporting to Canada.[36] But when auto plants were to convert to wartime production, surplus capacity disappeared, plants expanded and employment doubled.

In the immediate postwar years, pent-up Canadian demand camouflaged the serious loss of export markets as other countries adopted the Canadian-style import-substitution model. Dykes, in a popular treatment of the industry, writes: "most nations look on the automotive industry as a symbol of maturity" with no implication that he is thereby damning Canada with faint praise.[37] The record level of production of 1929 was broken in 1948, but in 1949 Canada was a net importer of passenger cars for the first time since 1914, a status that was to be matched by the US in 1957 (the same year that Ford introduced the Edsel!)[38] The United Kingdom took over second position as world producer immediately after the war; in the 1950s, France, Germany and Italy passed Canada, and in 1960, Japan. The heyday of the North American industry was over and Canada, as an exposed appendage of the American complex, felt the crisis first.

III

By the early 1960s, the growing trade imbalance in cars exacerbated Canada's current account deficits, there were fewer jobs than there might have been, prices were 10 per cent higher than in the United States and wages were 30 per cent lower. Whatever the alleged benefits of foreign ownership, in this most foreign-owned of Canadian industries, things were not working and threatened to give foreign ownership a bad name. The combination of foreign ownership and the tariff had culminated in a crisis; if foreign ownership was not to

go then the tariff had to and there were even mainstream economists prepared to advocate this.[39] But no government with a social
conscience or a desire to be reelected could contemplate free trade
without assurances as to what would survive by way of an auto industry in Canada. Free trade had been tried in agricultural implements
since 1944 and a once thriving industry had subsequently grown
more slowly than its American counterpart in spite of having strong
indigenous firms.[40]

The Diefenbaker Government had no choice but to act, if necessary unilaterally; it established the Royal Commission on the Automotive Industry, under the leadership of University of Toronto
economist Vincent Bladen, to consider the future of the industry.
There were really only two choices: either continental rationalization to achieve economies of scale and with exports offsetting
imports; or more efficient production within Canada market by reducing the number of models and, perhaps, even producing an all-
Canadian car. Faced with only these two possibilities, the American
automakers obviously would accept only the first; but either unable
or unwilling themselves to resolve the crisis in the Canadian industry, the United Autoworkers (UAW) played a larger role than one
might at first sight have imagined. Yates makes the point that in
postwar Canada "each sector of the economy had its own form of
regulation;"[41] perhaps, paradoxically, the union can play a larger
role in finding a solution when the sector is foreign-owned and the
national or Canadian interest eludes business and governments.

Canadian autoworkers, like their American counterparts, organized in the 1930s and, consistent with the tendency of Canadian
unionists to belong to American-based unions, ended up in the
UAW. More so than in most industries, this made a certain sense
given the overwhelming presence of American-based firms. The
Canadian UAW supported the continental rationalization option
with the hope that higher productivity would lead to wage parity; so
did the UAW in the US in order to prevent jobs from moving to
Canada.[42] Within the Canadian UAW, the Left Caucus pushed the
nationalist option but in the climate of the Cold War was unable to
mount a challenge to the union's leadership.[43] The nationalist
option was also supported by independent parts manufacturers
and the social democratic Government of Saskatchewan. The latter's brief to the Bladen Commission asked that "the industry give
consideration to the production of a Canadian automobile, an

automobile that would be more utilitarian, less subject to model changes, easier to repair and less expensive than the recent American mode."[44] It is poignant description of what is not a choice from multinational capital. Bladen was an old-fashioned economist who understood the argument, but wrote that we "must accept some features of the industry in the United States, such as the multiplicity of models and the frequency of model changes."[45]

Bladen shrewdly rejected both free trade and high protection and put forward an imaginative "extended content" provision whereby companies could earn duty-free entry of imports (mostly parts) by exporting (mostly assembled vehicles). He was impressed by the extent of scale economies: "if Canadian vehicle manufacturers were to adopt one type of automatic transmission for all models, the production of this part in Canada would not permit economies of scale such as now are obtained by a single United States producer of automatic transmissions."[46] But no action was taken on Bladen's proposals other than removing the excise tax, a belated recognition that the car was not a luxury.

The new Liberal government was sufficiently exercised about the state of Canadian industry in general that it created a new Department of Industry. It is a sign of how dependent the Canadian economy had become on the American, how irreversible that was, how non-viable the nationalist alternative already was, that even the greatest nationalist, Walter Gordon, reluctantly supported continental rationalization in the auto industry. "I did not like this [continental rationalization] in principle, but as three companies dominated the industry on both sides of the border, this acceptance merely acknowledged the existing fact."[47] More than that, to Gordon's intense unhappiness, he later had to agree to exempt *Time* and *Readers Digest* from proposed legislation on Canadian ownership of magazines because of concern that otherwise Henry Luce, the publisher of *Time*, might try to sabotage the Auto Pact. All in all, a depressing story about how dependency breeds dependency.

If the die was firmly cast within Canada for continental rationalization, the key was to convince Washington. With respect to the negotiations that culminated in the Auto Pact, Carl Beigie writes: "it became clear that the highest levels of administration in the US government attached a great importance to a successful conclusion. US officials realized that Canada was determined to do something about the poor prospects for its automotive industry."[48]

Stephen Clarkson adds: "When Lester Pearson sent peacekeeping troops to Cyprus in response to Lyndon Johnson's request, Johnson supported the Auto Pact in Congress as an exchange of favours."[49] The Pact included both an intergovernmental agreement and the companies spelling out the safeguards for Canada; it is not a figment of the Left's imagination that companies rank with countries – for some companies and some countries.

If the Auto Pact resolved the crisis that gripped the Canadian auto industry in the early 1960s, it did so by accentuating both the benefits and the costs of dependent industrialization. The intent of the safeguards was to increase Canadian production to more closely match Canadian consumption; but in fact, two-way trade flows increased dramatically (24-fold in 20 years) making the Canadian industry dependent on the American market rather than the Canadian market.[50] Prices fell in Canada, employment stabilized (as labour-shedding from increased efficiency was offset by increased demand from expanding production) and wages rose to nominal parity (the Canadian dollar was valued below the American dollar). But management and R&D functions were further centralized under the Pact to Canada's disadvantage and lower relative wages in Canada attracted a disproportionate share of the labour-intensive portion of the industry.[51] After twenty years of the Pact, two orthodox economists told us: "While Canadians are not hewers of wood and drawers of water, we are 'assemblers' of cars – a relatively low-skilled activity in which we compete with Korea, Taiwan and Brazil. Mexico produces more engines than does Canada ... All is not well in auto land."[52]

That the Auto Pact worked to Canada's advantage was certainly the American perception. Lyndon Johnson told Charles Ritchie, Canada's Ambassador to Washington, at the outset, "ooh, those Canadians. They got an Auto Pact and they're screwing us on that."[53] The US position was that the safeguards for Canada were transitional but even the notoriously pro-American, pro-free trade Canadian-American Committee was leery of that argument. There was too much discussion, it felt, of the balance of trade (which had moved in Canada's favour) and not enough of the balance of payments which took account of the remission of profits to the US. It asked, "Is there, as some Canadians contend, a southward migration of managerial and professional personnel out of the Canadian automotive industry as a result of the Agreement?"[54] US displeasure was such that in 1971, when its troubles led it to impose a temporary import surcharge, "President Nixon was on the point of abrogating the whole pact – only being dissuaded from such a drastic step by an impassioned intervention from the State Department an hour before the fatal step was to be taken."[55] But the Nixon administration did bring in the DISC (Domestic International Sales Corporations) program which created a tax advantage for producing in the US, and investments by automakers in Canada fell off sharply.[56]

By the late 1970s there were mounting deficits again in auto trade, and during the interlude of the Clark government, Trudeau committed the Liberals "to renegotiate the Auto Pact's disastrous imbalances." But as Clarkson documents so well, that was not to be. The rejuvenated Trudeau government brought in the National Energy Program and talked of NEPs in other sectors, but the election of the Reagan administration decisively ended the detente of the 1970s that had given countries like Canada at the margin a little room for manoeuvre. Fearing, excessively fearing, US protectionism, Canada tried to negotiate more sectoral arrangements, more Auto Pacts, with the US. The US was not receptive and with the election of the neo-conservative and highly pro-American Mulroney government in 1984, Canada moved to negotiating across-the-board free trade.

I V

During the negotiations of the FTA, Canada kept insisting that the Auto Pact was not on the table but it was and to Canada's detriment. The reality for some time had been that the North American industry was losing out to Japanese and then South Korean producers. In the early 1980s, the US responded to this unilaterally by negotiating voluntary restrictions on Japanese exports that encouraged Japanese companies to set up operations in the US. Canada moved tentatively in that direction with a production-based duty-remission scheme designed to encourage transplants in Canada.[57] But a concerted effort, led by the CAW and parts manufacturers, to extend Auto Pact provisions fully to the offshore producers came to naught with the election of the Mulroney government and the triumph of the ideology of deregulation over the national interest.[58] The FTA forbade Canada from extending the Auto Pact to offshore producers (other than GM's CAMI joint venture with Suzuki), phased out the duty remission scheme and precluded conditional subsidies to non-American automakers locating production in Canada. In effect, there is now a two-tier industry with American companies facing Canadian safeguards that are not applicable to the offshore producers.[59] The consequences for employment are disastrous: "If we compare the number of jobs provided by the North American-based companies relative to their sales with that provided by the major Japanese-based companies (Toyota, Honda, Nissan and Mazda), we find that the former provides ten times as many jobs ... If GM, Ford and Chrysler only had the same commitment to Canada as the Japanese multinationals, we would have 60,000 fewer jobs (even fewer if we included the parts manufacturing jobs)."[60]

Of course, the Auto Pact was not free trade *per se*, but *managed* trade, a critical distinction that was blurred during the great free trade debate of 1988. Grant Devine, the far-right and vehemently pro-free trade Premier of Alberta, went to Oshawa, the home of GM Canada, to declare that all of Canada would now get the alleged benefits of free trade which Ontario reaped from the Auto Pact. Ironically, what the FTA did was undermine the safeguards of the pact, since the duties which the companies had to pay as penalties for non-performance disappeared. Canadian-content rules – anathema to free traders – were replaced by North American content rules, with the problem for Canada that if the US plays hard ball, there is a risk that North American content *de jure* will be reduced to American content *de facto*. The North American industry was "protected" relative to the offshore producers but at a loss of protection for the Canadian segment. Canada is into a new variant of "imperial preference" with none of the promise of the first. Canadian nationalists who have always seen the Pact as a second-best-is the "managed trade" of the Pact economic nationalism or managed continentalism? – are compelled to rally to its defence and mostly fail in that effort.

NAFTA has only made the situation worse. Canadian production – including Canadian-owned parts manufacturing – can now shift to either the lower wage, less unionized states of the American south or to much lower wage Mexico. North American-content is increased from 50 to 62.5 per cent but there remains no Canadian-content rule and Mexican production has now to be included. After one cuts through the propaganda of governments and

neo-classical economists, commentators see Canada as having "lots
to lose, little to gain," particularly in parts production.[61] Still, they
may be prone to take too seriously the neo-conservative version of
the "competitiveness" model; in so far as public health insurance
and good highways for just-in-time production are determinants of
investment in the auto industry, Canada has an advantage which it
is likely to retain.[62] Absenteeism is less in Canadian plants, and
quality of production, as well as the return on investment "higher –
or so the union has claimed in the past."[63] With the new flexible-
production technology, GM has moved towards a regional production complex in southern Ontario.

Holmes argues that "The return to a more national alignment of
assembly and parts manufacturing is felt necessarily to reduce
vulnerability to outside forces" and he adds that "One source of
such vulnerability is the split in the union."[64] That Canadian autoworkers belonged to an American union seemed logical under
continental-rationalization model of the Auto Pact; but as Sam
Ginden observes (from the inside), "However much Canadian auto
workers were integrated in the continental economy, they were still
part of a different social formation."[65] The weakening of the American labour movement relative to the Canadian labour movement
and a growing sense of Canadian nationalism – in combination
with the move to post-Fordist production – led to the split, and
from that came the CAW that has played a catalytic role in energiz-
ing and restructuring the Canadian labour movement. Strong
unions, and progressive governments that invest in physical and social infrastructure – if Canada can maintain them in the face of the
powerful harmonizing effects of free trade – can be an advantage.
Yates writes of "Canada's continued preference as a good site for
building cars" and adds, "although it is impossible to predict the
CAW's success or failure in influencing the emergent mode of regulation, it is possible to state with certainty that any new regime, in
contrast to the Fordist experience, will be 'made in Canada.'"[66] To
reiterate a point made earlier, Canadian workers apparently make
more history than Canadian businesses.

v

Innis was concerned with the impact of media as technologies on
space and time. The automobile has become so pervasive in our

lives that we often overlook its influencing in shaping our very perceptions of space and time. But as Wilson reminds us: "The faster we drive, the flatter the earth looks ... [What we see] are events in 'automobile time' ... Distance is experienced as an abstraction; suburbs lie 'minutes from downtown' ... What we saw out the window of the speeding car – the Futurists were right after all, it is one of the greatest experiences of modern life – was the future itself ... The speeding car is a metaphor for progress. It is always moving ahead."[67] Moreover, the car pervasively privatizes. "It's hard," says Wilson, "to imagine a technology that better discourages communal activity ... The private car and the nuclear family have a parallel history."[68] This is perfectly captured in the phrase "the family car." It has been said that car and driver are "the dominant life-form roaming the countryside,"[69] and there is, Ursula Franklin points out, no population control for cars: "China can embark on a rigorous one-child-per-family policy ... But where in North America, western Europe or Japan is there serious discussion on the political level about ... the need for a one-*car*-per-family policy for the sake of the country's or world's future?"[70]

The book which launched Marshall McLuhan as Innis' successor in communication studies was *The Mechanical Bride*. "Sex, technology and death," which made up for McLuhan "the mystery of the mechanical bride," are what the car is manifestly all about,[71] the essence being captured by a recent headline, "Shun sex and fast cars, Vatican tells priests" – the better to free them up for the funerals, what with road accidents being the most common cause of death among white youths, aged 15 to 19, in America and traffic deaths outnumbering homicides six to one in Canada.[72]

If McLuhan is right, that each technology like the automobile is an extension of the human personality, then we research ourselves each time we drive, or even try to cross the street. When Canadians do so, there is cause to reflect not only upon our personal experience but also upon our industrial history and our economic relationship with the United States. The growth of the Canadian automotive industry was initially related to Canada's skilful exploitation of imperial preference arrangements and the development of Canadian-content rules which in due course culminated in the ingenious Auto Pact arrangement of the mid-sixties. In the face of the FTA and NAFTA, it has largely fallen upon Canadian autoworkers to defend the national interest in the industry. Even more so, the automobile has been a pervasive force in the continental rationalization of the North American economy generally, and with has come American cultural baggage and a tendency to political disintegration within Canada. Whether or not working people have the capacity to resist this occurrence is a question for more sombre reflection.

NOTES

1 Michael Bliss, *Northern Enterprise: Five Centuries of Canadian Business* (Toronto: McClelland and Stewart, 1987), 604. Charlotte Yates' book on autoworkers, *From Plant to Politics: The Autoworkers Union in Postwar Canada* (Philadelphia: Temple University Press, 1993), is much better than anything written about the auto industry in Canada. Tom Traves' chapter on "The political economy of the automobile tariff" in *The State and Enterprise: Canadian Manufacturers and the Federal Government, 1917–1931* (Toronto: University of Toronto Press, 1979) is the best that we have produced on the automobile tariff.

2 H.A. Innis, *A History of the Canadian Pacific Railway* (London, 1923; Toronto: University of Toronto Press, 1971).

3 A. John Watson, *Marginal Man: Harold Innis' Communication Works in Context* (PhD. Thesis, University of Toronto, 1981), 243.

4 Graeme Patterson, *History and Communications: Harold Innis, Marshall McLuhan and the Interpretation of History* (Toronto: University of Toronto Press, 1990), 8. He makes the telling point that "chapter one of the book deals with the river culture of the Nile and chapter two with civilization in relation to the Tigris and Euphrates" (10).

5 Given his obsession with deficits during the Great Depression, Innis merely noted that motor transportation was exacerbating problems of railway deficits. He also sat on the Royal Commission on Transportation that reported in 1951 and filed a Memorandum for inclusion in the Report; this was his chance to do what Brebner proposed, but in fact his Memorandum is almost exclusively concerned with the narrow issue of freight rates and their adverse impacts on regions outside of central Canada, a point which Innis had long insisted on. Nor does the index for Innis' "Idea File," compiled in the last seven years of his life, include any entries on transportation. See *The Idea File of Harold Adam Innis,* edited by William Christian (Toronto: University of Toronto Press, 1980).

6 James P. Womack, Daniel T. Jones and Daniel Roos, *The Machine that Changed the World* (New York: Harper Collins, 1990).

7 Perhaps the most oft-quoted sentences of *The Affluent Society* (Boston: Houghton-Mifflin, 1958) are these: "The family which takes its mauve and cerise, air-conditioned, power-steered, and power-braked automobile out for a tour passes through cities that are badly paved, made hideous by litter, blighted buildings, billboards, and posts for wires that should long since have been put underground. They pass on into a countryside that has been rendered largely invisible by commercial art ... They picnic on exquisitely packaged food from a portable icebox by a polluted stream and go on to spend the night at a park which is a menace to public health and morals. Just before dozing off on an air mattress, beneath a nylon tent, amid the stench of decaying refuse, they may reflect vaguely on the curious unevenness of their blessings" (199–200). Chapter 2 of *The New Industrial State* (Boston: Houghton-Mifflin, 1967), titled "The Imperatives of Technology" is the story of the Ford Motor Company.

8 The figure for personal consumption is from *The Machine that Changed the World*, 200; data on car-associated costs is cited in *Nation* (28 February 1994).

9 Alexander Wilson, *The Culture of Nature: The American Landscape from Disney to the Exxon Valdez* (Toronto: Between the Lines, 1991), 30.

10 George Ehring and Wayne Roberts, *Giving Away a Miracle: Lost Dreams, Broken Promises and the Ontario NDP* (Oakville: Mosaic Press, 1993), 187.

11 Harold Innis, "Significant Factors in Canadian Economic Development," in *Essays in Canadian Economic History* (Toronto: University of Toronto Press, 1956).

12 Maureen Appel Molot, ed., *Driving Continentally: National Policies and the North American Auto Industry* (Ottawa: Carleton University Press, 1993).

13 Garth Stevenson, "Transportation and Communication," in Mel Watkins, ed., *Canada* (New York: Facts on File, 1993), 450.

14 Stevenson, "Transport and Communication," 451.

15 Patterson, *History and Communications*, 185–6.

16 James Laxer, *Canada's Economic Strategy* (Toronto: McClelland and Stewart, 1981).

17 Michael E. Porter and the Monitor Company, *Canada at the Crossroads: The Reality of a New Competitive Environment* (1991).

18 Department of Regional and Industrial Expansion (DRIE), *Competitiveness Profiles* (Ottawa, 1986) and the National Advisory Board on Science and Technology (NABST), *Science and Technology, Innovation and National Prosperity: The Need for Canada to Change Course* (Ottawa, 1991) as cited in

David Crane, *The Next Canadian Century: Building a Competitive Economy* (Toronto: Stoddart, 1992), 121, 123.

19 Lorraine Eden and Maureen Appel Molot, "Continentalizing the North American Auto Industry," in Ricardo Grinspun and Maxwell Cameron, eds., *The Political Economy of North American Free Trade* (Montreal: McGill-Queen's Press, 1993), 300.

20 Paul Kennedy, *The Rise and Fall of the Great Powers: Economic Change and Military Conflict from 1500 to 2000* (London: Fontana Press, 1989).

21 Mira Wilkins, *The Emergence of Multinational Enterprise: American Business Abroad from the Colonial Era to 1914* (Cambridge: Harvard University Press, 1970), 96–7.

22 R.T. Naylor, *History of Canadian Business, 1867–1914* (Toronto: Lorimer, 1975), 2: 58.

23 W.A. Mackintosh, *The Economic Background of Dominion-Provincial Relations* (1939; Carleton Library, 1964), 100.

24 Mira Wilkins and Frank Ernest Hill, *American Business Abroad: Ford on Six Continents* (Detroit: Wayne State University Press, 1964), 44.

25 C.H. Aikman, *The Automotive Industry of Canada*. Montreal, McGill University Economic Studies 8 (1926): 18.

26 Aikman, *Automotive Industry of Canada*, 14; Sun Life Assurance Company, *The Canadian Automotive Industry* (a study prepared for the Royal Commission on Canada's Economic Prospects, September 1956); Herbert Marshall, Frank Southard Jr. and Kenneth W. Taylor, *Canadian-American Industry: A Study in International Investment* (1936; Carleton Library, 1976); Wilkins, *Emergence of Multinational Enterprise*, 97.

27 Wallace Clement, *Continental Corporate Power: Economic Linkages between Canada and the United States* (Toronto: McClelland and Stewart, 1977), 60. The ramifications of foreign ownership extended to other secondary industries, such as steel; years later the Bladen Royal Commission noted that in 1959 the Canadian steel industry sold about 6 per cent of its shipments to the automotive industry while the comparable American figure was 17 per cent (Royal Commission on the Automotive Industry, *Report* (April 1961), 24).

28 Yates, *From Plant to Politics*, 20.

29 Aikman calculates that factory prices ranged from 32 to 44 per cent higher in Canada than the US, while the actual cost to the consumer was 41 to 54 per cent higher (*Automotive Industry of Canada*, 27). Companies may well have taken advantage of the tariff in their pricing; Marshall *et al* note that Ford Canada, which imported practically no parts, "has been almost fantastically profitable throughout most of its history" (*Canadian-American Industry*, 64).

30 James Dykes, *Canada's Automotive Industry* (Canada At Work Series, 1970), 49; Marshall *et al, Canadian-American Industry,* 276.

31 These were actually Empire-, and later Commonwealth-content rules, but this distinction is of little significance since the only outside source of parts was the US.

32 Traves, *State and Enterprise,* 106.

33 Cited in Traves, *State and Enterprise,* 108.

34 Traves, *State and Enterprise,* 115.

35 Estimated by Marshall *et al, Canadian-American Industry,* 63.

36 Dykes, *Canada's Automotive Industry,* 49.

37 Dykes, *Canada's Automotive Industry,* 59.

38 K.J. Rea, *A Guide to Canadian Economic History* (Toronto: Canadian Scholars' Press, 1991), 234.

39 See, for instance, Harry Johnson's critique, "The Bladen Plan for Increased Protection of the Canadian Automotive Industry," in *The Canadian Quandary: Economic Problems and Policies* (Toronto: McGraw-Hill, 1963).

40 Peter Morici, "US-Canada Free Trade Discussions: What Are the Issues?" *American Journal of Canadian Studies* (Autumn 1985), 315.

41 *From Plant to Politics,* 238.

42 Robert White, *Hard Bargains: My Life on the Line* (Toronto: McClelland and Stewart, 1987), 72.

43 Yates notes that: "The Left Caucus in the Canadian UAW was especially open to attack, given the participation in the caucus of many Communists" (*From Plant to Politics,* 98).

44 Cited in the Royal Commission on the Automotive Industry, *Report,* 44.

45 *Report,* 21.

46 *Report,* 24.

47 Cited in J.L. Granatstein, *Canada 1957–1967: The Years of Uncertainty and Innovation* (1968), 207

48 Carl Beigie, *The Canada-US Automotive Agreement: An Evaluation* (Canadian-American Committee, 1970), 51.

49 Stephen Clarkson, *Canada and the Reagan Challenge* (Toronto: Lorimer, 1982), 283.

50 Tayce A. Wakefield, "The Canada-US Free Trade Agreement and the Canadian Auto Industry: Doing the Right Thing at the Right Time," in Marc Gold and David Leyton-Brown, eds., *Trade-Offs on Free Trade: The Canada-US Free Trade Agreement* (Toronto: Carswell, 1988), 285. This decoupling of domestic production from domestic demand gave the Pact a post-Fordist flavour.

51 ARA Consultants, *An Assessment of Three Existing Canadian Trade Agreements with the US* (September 1985); John Holmes, "Towards an Integrated North American Automobile Industry," in *Driving Continentally*, 26.

52 Melvyn Fuss and Leonard Waverman, "The Auto Pact and the Canada-US Free Trade Agreement," in *Trade-Offs in Free Trade*, 278.

53 Lawrence Martin, *The Presidents and the Prime Ministers* (Toronto: Doubleday Canada, 1982), 227.

54 Canadian-American Committee, *Toward a More Realistic Appraisal of the Automotive Agreement* (June 1970), 8, 11.

55 Clarkson, *Canada and the Reagan Challenge*, 130; see also Robert Bothwell, *Canada and the United States: The Politics of Partnership* (New York: Twayne Publishers, 1992).

56 Laxer, *Canada's Economic Strategy*, 136.

57 Simon Reich, "NAFTA, Foreign Direct Investment and the Auto Industry," and Molot, "Introduction," in *Driving Continentally*, 9.

58 Tates, *From Plant to Politics*, 211ff.

59 The FTA required that duty remissions be phased out by 1995 and precluded the granting of subsidies to automotive firms for the construction of plants conditional on provisions such as the level of Canadian content. Jon R. Johnson, "NAFTA and the Trade in Automotive Goods," in Steven Globerman and Michael Walker, eds., *Assessing NAFTA: Trinational Analysis* (Vancouver: Fraser Institute, 1993); N.B. Macdonald, "Will the Free Trade Deal Driving a Gaping Hole Through the Auto Pact?" *Policy Options* (Jan/Feb. 1993).

60 Sam Gindin, "The Auto Sector," in Duncan Cameron and Mel Watkins, eds., *Canada Under Free Trade* (Toronto: Lorimer, 1993).

61 Reich, "NAFTA," 89; Molot, "Introduction," 14; Holmes, "Towards," 54; and Eden and Molot, "Continentalizing," 308.

62 "Ford puts its 1990 health insurance expenses at $65 per vehicle in Canada, compared with $300 in US plants" according to the Office of Technology Assessment, Congress of the United States, *US-Mexico Trade: Pulling Together or Pulling Apart?* (Washington: 1992), 141–2. The report adds: "The problem is much greater for the Big Three than the transplants because Ford, GM and Chrysler must pay the full costs of health and benefits packages for an older and still aging workforce" (142).

63 White, *Hard Bargains*, 142–3, 245.

64 John Holmes, "The Globalization of Production and the Future of Canada's Mature Industries: The Case of the Automotive Industry," in Daniel Drache and Meric Gertler, eds., *The New Era of Global*

Competition: State Policy and Market Power (Montreal: McGill-Queen's University Press, 1991), 170.

65 Sam Ginden, "Breaking Away: The Formation of the Canadian Auto Workers," *Studies in Political Economy* (1989) 29: 69.

66 Yates, *From Plant to Politics*, 252.

67 *The Culture of Nature*, 34.

68 *The Culture of Nature*, 38. A major theme of Wilson's book is that "the private car [leads to] ... the private consumption of nature" (34) and the enormous expansion of tourism.

69 K.T. Berger, *Where the Road and the Sky Collide.*

70 Ursula Franklin, *The Real World of Technology* (Toronto: CBC Massey Lectures, 1989, 1990), 30.

71 Marshall McLuhan, *The Mechanical Bride: Folklore of Industrial Man* (New York: Vanguard Press, 1951), 101.

72 A popular history of the automobile in Canada by Robert Collins, published in 1969, was actually titled *A Great Way to Go.* The 1994 film *The Chase,* consists entirely of a two-hour car chase with a couple making love at one hundred miles an hour on a crowded expressway while being pursued by eight police cars and a helicopter.

PART THREE

Economics and Political Economy

The papers in this section offer striking insights into several aspects of Canada's recent intellectual history. They also involve a personal journey that continually placed Mel Watkins at the centre of the development of the new political economy in Canada.

The first of these papers, "The Dismal State of Economics in Canada," is a lament for the state of the discipline of economics in the wake of its "Americanization." In large part, Keynesianism arrived in Canada via the United States, where many Canadian academics received their graduate school training. This new orthodoxy, with its "general theory" and "universal technique" swept aside much of the indigenous approach to political economy and its emphasis on Canada's unique economic history and institutional setting. Extending this critique of neo-classic economics led to a consideration of "The Economics of Nationalism and the Nationality of Economics," and the opportunity to address the work of Harry Johnson, the acerbic Canadian who, despite his idiosyncratic views on Keynes,* had achieved iconic status in the economics discipline. Johnson's writings on the multinational corporation and nationalism, which represent the clearest statement

---

* For an interesting perspective on Johnson, see Tom Naylor's "Johnson on Cambridge and Keynes," in *Dominion of Debt* (Montreal: Black Rose Books, 1987).

of the neo-classical orthodoxy, are contrasted with developments in
the heterodox or dissenting literature. Counterposing the two approaches highlights the richness of a broad, political economy
framework and the constraints of the more narrowly defined economics literature. The pessimism of these papers stands in sharp
contrast to the third, "The Innis Tradition in Canadian Political
Economy." In reviewing the foundations of the Innisian approach,
Watkins defines the possibility for constructing a new political
economy in Canada.

The last three papers offer a commentary on the politics of the
Left in Canada and the appropriate role of the academic therein.
"Social Democracy" reviews the writings of the members of the Fellowship for a Christian Social Order and of the League for Social
Reconstruction during the 1930s and draws out two prominent
currents in Canadian social democratic movements. The first is the
ongoing debate over social reformism and, more particularly, the
extent to which the Canadian Left was "seduced by Keynesianism":
while Keynes provided the rationale for tangible gains in social welfare and a larger role for public ownership, the application of
Keynesian policies also inhibited a more thorough critique of capitalist relations. The second theme is the ambiguous stance taken towards American ownership of the economy, especially in light of
the "complacent attitude" expressed in the 1930s. "The Waffle and
the National Question" picks up on this second issue and lays claim
to the Waffle's legacy in terms of articulating a nationalist position
on the Left. The final paper, "The Intellectual and the Public," is a
fitting piece to conclude this volume since it is a personal reflection
on the relationship between the academic and political activism. It
addresses Innis's insistence that academics should refrain from political involvement, and his warning of the dangers of "present
mindedness" interfering with scholarly reflection. In light of Mel
Watkins' contribution to Canadian scholarship and his lifelong political engagement, it appears necessary to concede that, on this
one point, Innis was wrong.

11

The Dismal State of Economics
in Canada (1970)

"The voice of the economist is heard throughout the land." Harold Innis wrote these words in 1941, but their relevance today is clear. The concern of this paper is with the quality of that voice and whether there is, or could be, any Canadian content to it.

It might be agreed that there is a certain absurdity in the notion of mathematics for Canadians, but that it is hardly absurd to talk about Canadian art. In spite of its pretensions, economics is more art than science – in current American parlance, it is a "soft" rather than "hard" discipline – and therefore we can speak of *Canadian* economics in the sense of there being at least the possibility of an indigenous and distinctive national style. Indeed, the possibility became a reality in the writings of Innis and the so-called staple approach. In the main, however, Canadian economics means the application of universal technique, or at least free-world technique, to Canadian problems. Since Canada is better endowed with some problems than others – for example, resource development, international trade, foreign ownership – specialization will result and, with specialization, innovation and the potential for the export of ideas.

Similarly, to the extent that Canadian problems are unique, importation of ideas and technique will have its limitations: "Theories

Reprinted from Ian Lumsden (ed.), *Close the 49th Parallel etc.: The Americanization of Canada* (Toronto: University of Toronto Press, 1970).

developed and perfected in relation to the economies of Britain
and the United States, while perhaps intellectually satisfying, could
not by themselves be adequate instruments for analyzing the economic life and difficulties of Canada. Neither Marshall's *Principles*
nor Taussig's *Principles*, nor, later Keynes' *General Theory*, could be applied directly to a country where the price system, though no doubt
ultimately dominant, was complicated and distorted by significant
national peculiarities."[1] By way of example of the latter, Macpherson
cites "political rigidities such as the tariff." It is symptomatic of developments in the decade since he wrote that the present stance of
Canadian economists is to get rid of such distortions so that the
principles will apply; nature copies art.

   J.H. Dales has pointed out that, in fact, nearly the whole of
modern economic theory was developed by scholars working in
three countries: England, Sweden, and the United States.[2] His intent was to show the absence of Canada – about which there can
be no debate – but he unintentionally raises the question of the
legitimacy of the American contribution, an issue of some relevance to Canada given the present Americanization of everything,
including economics.

   In fact, there would be little disagreement with the statement that
economics was overwhelmingly British, rather than American, in
genesis until after the Second World War. Walter Heller has recently
listed five significant contributions to economics since the 1920s:
1) Keynes's "spectacular rescue ... of economics from the wilderness
of classical equilibrium"; 2) Hansen's "Americanization of Keynes";
3) Kuznetz' "seminal work on the concepts of national income and
gross national product"; 4) Samuelson's "neoclassical synthesis"; and
5) "computer-oriented economists whose qualitative work is increasing the scope and reliability of economic analysis and forecasting."[3]
Although apparently intending to do the exact opposite, he implicitly raises serious doubts about the importance and significance of
the American contribution, and anyone else since Keynes for that
matter. Hansen derives from Keynes; quantification and computer-
ization are hardly first-order activities – and econometrics is more
Dutch than American in origin; Samuelson's neoclassical synthesis is
little more than a transparent attempt to impose order on his best-
selling textbook. It would appear that the United States took the neo-
classical economics of Britain, including Keynes, and mathematized,

quantified, and computerized it. In the process, any indigenous roots, such as Veblen's institutionalism, were sloughed off.

At the risk of only slight exaggeration, it may be said that American economics, at present so dominant in the First and Third Worlds, is a fragment of British economics. The latter was predominantly liberal bourgeois, and the former more so; witness the greater intolerance toward Marxism in Cambridge, Massachusetts, than in Cambridge, England. Economics became respectable within the United States as Keynesian economics, demonstrating, incidentally, the inherent limitations of Keynesian economics. Once dismissed as the dismal science, economics has been riding high ever since. John Kennedy brought top economists into the White House. It is difficult to avoid the conclusion that the export of American economics reflects more the dominant position of the United States in the international economy and polity than innovation *per se*; the pen is not mightier than the sword. For reasons of power, that present American economics understandably ignores, the economics of the centre has become the economics of the margins.

The state of economics in general, then, consists of neoclassical and Keynesian economics filtered through American technocracy, and this has profound implications. Political economy, slowly dying in the hands of the British, was decisively transformed into quantitative economics. American economics is the quantification of quantification. In the process, the theory economists use has been emptied of the political.[4] The modern economist sees himself as concerned with allocating scarce means among competing ends. He sees economic theory as a set of techniques that gives the best solution to this "fundamental" problem. The answer invariably turns out to be the use of markets, and endless energy is devoted to discovering their minor imperfections and to fighting false battles with businessmen and civil servants openly committed to the free enterprise ideology.

In the process what is ignored is that the market economy is not a neutral mechanism that can be allowed free reign in a society without the most profound political and social implications which, in their turn, constrain the solutions which economists can put forward. The market economy creates the market society and thereby a set of institutions and values which are anything but neutral. Suddenly, important things like the distribution of income and wealth become sacrosanct, for to challenge them would undermine the incentives requisite for the operation of the market economy – that is, it would undermine the power elite which has most to gain from the operation of the market economy. Economists become, without quite being aware of it, rationalizers of the *status quo*.

Even that is not the end of the matter. Economics has become increasingly a technology characterized by great abstraction and high-powered technique. Jacques Ellul has written about the triumph of technique and its increasing autonomy from social and human considerations.[5] As he makes clear, economics is a leading example of this disease. If economists say sensible and humane things, as they sometimes do, it is in part by accident, by a process of random truth. In politics, we speak of the radical right and the radical left. Abe Rotstein has suggested that modern liberal economists belong to the radical centre. As intellectuals and citizens, they are usually in the centre of the mainstream, or at most slightly to the left. But as technocrats, using techniques increasingly developed out of the exigencies of economic theory or adapted from the physical sciences, they may build models and propose policies which are genuinely radical in the sense of the social disruption that would result from their serious application. A case in point is that, in a world of tariffs, there is an almost universal commitment of economists to free trade, including its unilateral pursuit. In this fashion, economists tend either to support the status quo by their irrelevance and absurdity, or to contribute to the further disruption of a world that is already out of control.

Consider poverty as a case in point. In the last decade it has suddenly become visible in North America. The only economist who played any significant role in this discovery was John Kenneth Galbraith, and he is not highly regarded within the guild. The oversight is not surprising, for economists for at least the past century have not had anything important to say about the causes of poverty. Unwilling or unable to diagnose, prescription becomes haphazard. Economists talk about the poor as if they were dealing with dropouts who need a little help in shaping up. The possibility that industrialization, at least under capitalism, creates the poor in the very process of creating the affluent – or, worse still, that the affluent owe some considerable portion of their affluence to their ability to exploit others at home and abroad – is rarely perceived. The absence of perception, combined with the technocratic bias, is fatal to policy. Elaborate proposals to reform tax systems[6] or apply cost-benefit techniques to poverty programmes,[7] mask the distinct possibility that liberal democratic societies, like Canada, are unable, because of their power structure, to do anything serious about correcting poverty.

If the economist is a technocrat, then what manner of intellectual is he? A distinction must be made between the expert as traditional intellectual and the expert as organic intellectual. The former devotes himself to a critique of the way it is. The latter devotes himself to working for the system, not only, or even primarily, by helping in his small way to solve its problems – which is largely legitimate and proper – but rather by rationalizing its operation; by developing theory which ends up proving that this is really the best of all possible worlds, by endlessly debating minor differences in policy so that everyone forgets, partly through fatigue, that there may be major alternatives that no one is ever taking the bother to try to conceptualize. The economist today, with rare exceptions – the latter notable being Marxists such as Baran and Sweezy[8] – is an organic intellectual; fundamental criticism is passe.

To perceive the nature of present-day economics yield insight on the state of economics in Canada. If economists exist to rationalize or justify the economy, then those in a branch-plant economy rationalize the neo-colonial situation. The status of the Canadian economy is hardly in doubt. Its efficient functioning rests on the turning out of branch-plant intellectuals, or organic intellectuals twice removed from the seats of power. As the Canadian economy has become Americanized, it follows, with only a short lag, that its economics must be Americanized as part of the broader process of Americanizing the educational system, both as institution and technique. John Porter has shown how the Canadian elites systematically neglected higher education so as to remove potential threats to their power; in the process they neglected even their own education and contributed to the drain of power outward to the United States.[9]

It would appear, indeed, that they failed even to run the branch plants efficiently, much less to create any kind of independent economy with a capacity to generate growth on its own. The great educational push in Canada in recent years is intended to improve the efficiency of the branch-plant economy. The process has been abetted by the importation of American academics, particularly in the social sciences. Rhetorical support for reformist measures to improve the performance of the branch-plant economy without changing its structure has been offered by the Economic Council, itself an emasculated version of the United States Council of Economic Advisers, with its research often done by economists otherwise employed by the Canadian-American Committee, a lobby group for North American economic integration, that is, for Canada's political disintegration. Canadian economists have made their contribution by, with few exceptions, demonstrating that the benefits from foreign investment are large and positive and, to the extent they are less than they might be, should be increased by abandoning the Canadian tariff. As apologists for the American-based multinational corporation, they are outranked only by American economists in the employ of American business schools. The Canadian case is no exception to the rule that an economy gets the economists it deserves.

Separate departments of political economy did not emerge in any significant way in Canada until the last decade of the nineteenth century. The initial tendency was to import scholars. As J.J. Spengler observes in the preface to the only book-length study of Canadian economic thought, by C.D.W. Goodwin: "Not until after World War I did Canadian scholars begin to contribute to the progress of economic science in general."[10] Following Goodwin, an examination of the appointment of W.J. Ashley to the first chair in political economy at the University of Toronto is illustrative of persistent phenomena. Ashley was an economic historian, not a theorist. When he came to Toronto, economic theory, especially as applied to commercial policy, was a source of bitter controversy in Canada consequent on Macdonald's National Policy in defiance of British free trade. Ashley was interviewed by the provincial premier, and it was clear that, being an economic historian, it was anticipated that he would not adopt a doctrinaire position; in fact, he did not disappoint. Nor was it an accident that economic historians were reliable protectionists, for economic history, as born in Germany and England, was a reaction to the laissez-faire bias of classical economics. In the event, Canadian economics, particularly at Toronto, was biased for the long run towards economic history. The occasional indigenous character of Canadian economics can be seen as an unexpected benefit of the tariff; when Dales refers to "the sad effects on Canada's intellectual life of the duel in the dark between commercial protectionists and their opponents," he is in the curious position of an economic historian created by the tariff and now attacking it.

Goodwin makes a number of useful observations on the effects of the tariff, as symbolic of the economy, on Canadian economics. On the one hand: "the widely-held conviction that orthodox political economy was no more than laissez-faire propaganda became for more than half a century the most powerful check on the development of Canadian economics." On the other hand: "After Confederation the Liberal party, in opposing the National Policy of high tariffs, treated political economy practically as revealed truth. It is easy to understand why for most people there was no distinction between the study of economics and a policy of laissez-faire." Finally:

In the 1880s and 1890s a combination of circumstances gave life to economics. Industrialization, westward expansion, and a new national consciousness resulted in unprecedented public awareness of economic problems; at the same time controversies over commercial policy (which for fifty years had made economic science unpopular) abated, and attention focused on labour legislation, land taxation, industrial combinations, and a government currency. By the turn of the century powerful social groups which formerly had regarded economics with distrust as an obstacle to tariff protection came to view the science with approval because it provided arguments against trade unions and government intervention."

The tendency for economics to reflect the economy is clearly evident.

The implication, by Goodwin and Dales, that the tariff inhibited economic scholarship is fair enough, but the hopelessness of the dilemma needs to be understood. On the one hand, protective tariffs were inevitable in areas entering upon industrialization; for Canada, there were the powerful examples of the United States and Germany. On the other hand, the imperialism of British classical economics was the counterpart of British imperialism for free trade. Intellectual imperialism is real, but reactions to it in marginal areas typically produce mediocrity – though the judgment is largely internal and tautological.

The breakdown of the British empire in the interwar period permitted economics to develop at the margin. "Economics came of age in Canada in the 1920s" (Dales). The so-called Toronto school

of economics, associated particularly with the work of H.A. Innis
and to a lesser extent with W.A. Mackintosh of Queen's University,
emerged as the first and last evidence of an indigenous Canadian
economics. Dales has maintained that Innis' monographs on the
fur trade and the cod fisheries are the only outstanding works in
economic history that relate to a non-European country. The
unifying theme was the emphasis on staple production for export
in new countries:

Concentration on the production of staples for export to more highly industrialized areas in Europe and later in the United States had broad implications for the Canadian economic, political and social structure. Each
staple in its turn left its stamp, and the shift to new staples invariably produced periods of crises in which adjustments in the old structure were
painfully made and a new pattern created in relation to a new staple.[11]

As economics, it was necessarily political economy: "The so-called
Staple Theory, which is commonly used to explain economic
growth in Canada, is really a pseudonym for a kind of imperial relationship."[12] Innis was creating not only a new economic history that
would go beyond the traditional constitutional bias to focus on the
interaction of geography, technology, and institutions, but also a
new history of Canada – *vide* particularly the writings of A.R.M.
Lower, the early Creighton, and the so-called Laurentian school –
and ultimately a new economics, at least in the negative sense, of
dissent from the mainstream.

   Innis, the Canadian Veblen, rejected both Marshallian equilibrium analysis and Keynesian short-run monetary analysis. He was
able to exploit the already established bias toward economic history
at Toronto, the peculiar weakness of economics generally as a discipline in the 1920s – its sterility between Marshall and Keynes, with
the latter saving the discipline from the worst of all fates, irrelevance – and the momentary freedom as Canada moved from the
British to the American empire. Briefly, novelty was possible.

   Though after 1940 Innis was to turn from Canadian economic
history to universal history, there are numerous trenchant observations by him on the consequences of American imperialism for
Canada and an implicit recognition of the futility of Canadian economics. His death in 1952 ended a dominance over Canadian social science that was more than intellectual – he both chaired the

Toronto Department of Political Economy and was Dean of the
Graduate School – and facilitated an Americanization of Canadian
economics that has virtually obliterated his own work. It is tempting
to assign the blame to his disciples who too often paid him only lip
service and dismissed his analysis with that great Canadian cliche,
"anti-Americanism."[13] But Daniel Drache has recently demonstrated an inherent weakness in Innis' work that is symptomatic of
(non-radical) attempts to dissent within the American system.[14] Innis was a liberal nationalist for whom Canada, having sprung from
liberalism, must develop its own national version. He recognized
liberal (American) imperialism, but he did not abandon his faith in
Canadian liberalism. The resulting tension made him personally
highly productive but socially increasingly irrelevant. His contemporaries, unable to accept his analysis of liberal imperialism, became
continentalists. Significantly, a present revival of interest in Innis,
of which Drache is the most relevant example, is found among
young socialist scholars. Innis, convinced that the price system was
the basis of liberal culture and a fundamental protection for the individual, was unwilling to recognize positive government and hence
precluded the possibility of adequate defence against Americanization. For those without that conviction, Innis' anti-imperialism
argues powerfully for the necessity of a Canadian nationalism of
the left.

In the period since the decade of the 1920s, the key event in economics at the global level is, of course, not Innis but Keynes. The
combination of Keynesian economics and American imperialism
made economics relevant and choked off independent developments in peripheral areas such as Canada. Canadian economics in
the wake of the Keynesian revolution returned to its historic mediocrity; Innis survived by transcending the discipline but at the necessary price of irrelevance and neglect. From a low point in the
mid-1950s, Canadian economics has recovered via Americanization.
Significantly, the critical discovery was that the Canadian economy
was a miniature replica of the American economy, with its lesser
efficiency attributable to inappropriate Canadian policy. To stress
the commonality of the American and Canadian economies at a
time when the latter is a satellite of the former is to offer the most
convincing evidence possible of how the political has been drained
out of political economy. Innis as doyen of Canadian economics
gave way to Harry Johnson of the University of Chicago and London

School of Economics, seats of the new and the old imperialism. Where Innis had resisted and Canadianized, Johnson promoted and Americanized.

That there are benefits, albeit of a second order, from being safely ensconced within the paradigm, should be obvious; the contributions of Canadian economists to the American-dominated discipline have been ably, even generously, detailed by Johnson, and the interested reader is referred thereto.[15] In the days of the British empire, Canadian insistence on a protective tariff inhibited the importation of British classical economics. The result was not creativity but backwardness and mediocrity. In the days of the American empire, the rhetoric of pro-imperialism may be less, but the reality in terms of economic policy greater. The inhibitions once imposed by the tariff have been transcended, directly by a spate of monographs both beating the tariff to death in its own right and attributing any alleged costs of foreign ownership – the new concern of the masses – to the tariff, and indirectly by opting in the American tradition for technique over relevance. Mediocrity has given way to competence, and the Canadian economist as technocrat has earned the respect of his American counterpart. By accepting the imperial rules of the game, he can, as in the case of the Carter Commission on Taxation, work out policies of a purity and rationality denied to those who work in the less tidy and more pathological seat of power.

But quantity and competence are not to be confused with creativity. If economics in Canada is to become something other than a rationalization of a satellite economy, then, short of the liberation of the economy and the consequent liberation of economics – admittedly the reliable though improbable route – Canadian economists must begin the struggle of coming to grips with the power structure within which the economy is imbedded. By ignoring power, the economist, in Canada and elsewhere, claims to be apolitical. Unfortunately, he seems simply to be trapped in the existing constellation of power and ideology, and to be deeply political in a sense that only the innocent can be.

It must be conceded that the future of economics lies largely outside our hands, though the revival of Innis is a useful technique of resistance for the sake of a Canadian economics. The revival of interest within the United States in Marx, as the last political economist, is a more hopeful development, not only because of the immediate relevance of even a fossilized Marxism, but primarily because it implies a subversion of the present paradigm that is a prerequisite for a new synthesis and leap forward.

Ultimately, however, there can be no escape from the rule that economics follows the economy. The increasing contradictions of American capitalism and, less certainly, the mounting concern for Canadian independence, suggests the possibility that economics in the 1970s may at least return to the creativity it demonstrated, at both the centre and the margin, in the interwar period. Until that happens, however, the non-economist heeds us at his peril.

NOTES

1 C.B. Macpherson, "The Social Sciences," in Julian Park, ed., *The Culture of Contemporary Canada* (Ithaca and Toronto, 1957).
2 "Canadian Scholarship in Economics: Achievement and Outlook," in *Scholarship in Canada, 1967*, edited by R.H. Hubbard (Toronto, 1968).
3 *New Dimensions of Political Economy* (New York, 1967), 4.
4 The remainder of this section draws in part on the author's "Economics and Mystification," *Journal of Canadian Studies* 4 (Feb. 1969): 55–9.
5 *The Technological Society* (New York, 1964).
6 *Royal Commission on Taxation, Report* (Ottawa, 1967); for a detailed critique of the Carter report in these terms, see Stephen H. Hymer and Melville H. Watkins, "The Radical Centre – Carter Reconsidered," *Canadian Forum* (June 1967).
7 Economic Council of Canada, *Fifth Annual Review* (Ottawa, 1968).
8 See, for example, Paul A. Baran and Paul M. Sweezy, *Monopoly Capital* (New York and London, 1966).
9 *The Vertical Mosaic* (Toronto, 1965).
10 *Canadian Economic Thought* (Durham, NC, 1961).
11 H.A. Innis, *Empire and Communications* (Oxford, 1950).
12 C.W. Gonick, "The Political Economy of Canadian Independence," *Canadian Dimension* (May-June, 1967).
13 An important exception is Donald Creighton; see his *Harold Adam Innis: Portrait of a Scholar* (Toronto, 1957).
14 "Harold Innis: A Canadian Nationalist," *Journal of Canadian Studies* 4(2) (1969): 7–12.
15 Harry G. Johnson, "Canadian Contributions to the Discipline of Economics since 1945," *Canadian Journal of Economics* 1 (1968): 129–46.

12

The Economics of Nationalism and the Nationality of Economics: A Critique of Neoclassical Theorizing (1978)

Such was the productivity of Harry Johnson that he is said to have published more articles in professional journals than any other economist.[1] This is a remarkable and laudable achievement, and one that would have been even more impressive were it not for his untimely death. In the face of such prodigious output, it can be argued that the minimum number of economists required to assess his contribution is six, with each of us (perhaps even all of us together) being, in the nature of the case, less productive than Johnson. As well, Johnson's work ranged over many of the sub-disciplines within economics; unlike him, we are again lesser men who practice the finer division of labour. When asked to assess his work on the multinational corporation (MNC) and nationalism I was told I would receive a bibliography of his writings relevant to my topic; on receiving it felt like the apocryphal student in this age of declining literacy who thought the reading of the reading list a sufficient assignment.

Harry Johnson was a neoclassical economist, indeed the most creative practitioner thereof that Canada has produced in recent

A revised version of a paper by the same title that appeared in the *Canadian Journal of Economics* 11 (1978): S87-S120. The original paper was one of six presented at the "Harry Johnson Memorial Symposium" organized by the Canadian Economics Association.

times, and a committed internationalist, or anti-nationalist.[2] I am none of these things, but rather a Marxist and a nationalist. I could have chosen to focus on the first of these differences (neoclassical versus Marxist) and to some extent I must; but a Marxist critique of neoclassical theorizing struck me as unproductive at least at the margin both because it has about it the character of a dialogue of the deaf and because it has been done many times already and is likely to be subject to diminishing returns.[3] I am also acutely conscious of the inherent dilemma posed by Kuhn: "When paradigms enter, as they must, into a debate about the paradigm choice, their role is essentially circular. Each group uses its own paradigm to argue in that paradigm's defense ... To the extent that two scientific schools disagree about what is a problem and what a solution, they will inevitably talk through each other when debating the relative merits of their respective paradigms."[4] I could have brought to bear the writings of Marxists on imperialism which are at least as vast and complex as those of neoclassicists on the MNC, with the additional difficulty that Johnson, though he sometimes railed against Marxism, did not, so far as I know, ever cite their works in his works and may simply have never read them. In this sense, as in others, Johnson was, one suspects, very typical of the mainstream of our profession. As Macpherson has observed: "Ignorance of Marxism is no sin in an economist."[5]

A nationalist critique of neoclassical theorizing and particularly of the Johnsonian version, albeit from a Marxist stance as well, is potentially a more productive exercise.[6] As Rotstein argues, both the neoclassical and the Marxist paradigms have great trouble with nationalism; given the reality of nationalism, this suggests that my topic is the one where the intellectual action is, or should be.[7] To admit the existence of nationalism as a general phenomenon is necessarily to acknowledge its relevance to ideas or knowledge or technique, including economic theorizing itself. Johnson denounced nationalism in the academy more vehemently than any other manifestation of nationalism, but that is not the only possible stance. A nationalist perspective may enable me at least to raise questions that are much neglected by our profession and highly relevant to any assessment of Johnson's writings on what he chose to think of as timeless "scientific economics" and to his role as a reputable intellectual who never fully transcended the dilemma of the "colonial intellectual"[8] that inheres in being Canadian.

My subtitle will make it evident that this paper is fundamentally a
critique of neoclassical theorizing, and thus a critique of Johnson
precisely because of his great proficiency as a neoclassical theorist.
We should be honest and recognize that one's position on Johnson's
work is mostly predetermined by one's allegiance, or lack of it, to the
orthodox paradigm within which he prospered. I am able to insist
on this point since, in a previous incarnation as a liberal anti-
nationalist economist, I favourably reviewed *The Canadian Quandary*.[9]

I

Johnson's writings on the MNC proper can fairly be described as
representing evolving orthodoxy. Initially, his focus was Canada;
the relevant essays, as collected in *The Canadian Quandary*, contain
little of analytical interest and reflect the general impoverishment
of economic analysis in this area at that time. Change came with
the slow spread of the analysis in Stephen Hymer's path-breaking
1960 dissertation, that other Canadian economist who chose to
pursue his career outside Canada and also met an untimely
death.[10] Johnson accepted Hymer's analysis, wedding international
economics and industrial organization, directly in its own right and
indirectly as later adumbrated by Caves but argued, typically, that
recognition of imperfect competition did not alter policy conclusions based on models assuming perfect competition.[11]

Vanderkamp, in a brief obituary notice, observes that Johnson
was "a professional social scientist who was prepared to change his
opinion in the face of new theoretical developments and new
factual evidence" and cites, by way of example of "this intellectual
evolution," Johnson's "more recent balanced treatment of the benefits and costs of foreign direct investment, in *On Economics and
Society*."[12] This is true, but in a rather limited sense. There is no evidence that Johnson altered his earlier views on Canada and the
Preface to the Carleton Library reissue of *The Canadian Quandary*
(1977) concedes nothing to the nationalists. He held firmly to the
position that foreign ownership was not a problem in its own right
independent of the Canadian tariff and the solution was to abolish
the latter. He was not influenced by claims to the contrary and, for
example, tartly dismissed the Gray Report.[13] His views were, and
still are, the mainstream position of the profession. As well, in the
worst hinterland neo-classical tradition, Johnson found it easier to

make jibes about the inadequacies of Canadian businessmen – "the small, smug mind and large larcenous hands of Bay Street"[14] – than to pose the question, much less attempt to answer it, about the reasons, which just might include the stultifying effect of foreign ownership, behind the deficiencies of Canadian entrepreneurship.[15]

A case can be made that Johnson became aware of the limited benefits of foreign direct investment (FDI) to developing countries:

[The MNC's] need for profitability ... is likely to conflict sharply with mounting concern about social justice in the distribution of income ... In concrete terms, reliance on [FDI] to promote development is likely to mean highly uneven development ... [The MNC's] purpose is not to transform the economy by exploiting its potentialities (especially its human potentialities) for development, but to exploit the existing situation to its own profit by utilisation of the knowledge it already possesses, at minimum cost to itself of adaptation and adjustment ... The main contribution of FDI to development will be highly specific, and very uneven in its incidence. In particular, the direct and visible impact is likely to be the training of a relatively small number of native employees for jobs on the factory floor and in the company offices, and the creation of a relatively tiny elite of higher-income people in a general environment of low income and heavy unemployment.[16]

But lest an unwary reader of these selected quotations infer that Johnson had switched sides it must be pointed out that all of them are preceded by the prediction that "the emphasis in development policy is likely to shift more and more towards increased reliance on private competitive forces" and "such a shift of emphasis will, if it is to work effectively to promote development, require fundamental changes of attitude in the developing countries." The implication seems clear: FDI may not be all it is sometimes touted to be, but it is the only game in town, and one had better learn to play by the rules.

In general, it can be argued that Johnson was not sufficiently sensitive to two issues in the literature that have recently attracted increasing attention: the importance of intra-firm transactions rather than market transactions proper; and the effects of FDI on employment and working conditions in the host countries.

On transfer pricing, Johnson ignored a necessary inference of Hymer's analysis that the market was being suppressed. Analytically, the phenomenon has been known at least since the seminal article by Coase and, in light of the accumulated evidence on its quantitative importance, it was distinctly unhelpful simply to go on assuming the contrary.[17] Helleiner's study of primary commodities places Johnson's "doctrinaire" view that less developed countries should not interfere with the operation of "free" markets against Malmgren's observation that "large corporate systems are really central planning entities which frequently substitute internal administrative arrangements for market forces" and comes down distinctly on the side of Malmgren.[18] A long-standing critique of orthodox liberal theory, of which Karl Polanyi's *The Great Transformation* is an outstanding example, is that it assumes markets while what needs to be explained is the institutionalization of markets. What is evident is Johnson's willingness to go on assuming what may no longer exist and chastise those who do not share the illusion. The issue is important for the ability of the host country to tax foreign subsidiaries; indeed, Johnson consistently cited this fiscal benefit first in the list of benefits of FDI to the receiving countries, though neglecting how prices relevant to the tax calculation are determined.

On the second issue, employment and its ramifications, the later Johnson was not inclined to exaggerate the benefits of FDI to the developing countries, especially in the face of their population growth and abundant labour supply. But the appropriate response was not to "interfere" with the operations of the MNC, much less replace it with an alternative geared to the human needs of the masses of people. Rather "the fundamental solution to this problem obviously lies in control of population growth in the less developed countries."[19] While the MNC was not a panacea of job creation, Johnson seems never to have been in doubt that it did at least create jobs, both directly and indirectly through spread effects, including training.[20] While this is the conventional view, surprisingly little of the vast literature on the MNC speaks directly to this question. In an impressive recent study, part of the ILO World Employment Research Programme, Vaitsos writes of "an employment illusion": foreign firms appear to create employment, but they instead displace more appropriate national activities and distort the process of industrialisation in such a way as to continually reduce employment and aggravate poverty in developing countries.[21]

Broadly conceived, the interrelationship of the MNC and jobs is, in conventional parlance, the issue of the international division of labour or, more accurately, the occupational hierarchy of contemporary capitalism as a world system. Johnson certainly saw an integrated world economy as already substantially in existence and advocated more of the same. He was also aware of the "unevenness" of development. But being unconcerned with the hierarchical character of the corporation, Johnson had no cause to question the international hierarchy of decision-making that flowed from it.[22] If this mode of analysis is pushed far enough, one can transcend the neoclassical paradigm, which necessarily begins (and ends) with the exigencies of capital, by taking labour and its needs as the starting point; *its* inherent antagonism with capital is then *the* motor of contemporary capitalist development under the aegis of the MNC. The analysis suggests the necessity for the nation-state to respond to the (nationalist) demands of its own mostly immobile labour force, as well as to the demands of foreign and domestic capital, this being the essential dilemma of contemporary "national policy." Hence, it offers a rationale for the nation-state that is often ignored, that is, to attempt to resolve the specific conflict between immobile (national) labour and mobile (transnational) capital within the context of the general antagonism between labour and capital. At the same time it provides a fresh explanation for international conflict and rivalry – rather than for the harmony and cooperation that neoclassical theory presumes to inhere in the international economy – by showing how class conflict translates itself into conflict between nations.[23]

On matter of technology transfer, Johnson held that there was an economics to technology "just as there is to any phenomenon." Given the "institutional embodiment [of technology] in the multinational enterprise," the economics of technology becomes for Johnson little more than an exercise in further elaborating the imperatives of the corporation. The conclusions are equally dreary: "imitation is the cheapest means of improving technology: and thus it is worth the social price of learning to conform. All that society and politics can do is to raise the price of conformity or subsidize the cost of non-conformity."[24] Other views are possible, both as to the nature of the phenomenon and the alternatives. For Vaitsos, what occurs is not the transfer of technology from one society to another, but "the captive use of knowledge by the [MNC's] internationally," and he points ironically to one of the specific realities that flows from the process that was so rational for Johnson:

developing countries end up exporting engineers and importing engineering.[25] Amin argues, from a Marxist and Third World perspective, that "industry must be made to serve the poor urban masses and no longer be guided by the 'profitability' criteria which favor the privileged local market and exports to the developed centers ... This kind of remodelled industry cannot find its technological models ready-made in the developed countries ... The real issue is not the conditions of 'transfer of technology, but the creation of conditions conducive to creativity in this field, not out of motives of 'cultural nationalism' but for objective reasons."[26]

Finally, Johnson, though a Canadian and a student of Innis, appears completely uninfluenced by a Canadian intellectual tradition – led in their different ways by Innis, McLuhan, Grant and Rotstein – that has generated profound insights about mankind's fate in the face of a technology outered from ourselves and alienated to corporate monopolies. These are, perhaps, insights from the hinterland inaccessible to those who too deeply embrace the metropolitan paradigm.

II

A recurring theme in the literature is that of the MNC versus the nation-state. It is not one, however, that has been particularly productive of insight, at least in the mainstream literature. By and large it is an area where it is difficult to distinguish between belief, or wishful thinking, and analysis; *obiter dicta* abound. That is certainly the case with Johnson, for whom it was an article of faith that the MNC was the wave of the future, the nation-state the dead hand of the past.

In his early writings on Canada, he dismissed what he saw as "this vague anxiety about the closeness of Canadian economic relations with the United States" as "an anachronism, a hangover from history."[27] In his later writings on technology, "not the least" of the problems that he saw in prospect from technology and its increasing complexity was "man's archaic clinging to the nation state as his unit of social organization."[28] On the issue of extraterritoriality as an area of tension between the MNC and the nation-state, he states: "The issue necessarily brings national states into conflict with one another and should be seen, not in terms of the traditional categories of 'American imperialism,' 'colonialism' and so forth, but in terms of a more general and fundamental problem of reconciling the traditional and anachronistic conception of the 'isolated state' with the economic – and political – facts of a rapidly integrating world in which there is increasing mobility of goods, capital, labour (at least educated labour) and knowledge. In the long run, we shall have to become one world, politically as well as economically."[29] For Johnson the assumption that the nation-state was obsolete served in conjuring away such nasty things as imperialism and colonialism; on the few occasions that they are alluded to, he puts them in quotation marks or precedes them with "alleged." The final sentence is only one of the countless examples of Johnson's conviction that there already was a world economy and it was time the world polity got in step.

There is much to object in these simplistic views. The first is how anything so obsolete as the nation-state can still be tolerated, much less actually supported, by so many of the ordinary people of this world. Neoclassical economists are but the slightest fraction of the world's population; how is it possible for so few to be so right and so many to be so wrong? It is, to say the least, puzzling: "Some cry, anachronism – but if so the question remains, how come such a flourishing anachronism?"[30] And what is meant by "archaic?" Johnson and others use it mostly as a pejorative term, a tendency which is distinctly unhelpful. Kindleberger tries to be understanding but, perhaps precisely because of his lucidity, only manages to demonstrate the extreme limitations of the neoclassical paradigm when confronted with a truly complex phenomenon. "Scratch any of us deeply enough," he tells us, "and you will find instinct of nationalism or xenophobia, overlain though they may be with layers of civilizing repression." People react instinctively to "the fact that the activities of institutions within their economy and polity are 'controlled' from outside the political unit … The reactions are understandable, but are not on that account to be approved." Nationalist sentiment is "non-economic," an example of "irrational instincts which the study of economics is perhaps designed to eradicate."[31] Economics, it would appear, is part of those "layers of civilizing repression," part of the hope that the nationalist hordes can be converted to reason. I risk being facetious, but surely the transformation of economics from science into magic is striking.

If this seems too strong a charge, bear in mind what has been done. Nationalism is variously described as anachronistic, or archaic, or instinctual (though these words in fact do not all have the same meaning). It is then labelled irrational, because it represents non-economic behaviour, in the sense of not maximizing material gain. Being archaic and irrational, it must be condemned.

What does the term archaic imply? Régis Debray argues that the nation-state is a historical creation that expresses the cultural organization of the human collectivity. Against the tendency to disintegration, it seeks to survive by reproducing its own identity in space and time. In this sense, that the "hard core" of the nation-state is always archaic makes it more resistant and resilient: born with capitalism, now in bed with communism, it may have staying power equal to either.[32] The difference between Debray's mode of reasoning and that of neoclassical economics is so vast that it is not easy to make a connection, but it should put all of us on our guard against facile predictions, such as Johnson's that "the long-run trend will be toward the dwindling of the power of the national state relative to the corporation."[33]

Debray's allusions to man's fundamental notions of time and space will recall how the later Innis also used these dimensions as the warp and woof of history to try to get at the mysteries of empires as political entities.[34] These themes resonant in Canadian writing, significantly in the discussion of nationalism. Grant spoke to the temporary dimension in his lament for Canada: "I lament it as a celebration of memory; in this case the memory of that tenuous hope that was the principle of my ancestors," and his lament was in turn to feed fresh hopes.[35] Rotstein sees English Canadian nationalism as a spatial phenomenon "confined to a single dimension of political concern: the integrity of Canadian territory from sea to sea, and the integrity of legal jurisdiction and social order on that territory." From this it draws what little strength it has in resisting American penetration, and hence there is minor virtue; but from this it also draws its obsession with national unity and its inability to relate to Quebec's nationalism with its much deeper historical, or temporal, roots, and here lies its "grave liability."[36]

What is there to say about the matter of "irrationality?" Nairn describes nationalism as an apparently "irrational" mass response to the rapid industrialization of the 18th Century, an industrialization destructive of all traditions and customs. Nationalisms resisted industrialization by looking to the past, but at the same time were transformed by the "ordeal of development." In this context, neoclassical theorizing on nationalism is best understood as a "metropolitan fantasy" that serves the imperatives of the grand bourgeoisie (now the MNCs) of the metropolis. But in the nature of the case, that is, of imperialism, it also serves the interests of comprador bourgeoisies (allied to metropolitan capital) in the hinterlands; hence the fantasy must thrive as well among the intellectuals of the hinterland.

In the Canadian context, Rotstein – who is unquestionably the leading English Canadian theorist of nationalism – uses a Polanyi-like framework that has anticipated important aspects of this nationalist counter position. "The new MNCs threaten the survival of the indigenous cultures and political integrity of countries which they penetrate ... [by shifting] the locus of decision-making outside the borders of the host country ... For those concerned with the issue of national independence . . at stake is the integrity of the apparatus of the nation-state as a means of implementing the growing number of tasks assigned to it by its citizens ... In an age of rapidly spreading global corporations, only the nation-state remains as a regulatory power and safeguard of sufficient strength against the vast reorganization of resources and global planning carried on by these corporations in their own interests."[37] Johnson, though highly critical of Rotstein's work, never took it sufficiently seriously to detail what he thought wrong with the analysis. This would have required him to theorize about non-market activity and not to pretend that all activity is reducible to market-like activity.[38] The cost of doing otherwise is high, for it means (in this case) that economic theory threatens to destroy the possibility of the serious study of nationalism. Innis once wrote of the need "to rescue economics from the present-mindedness which pulverizes other subjects and makes a broad approach almost impossible" and advised that "the use of economic theory as a device for economizing knowledge should be extended and not used to destroy other subjects or an interest in them."[39]

III

Any theorist of nationalism therefore faces an awesome task; this needs to be borne in mind as we turn to an evaluation of the Breton-Johnson model. The core of the model is due to Albert Breton.[40] Nationalism is seen as a collective, or public, good in which societies can invest. Such an investment is not profitable for everyone. The monetary return takes the form of higher income jobs for a new middle class which uses nationalism to accede to wealth and power; non-monetary rewards accrue to the working class which supports nationalist policies despite the fact that income is redistributed to its detriment. Investment in nationalism, then, primarily entails income redistribution rather than income creation (and from a social point of view the rate of return in terms of income is lower than if the resources were invested in alternative uses). The model is then tested with respect to the nationalization of hydroelectric companies in Quebec in the early sixties and found valid. Therefore "nationalization and government ownership in Quebec today are a form of public works for the middle class."[41]

Johnson fleshes out Breton's analysis from two sources.[42] First, he appeals to Becker's economic theory of discrimination and derives the analogue to Becker's "taste for discrimination" (the sacrifice of economic gain by discriminators for a psychological gain) in a "taste for nationalism."[43] Second, he appeals to Downs's economic theory of democracy in order to argue that although the net benefits of nationalist policies are negative there is an asymmetry in the distribution of benefits and costs. The former are concentrated in the hands of specific producer interests and the latter are thinly dispersed over the mass of consumers, which works to facilitate political support for such policies.[44] Taken together, the Breton-Johnson model is, in effect, a bread-and-circuses model, with the state run by the middle class to provide itself with bread and the working class with enough circuses to elicit its support.

The central proposition in the model is that nationalism is income-distributing, not income-creating in *material* terms, that is, the middle class gains and the working class loses. As Clarkson notes, this aspect of the model gives it a "progressive" flavour, for it casts the nationalist in the role of favouring, or at least tolerating, a regressive redistribution of income.[45] If, however, nationalist policies create jobs or otherwise improve on the quality of labour or its mobilization for development, then the predictive value of this theory becomes problematic. Both the middle class and the working class could then gain and any redistributive effects would cease to figure so predominantly in the discussion. With respect to Quebec, if we accept the possibility that the immobile factor loses from open-door, free-trade, policies and would gain from nationalist policies, and that labour is generally less mobile than capital, it can be seen, contrary to Breton, that Francophone labour in Quebec could gain from independentist policies.[46]

With respect to the automotive industry, Wilton shows that the 1965 Automotive Agreement lowered retail prices in Canada and raised output and production worker employment in the Canadian industry. Significantly, "the only reservation would appear to be the failure of managerial-technical employment to keep pace with the accelerated growth in the Canadian subsidiary industry."[47] In the absence of proof of adverse income-redistributive effects and evidence of job-creation through nationalist policies, one is entitled to endorse a point made by Smith that "the assumption that antinationalists have a monopoly on concern for the Canadian wageearner is arrogant and unwarranted;"[48] indeed, Walter Gordon, the pre-eminent nationalist who was Harry Johnson's favourite target, has been consistently in the left wing of the Liberal party on such matters as medicare, unemployment, and tax reform.

Some light is cast on this latter issue in the only full-scale test of the model by Daly and Globerman in connection with Canadian tariff policies. On the key prediction of the regressive income-redistribution effect in favour of a managerial class, their conclusion is stark: "The data on incomes do *not* support the possibility of any financial gains to managers in Canada."[49] The reason why the model fails to yield the correct prediction is succinctly stated by Jenkins when he argues that it is implausible, "in view of the substantial (tariff-induced) foreign control of Canadian industry, that tariffs provide greater scope for decision-making by Canadian industry, that tariffs provide greater scope for decision-making by Canadian managers."[50] Whereas Daly-Globerman assume that management is the scarce factor that will gain from nationalist policies, the straightforward presumption is that foreign ownership and the tariff have together disadvantaged the Canadian managerial class. Clement shows that access to the elite is more difficult in Canada than in the United States because of, not in spite of, foreign ownership; and he documents what casual observation tells us, namely, the emigration of Canadian-born managers to the United States in the face of limited economic opportunities in Canada.[51]

Moreover, the Breton-Johnson model, at least in its formal presentation, is a static one which fails to capture the potentially dynamic effects of nationalist policies. As Paquet argues, nationalism can be integrative or mobilizing in the development process, and thereby can increase the quantity and improve the quality (or effort) of factor inputs: "In such a case, 'national independence' might be regarded as influencing the social technology in a way analogous to the effect of a technical advance on the physical technology … As such one can speak of an optimal amount of "national independence" different from zero."[52]

Up to a point Johnson recognizes this possibility, but he does not appreciate how it damages the model. He admits that nationalist policies, by strengthening the middle class, might be a prerequisite for creating a viable, stable, and democratic nation-state. "The problem, however, belongs in the spheres of history, sociology and political science rather than economics."[53] One might be inclined to agree with this position were it not for the fact that presumably the whole point of an *economic* theory of nationalism is to obviate that necessity. For the theory to break down on such a critical matter as the creation of stability, democracy, and a viable nation-state sows grave doubts as to its relevance to the study of the nationalism of the new nation-states in developing countries to the persistence of nationalism within such established nation-states as, say, Canada.

From a Marxist perspective, the most striking feature of the model is the discovery of classes since the hallmark of the neoclassical paradigm to deny their existence. The model is about what is variously called the "technocratic elite," the new technocratic petty bourgeoisie or, more narrowly, the state middle class (as a fraction of the new middle class). So understood, one is inclined to see merit in the model as an elucidation of the behaviour of a new strata of middle-range technocrats. Given the degree to which Quebec nationalism is now seen across a broad spectrum of scholarship as a weapon of the new technocracy of Quebec, Breton deserves recognition for making this point very early on.[54] But this observation alone tells us more about elitism than nationalism. As Clarkson observes: "That private jobs are bought with public funds is, of course, generally true about elitist political systems whether capitalist or socialist. The failure to distinguish statements about nationalism from statements about elitism makes this line of analysis very blunt."[55]

But the Breton-Johnson model is a most impoverished class model, the kind of crude caricature of class analysis that many neoclassicists charge inheres in Marxism.[56] There are only two classes, the middle class and the working class, and what is meant by the middle class after much re-reading remains unclear.[57] Nor is there any recognition of class *fractions* beyond Breton's distinction between an old (Anglophone) and a new (Francophone) middle class in Quebec, with the nationalism of the latter being merely ethnic discrimination. Had they allowed for divisions within the middle class along lines other than language, they would have seen, as many writers have, that the Francophone middle class consists of both a federalist fraction (led politically by Trudeau) and a separatist fraction (led politically by Levesque). The truth of the matter – the secret that the nationalists have been unable to keep to themselves – is that most of the Canadian middle class is *not* nationalist. For those inclined to see everything as a matter of taste, what needs to be explained is not a "taste for nationalism" but a "taste for continentalism."

Even if we assume both a homogeneous middle class and that it benefits from nationalist policies, to infer that its behaviour is explained by the fact of benefit (and *ex post* benefit to boot) is to risk falling victim to conspiracy theories based on the *cui bono* maxim.[58]

More important, why are workers receptive to nationalism even if all they receive are psychic benefits? Can they not play a leading role themselves, at least in the sense of being more nationalist than the middle class? After all, they are human beings, not mere receptacles into which bad ideas are poured.[59] What is ultimately at issue, theoretically, in this matter of psychic benefits for the working class is the very thorny problem of false consciousness. Breton-Johnson see workers as anti-nationalist but somehow conned, and Johnson relies upon Downsianism by way of explanation.[60] (It is hard not to see an analogy with certain tendencies in Marxism which see workers as anti-capitalist but somehow deceived.) But it is possible that workers are nationalist and that their ideas spring from the material reality of the harm suffered by the unevenness of international development. This is not to deny Clarkson's point that workers typically only get to choose among options defined by elites, and that in both Quebec and Canada there is no effective organized working class politics.[61] It might be argued in both of these cases (and particularly Quebec) that the workers are more nationalistic than their actions suggest because they are constrained by their (rational) perception of short-run economic costs. In such an event, the issue would not be nationalism as propaganda from above, but the conscious constraining of inherent nationalist feelings.[62]

The more obvious shortcoming of the Breton-Johnson model is that there is no capitalist class or, at the very least, an "upper class." Johnson seem not to understand that his views are the majority sentiments of the more powerful Canadians. He explains the nationalism of Walter Gordon in a way that presumes *all* Canadian businessmen are nationalists; a theory that incorrectly predicts in nine cases out of ten – or is it ninety-nine out of a hundred? – is not defensible by that elementary test so appealing to positivists.[63] Breton and Johnson see nationalism under every non-working-class bed, an error made truly ludicrous by Daly-Globerman when they conjure up, at one end of the nationalist spectrum, "right-wing bankers."[64] This failure of understanding leads to a certain tendency to cry wolf. As Rotstein has put it: "To warn a country that it is in danger of becoming too nationalist when 58.1 per cent of its manufacturing is already in foreign hands, as well as great stretches of its natural resources, is about as gratuitous as warning St. Francis of Assisi not to become a possessive individualist."[65]

Embedded in all this discussion of nationalist policies, whether viewed from a neoclassical or a Marxist perspective, is necessarily a theory of the state. Johnson parodies "the Marxist concept of the state as an instrument of the ruling class," while writers like Downs and Breton represent "a recently emerging school of theorists [which] has been absorbing political into economic theory" with the "concept of the state as a type of market process."[66] Yet what is this new-fangled notion of a state that represents "producer interests" except a rediscovery of that tired cliché of "vulgar Marxism" – against which Johnson has just warned us – that "the state is an instrument of the ruling class?" His early position – frequently reiterated in *The Canadian Quandary* – was that the host country state was "sovereign," and if there were problems from foreign control (though there were not) the state would, and could, act. Rotstein commented at the time on the apparent gap between "Professor Johnson's vaunted sovereignty" and "effective policy,"[67] and Vaitsos and many others have commented on the ability of transnational corporations to influence the policy of host countries pervasively and – notwithstanding the propensity of neoclassical economists to see the transnational corporations as rational and pacific – not always subtly, as the case of ITT in Chile demonstrates.[68]

There is a specific aspect of the state of great importance in understanding Quebec and Canada and other cases that are nowhere to be found in the Breton-Johnson model. Petras argues that the hinterland state is formed by imperial capital to serve metropolitan imperatives, but the process is dialectical and, particularly in the face of any "nationalist" tendencies, imperial capital acts to constrain and "disaggregate" the hinterland state.[69] This tendency of the "external threat" to exacerbate the "internal threat" is a major theme of Canadian Historiography. Gilpin has adumbrated the Quebec/English-Canada confrontation within the context of the North American triangle (of Quebec, English-Canada, and the United States), with the "separatist" fraction continuing to argue the case for mediating the Quebec-US relation through Ottawa and Toronto.[70] Presumably Breton-Johnson cannot see any of this because they actually have a theory of nationalism that, not admitting imperialism, cannot recognize the strategy of divide-and-conquer.

This also casts the issue of discrimination in a different light. Do nationalist policies in themselves constitute discrimination *against* foreigners or do they rather correct existing discrimination *by* foreigners? Johnson finds it difficult to determine "whether the employment of non-nationals represents discrimination against nationals or reflects their inferior quality," but "under competitive conditions" (an assumption he was always willing to make) "there is a presumption in favour of the latter assumption."[71] Given the pervasiveness of colonialism there is a powerful presumption that what nationalism is reacting to is discrimination consequent on colonialism, and that nationalist policies should be understood not as as "reverse discrimination." Whether Quebec has been "backward by choice" or "backward by imposition" as a consequence of colonialism, is a fundamental issue in the warring schools of Quebec Historiography. A famous unpublished research report for the Royal Commission on Bilingualism and Bi-culturalism found that 60 per cent of the income differential between English Canadian and French Canadian Montrealers in 1961 was due to a clear preference of Anglophone employers for English Canadian over French Canadian employees. If this reflects the existence of colonialism, a more sympathetic understanding of Quebec's language policies to the extent that they are intended to correct this discrimination.[72]

All things considered, Rotstein is eloquent in exposing the folly of the assumptions and implications of a Breton-Johnson-type position:

A great deal of nonsense has been written on the subject by people who should know better, but who have become victims of their own antiquated dogmas, that nationalism is merely the protectionist armour for an incompetent middle class. It takes only the briefest acquaintance with the realities of the Canadian scene to appreciate that the middle class in this country has been the spearhead of the great sell out. No other business class in an advanced industrial society has presided so gracefully over its own liquidation. No other university establishment in an advanced country had flooded its ranks with so many non-Canadians to the point where the preservation of a Canadian intellectual tradition, or a social science addressed to contemporary Canadian problems, is now in grave doubt. No other trade union movement in the world is as dependent on direction from abroad. Had the middle class put its weight solidly behind Canadian nationalism, this erosion of national control would have been substantially impeded.[73]

The Breton-Johnson model is a most vulgar class model, yielding "insights" on contemporary nationalism that rank with those of the mechanistic and dogmatic tracts of the most doctrinaire ultra-left sects. This raises the possibility that the theory has little value other than to serve the ideological function of discrediting nationalism.[74] "Small" models may be appropriate to the undertaking of "small" tasks, but they fail dismally when applied to large questions, and nationalism is a large question. Innis warned that "We have failed to realize that the social sciences have been disastrously weakened by the neglect of the study of their limitations."[75] We cannot (if we understand Polanyi, not to speak of Marx) create society as an aggregation (through the market) of the logic of individual, or micro-level choice. Concretely, nationalism does not exist because it is in the self-interest of some people to be nationalists. The neoclassical view is the *reductio ad absurdum* of behaviouralism. Rather, some people are nationalist, and some are not, for a complex of reasons that grow out of "the machinery of world political economy."[76] In the nature of the case, we can only get at this by being political economists.

I V

If nationalism is "for real" its consequences will be pervasive, and ideas in general and economic theory in particular will not escape unscathed. Exactly because nationalism exists there is an economics of nationalism which, in turn, implies that there must be a nationality of economics.

A curious feature of Johnson's writings was the tenacity of his conviction that there is a timeless-and-spaceless scientific economics while those who dissented in any way were seen by him as the victims of the particularities of time and space and of vested interests. He accused Keynes and "his followers – which means the profession at large" of elaborating "his history-bound-analysis into a timeless-and-spaceless set of universal principles," whereas the truth of the matter (for Johnson) was that *The General Theory* was "one eccentric *English* economist's rationalization of his local problem."[77] He applied the same kind of reasoning to "Central European intellectuals" (he specifically mentions Mandelbaum, Kaldor, Rosenstein-Rodan, and Balogh), who falsely "presented as universals" concepts which were "fundamentally concerned with policies for developing the Balkan states on the German model." He blamed them for infecting the "Anglo-Saxon tradition" and, in due course, the developing countries with "the fictional concept of the nation as an economic entity endowed with consistent objectives and a consensus in favour of realizing them by national economic policy" and generally of implanting "the habit of thinking in nationalist rather than cosmopolitan terms."[78]

Canadian nationalists (like myself) – who he saw as essentially second-rate academics that mysteriously chose (even when proclaiming socialism) to get into bed with second-rate Canadian businessmen – were the symptom of a disease that manifested itself in the particular circumstances of the periphery. In striking contrast, he wrote of the United States as *the* place where one came into contact with "real scientific economics" and, asking why there are no rivals, answers:

The technique is easy – any intelligent young man can learn mathematics and statistics – the real problem is to learn to observe and try to understand the economic system, not as it functions in one's own country, where one's vision of its functioning may be highly distorted by governmental policies that, as a citizen, one does not question, but as it functions in general. For that, one has to go to the United States, the only country where governmental policies are still not regarded as sacrosanct and where a man is not only free but encouraged to think of government policies as arbitrary interferences rather than unquestioned national necessities.[79]

Aside from the incredible naïveté in such a conception of the American state, it is remarkable that Johnson nowhere explicitly admits the possibility that the hegemony of American-centred economics may tell us more about the actual distribution of power globally than it does about the inherent correctness of the economics. Ideas from the imperium are, for Johnson, superior to those from anywhere else; indeed, the former and only the former are truly scientific and partake of the quality of universal truth. The rest, except to the extent that they derive from the metropolitan paradigm, are in error, although only a moment's thought should be sufficient to appreciate that the definition of "error" is necessarily suspect when the defining is done by those who are by definition "correct."

Johnson seems not to have understood that if he could (rightly) characterize even Keynes as being the product of particular circumstances and experiences and a particular intellectual tradition, the same charge might apply to the neoclassical paradigm in general and Johnson's articulation of it in particular. Rotstein places Johnson's arguments "as emanating from the nineteenth century debate on free trade in England [now] misapplied to serve the interests of a continentalist establishment and the unimpeded spread of the new mercantilism."[80]

Johnson's belief is contradictory and self-serving, but it has a further and deadly consequence which is to suppress dissent from the ruling orthodoxy. One cannot avoid being struck by the paradox that Johnson believed in the competition of everything but ideas. So it is that the paradigm of the competitive economy and of free trade becomes a monopoly of knowledge, and a paradigm based on the "logic of choice" is used to discredit dissent and limit choice. To know of the nature of paradigms is not to be surprised by this, though still the extent of the contradiction with the core assumptions specific to neoclassical theory can only be described as puzzling. The phenomenon was well understood by Innis, and he was not unwilling to use the language of economics against economics itself to expose its limitations and guard against its pretentiousness: "imperfect competition between economic theories hampers the advance of freedom of thought."[81]

Johnson's position denied a fundamental tenet that Innis enunciated in theory and applied in practice throughout his life's work: the need for a distinctive *Canadian* economics. "The application of the economic theories of old countries to the problems of new

countries results in a form of exploitation with dangerous consequences. The only escape can come from an intensive study of
Canadian economic problems and from the development of a
philosophy of economic history or an economic theory suited to
Canadian needs."[82] The early Johnson (correctly) chided the Gordon Commission for having no "consistent philosophy of resource-
oriented growth."[83] But such a "philosophy" was of course precisely
what Innis and his school had offered in the staples approach, and
Johnson seems not to have understood that the intensification of
the penetration of the neoclassical paradigm in Canada had
worked powerfully to suppress the Innis tradition and to substitute
lip-service to Innis as a person for the scholarly attention that alone
could have assured a living Innisian economics. Nor was Johnson
guiltless in this process, for he proselytized in Canada for the neo-
classical paradigm with evangelical zeal, with all the legitimacy that
accrued to him as a Canadian who had "made good" in what were,
for English-speaking Canadians, the two great metropolitan centres. He was, after all, with his university appointments in both the
United States and the United Kingdom and his frequent visits to
Canada, the very embodiment of the North Atlantic Triangle.

Innis refused a university appointment in the United States (in-
terestingly also at the University of Chicago) and went to Britain
in his later years to warn of American imperialism, but it would be
too easy simply to see Innis as the truer Canadian and to ignore
how very Canadian it has long been to do what Johnson did.
Berger writes perceptively of the Canadian-born historians who
went to the United States, and his analysis is helpful in understanding a phenomenon that transcends that discipline. He quotes
James T. Shotwell, who went to Columbia from Toronto in 1898:
"I suppose that I think of the academic world as one that has no
territorial frontier;" while J.B. Brebner (who also left Toronto for
Columbia, in his case via Oxford) held, according to Berger, "the
same internationalist conception of the world of learning." But,
says Berger, there was "another side to this generous elitism":

While in the twenties and thirties the academic exodus from Canada was
often regarded as an example of intellectual internationalism ... the phenomenon was later described for what it really was: an exile of some of the
nation's most talented people and a testament to Canada's material society
and cultural meagreness. Brebner said Canada exported men and women

just as it exported fish, fur, lumber and wheat. Some of those who remained in the United States displayed an impatience with traditional Canadian attitudes and a patronizing treatment of Canadians who remained in the Dominion ... Canadian-born academics in the United States were on the whole the most receptive to the idea of continental history, because its truth seemed confirmed by their own experience. The discovery of North America was in a sense the discovery of themselves.[84]

Berger adduces no evidence from historians, nor does he himself make the point, that Canada's "material scarcity and cultural meagreness," might have something to do with its dependent and colonial status and that the continentalism they espoused might have exacerbated and perpetuate the provincialism they disliked. To admit that possibility would, in its turn, compel recognition that the solution for Canada might lie not in a deeper dependency (called North American integration) but in a lesser dependency.[85]

By Johnson's time, top Canadian intellectuals discovered an even broader world than North America. As with top managers, the world was now potentially their oyster. Hence they could recreate themselves not simply as North American but as members of the international elite. Johnson himself wrote of "the gradual change in the attitudes of corporation executives toward, and loss of respect for, the politicians and officials of national governments – including their own – as their horizons expand to comprise the international economy as the sphere of their operations, and they become impatient of those whose vision and responsibilities are limited to the territorial domain of a particular nation-state."[86] Clement, in his analysis of the composition of the US corporate elite, finds only two Canadians who made it to the top of the American, and hence global, pyramid of decision-making.[87] No analogous study has been made of Canadian-born intellectuals, but one guesses that few have matched Johnson's achievement in getting to the top of the intellectual pyramid of scholarship. It is not surprising that Johnson too "became impatient of those whose visions ... are limited to the territorial domain" of Canada.

All this needs to be situated in a broader strand of writing (and behaviour) associated with the new era of global, but American-centred, corporate capital. Brzezinski, a leading ideologue of the Trilateral Commission and now of the White House, has written of "the emerging international consciousness" as a new rational humanism that goes beyond purely nationalistic concerns.[88] But as the journalist Robert Collison observes, this is not news for any student of Canada but "one of history's more unexpected paradoxes, the Canadianization of this planet: Pax Canadiana. The world is soon to be run by an internationalized elite, the way Canada has always been run."[89] Whether or not this becomes so in the long run, it is clear that Johnson was in the vanguard of a powerful tendency.

Johnson was both a metropolitan intellectual and a Canadian intellectual. But he was no more able than the rest of us to transcend our contemporary fate: that we cannot avoid taking sides for or against the American-centred style of theorizing. At the limits we risk on the one side the comprador role and on the other being read out of the profession. Most will choose, with quiet competence, putting some Canadian content into the metropolitan paradigm. Johnson, in part because he was capable of more than that, chose exile, which has the prospect of transcending the problem by escaping it. But he also maintained a central interest in Canada, which meant that he remained to some extent impaled on the horns of the dilemma and a victim of the underlying forces. He opted fully for the metropolitan paradigm and was highly creative within it, but he could not resist the role of missionary to those who stayed at home.

If Innis can be seen as a creative colonial intellectual, Johnson might be described as chiefly a creative metropolitan intellectual, but also in some part a "neo-colonial intellectual" who, situated in the metropolis, acted as a go-between, mediating between central and peripheral (Canadian) scholars.[90] It is, I hope, clear that in saying these things, that I am not ascribing motives or otherwise engaged in *ad hominem* argument, but talking about how all of us (Johnson included) have little intellectual room to manoeuvre within the powerful imperatives laid down by transnational capital.

We should accept that side of Johnson which understood the nationality of ideas while rejecting the side that refused to see the imperialism of ideas. Johnson spoke of "a golden age terminated by World War I, when literally a small handful of economists in each of the European countries and imperial powers was struggling to understand the characteristics and laws of operation of industrial capitalism as it emerged in his own society, and to translate these into principles comprehensible to his fellow countrymen."[91] Some might imagine that this was not such a bad way to spend one's time, but Johnson felt otherwise. These national schools, he argued, had been replaced by three schools: scientific, Marxist and development economics. For Johnson the latter two were comedies of errors, so that there was, predictably, only one proper school. But a consideration of the deeper political economy suggests that the national schools grew out of an era of international rivalry, while scientific economics in its earlier British and its later American manifestations resulted in each case from the dominance of a single and hegemonic imperium.

If this be so, it matters, for we are once again to be in a period of rivalry. This new reality was much noted by Johnson and he worried whether freedom of trade and mobility of factors would survive it. In these circumstances we are likely to see more chinks in the armour of the American-centred neoclassical paradigm, including the possibility that national schools will reassert themselves, concerned with "the characteristics and laws of operation of industrial capitalism" as they operate in each society. That is to speak to the possibility of the rediscovery of political economy, not without the neoclassical paradigm, because that has already happened, but within it. In any event, the issue to which Johnson spoke, and on which I have used his premises to draw different conclusions, is no abstract matter but likely (whether we like it or not) to be increasingly an issue within our profession. And here, at the periphery, political economy will necessarily reassert itself around the question of Canadian dependence; it will not be helpful if it is dismissed as more "mindless nationalism." "Not to be British or American but Canadian is not necessarily to be parochial."[92]

V

I am conscious of the honour that has been done me by asking me to be on this panel and thereby to address a plenary session of this Association. I accepted the assignment with reluctance. I would, like all of us here, have preferred different and happier circumstances, but on this matter we have no choice. While I have offered a sustained critique of Johnson's work, I would ask it to be understood that to take a man's work seriously (as I have) is to recognize his importance; indeed, it is the highest tribute one can pay a scholar. Johnson was a creative and influential economist. It was Canada's loss that he did not stay in Canada – as Innis once wrote

"Canada becomes a headless nation with its brains scattered over other countries"[93] – but one cannot hope but be impressed by his continuing attachment to Canada and the frequency with which he alludes in his writings to the fact that he was a Canadian citizen. In general Johnson never hesitated to state his bias, and that is commendable: it is an honest approach that also adds a certain excitement to scholarship, and acknowledges the constraints on the freedom of thought that inhere in paradigms as intellectual modes of production. Let me again cite Kuhn as a way of getting at the necessary dilemma of my task: "the proponents of competing paradigms practice their trades in different worlds ... Practicing in different worlds, the two groups of scientists see different things when they look from the same point in the same direction."[94] The last word I will give to Innis, who taught both Harry Johnson and myself, and who Johnson very rightly consistently lauded. It is useful advice to all of us who practise our profession in the university: "The University lent her ear to those who on all sides told her they had discovered truth, and she forgot that her existence depended on the *search* for truth and not on truth."[95]

NOTES

1 Harry G. Johnson, "Biographical Note," *Technology and Economic Interdependence* (London: Macmillan, 1975).

2 "I adopt a cosmopolitan liberal position and regard nationalism as one of the least pleasant vices in which mankind indulges itself, or as one of the characteristics of childish immaturity out of which I hope the people of the world will ultimately grow" (Johnson, "Bibliographic Note," 91).

3 See, for example, Marc Linder, *Anti-Samuelson* (New York: Urizen Books, 1977), a two-volume critique of Samuelson's one-volume introductory text.

4 Thomas S. Kuhn, *The Structure of Scientific Revolutions* (Chicago: University of Chicago Press, 1962), 93, 108.

5 C.B. Macpherson, *Democratic Theory: Essays in Retrieval* (London: Oxford, 1973), 156. Johnson's critique of Macpherson's paper in T.N. Guinsberg and G.L. Reuber, eds., *Perspectives on the Social Sciences in Canada* (Toronto: University of Toronto Press, 1974) concludes on what can only be described as an ugly note. Macpherson's reasoned critique of Johnson's contribution to the same volume observes that on Marxist economics Johnson "has nothing but shrill ill to say" (127).

6 By a nationalist critique I mean either (or both) of two rather different things: on the one hand from the perspective of a nationalist of a specific time and place; on the other hand from the perspective of a political economist who regards nationalism as being one of the essences of our contemporary being, and therefore a phenomenon impervious to reductionist analysis or other tricks to conjure it away, but rather warranting the most serious scholarly analysis.

7 Abraham Rotstein, *The Precarious Homestead: Essays on Economics, Technology and Nationalism* (Toronto: New Press, 1973), 64.

8 The term is from John A. Watson, "Harold Innis and Classical Scholarship," *Journal of Canadian Studies* 12(5) (1977): 45–61.

9 Harry G. Johnson, *The Canadian Quandary: Economic Problems and Policies* (Toronto: McGraw-Hill, 1963); Melville H. Watkins, "The Canadian Quandary," *Canadian Forum* 44 (1964): 79–80.

10 Stephen H. Hymer, *The International Operations of National Firms: A Study of Direct Foreign Investment* (Cambridge, Mass: MIT Press, 1976).

11 Harry G. Johnson, "The Efficiency and Welfare Implications of the International Corporation," in C.P. Kindleberger, *The International Corporation: A Symposium* (Cambridge, Mass: MIT Press, 1970), 35–56; *On Economics and Society* (Chicago: University of Chicago Press, 1975). Richard E. Caves, "International Corporations: The Industrial Economics of Foreign Investment," *Economica* 38 (1971): 1–27. Caves's article is essentially a taxonomic treatment of Hymer's analysis but it contains only one perfunctory reference to Hymer.

12 J. Vanderkamp, "Harry Johnson: A Brief Tribute," *Canadian Public Policy* 3 (1977): 267.

13 *Technology and Economic Interdependence* (London: Macmillan, 1975), 167–8.

14 *Canadian Quandary*, 115.

15 Johnson on one occasion raises, though only parenthetically, the possibility that the entry of foreign firms "somehow suppresses domestic entrepreneurship" but cites Caves's empirical work to conclude that "the probabilities" are against this (*On Economics and Society*, 306). In contrast, he dismisses Kari Levitt, *Silent Surrender: The Multinational Corporation in Canada* (Toronto: Macmillan, 1970) and Ian Lumsden, ed., *Close the 49th parallel etc.: The Americanization of Canada* (Toronto: University of Toronto Press, 1970) "as distinguished by the unscholarly Marxist tradition of purporting to prove that something is a fact by quoting someone else who claims it is a fact" (*Canadian Quandary*, ix).

16 *Technology and Economic Interdependence*, 78–80.

17 Chung estimates that sales by US majority-owned affiliates from all areas to the United States in 1975 were 32 per cent of total US merchandise imports (the figure for Canada is a staggering 58 per cent, much higher than that for any other area) while, according to Helleiner, 45 per cent of total US imports in that year consisted of related-party trade (William K. Chung, "Sales by Majority-Owned Foreign Affiliates of U.S. Companies, 1975," *Survey of Current Business* 57 (1977): 2).

18 G.K. Helleiner, "Freedom and management in primary commodity markets: U.S. Imports from Developing Countries," *World Development* (1978) 6: 23–30; Harry G. Johnson, "Commodities: Less Developed Countries' Response," in Jagdish Bhagwati, ed., *The New International Economic Order: The North-South Debate* (Cambridge: MIT Press, 1977); Harold B. Malmgren, "The Raw Material and Commodity Controversy," *International Economic Studies Institute, Contemporary Issues,* no. 1 (Washington, 1975).

19 Johnson, *Technology and Economic Interdependence,* 150. In the face of such a gross interference with freedom of choice, otherwise so sacrosanct in neoclassical theorizing, Johnson quickly adds "pending ultimate arrival of the state of development at which procreation is controlled by voluntary choice of the number of children the parents can afford to feed, house and educate to their own or better standards of productive contribution." Those less inclined than neoclassical economists to think of people as "human capital" reproducing itself to serve higher imperatives, may find the ultimate solution as chilling as the immediate one. For an excellent statement of the need for an alternative, see Samir Amin, "Self-Reliance and the New International Economic Order," *Monthly Review* 29(3) (1977): 1–21.

20 Johnson did recognize that there could be problems for the home country: "There is ... a fairly solid theoretical basis for concern on the part of labour groups in the advanced countries about the implications for them of large-scale outflows of foreign direct investment" (*On Economics and Society,* 307). In a language uncharacteristic for him, he argued that "the solution to that problem will not be facilitated by blind insistence [on] the principle of free trade and maximum efficiency in the use of world resources" (*Technology and Economic Interdependence,* 158).

21 Constantine V. Vaitsos, *Employment Problems and Transnational Enterprises in Developing Countries: Distortions and Inequality (with particular reference to Andean Pact Countries).* Working Paper, World Employment Research Programme (Geneva: ILO, 1976), 52. For a synthesis of the evidence that the Canadian branch plant economy limits, even destroys, jobs, see James Laxer and Robert Laxer, *The Liberal Idea of Canada: Pierre Trudeau and the Question of Canada's Survival* (Toronto: Lorimer, 1977).

22 For the latter link we are again indebted to Hymer, whose work genuinely
   evolved, though in a Marxist direction. See Stephen H. Hymer, "The Effi-
   ciency (Contradictions) of Multinational Corporations," *American Economic
   Review* 60 (1970): 441–8; "The Multinational Corporation and the Law of
   Uneven Development, in J.W. Bhagwati, ed., *Economics and World Order* (New
   York: World Law Fund, 1971), 113–40; "The Internationalization of Capi-
   tal," *Journal of Economic Issues* 6 (1972): 91–111; "International Politics and
   International Economics: A Radical Approach," *Monthly Review* 29(10)
   (March 1978), 15–35; and Stephen H. Hymer and Stephen Resnick, "Inter-
   national Trade and Uneven Development," in J.W. Bhagwati, R.W. Jones,
   R.A. Mundell, and Jaroslav Vanek, eds., *Trade, Balance of Payments and Growth*
   (Amsterdam: North Holland Publishing, 1971).

23 On the other hand by beginning with capital and labour it runs the
   grave risk of exaggerating their existence as two great *world* classes to the
   detriment of the real world of classes imbedded without nation-states;
   sadly, we cannot know how Hymer would have resolved these contradictory tendencies.

24 *Technology and Economic Independence*, xiv.

25 Vaitsos, *Employment Problems*, 41.

26 Amin, "Self-Reliance."

27 *Canadian Quandary*, 102.

28 *Technology and Economic Interdependence*, 148.

29 *Technology and Economic Interdependence*, 86.

30 Immanuel Wallerstein, "The present state of the debate on world inequality," in Immanuel Wallerstein, ed., *World Inequality: Origins and Perspectives
   on the World System* (Montreal: Black Rose Books, 1975), 12–28.

31 Charles P. Kindleberger, *American Business Abroad: Six Lectures on Direct
   Investment* (New Haven: Yale University Press, 1969), 6, 5, 257, 263.

32 Régis Debray, "Marxism and the National Question: Interview with Régis
   Debray," *New Left Review* 105 (1977): 26–8, 34.

33 *Technology and Economic Interdependence*, 34.

34 It is relevant to remind ourselves that Innis was a nationalist in the specific
   and critic sense that, as a Canadian in the era of the origins of the Cold
   War, his studies led him to have grave doubts about U.S. imperial strategy
   and to warn his fellow-citizens: "We can only survive by taking specific action at strategic points against American imperialism in all its attractive
   guises" (H.A. Innis, *The Strategy of Culture* (Toronto: University of Toronto
   Press, 1952), 2.

35 George Grant, *Lament for a Nation* (Toronto: McClelland and Stewart,
   1965), 5.

36 Abraham Rotstein, "Is There an English-Canadian Nationalism?" Walter
Gordon Lecture Series, 1978, 15. See also his *The Precarious Homestead* and
"Canada: The New Nationalism," *Foreign Affairs* 55 (1976): 97–118.

37 Rotstein, *The Precarious Homestead*, 187, 19, 119.

38 It may be objected that neoclassical economics, as in the "new institutional" work of Douglass North and others, does theorizing about non-
market activity. But by and large it is not being done in such a way as to
enable getting at the political dimension.

39 H.A. Innis, *Political Economy in the Modern State* (Toronto: Ryerson, 1946),
101.

40 Albert Breton, "The Economics of Nationalism," *Journal of Political Economy*
72 (1964): 376–86.

41 Breton, "Economics of Nationalism," 385. There is a brief glance at Canadian policy toward the United States in the area of broadcasting, periodical
publishing and the automotive industry (the latter with specific relevance to
the Bladen plan), and again the model is said to predict accurately.

42 Harry G. Johnson, "A Theoretical Model of Economic Nationalism in New
and Developing States," *Political Science Quarterly* 80 (1965): 169–85; and
"Introduction," "A theoretical model of economic nationalism in new and
developing states," "Economic nationalism in Canadian policy," and "The
ideology of economic policy in the new states," in Harry G. Johnson, ed.,
Economic Nationalism in Old and New States (Chicago: University of Chicago
Press, 1967), v-xi, 1–16, 85–97, 124–41.

43 Gary S. Becker, *The Economics of Discrimination* (Chicago: University of
Chicago Press, 1957).

44 Anthony Downs, *An Economic Theory of Democracy* (New York: Harper,
1957).

45 Stephen Clarkson, "Anti-Nationalism in Canada: The Ideology of
Mainstream Economics," *Canadian Review of Studies in Nationalism*
5 (1978): 45–65.

46 Both Treddenick and Gilpin emphasize the immobility of French Canadian workers, such that the purpose of protectionist policies is to relocate
jobs in Quebec. Nevertheless, Gilpin endorses Breton's simplistic analysis
of Quebec "separatism" as merely middle class. See J.M. Treddenick,
"Quebec and Canada: Some Economic Aspects of Independence," *Journal
of Canadian Studies* 8 (1973): 21–2; and Robert Gilpin "Integration and
Disintegration on the North American Continent," *International Organization* 28 (1974): 871.

47 David A. Wilton, "An econometric model of the Canadian automotive
manufacturing industry and the 1965 Automotive Agreement," 1972, 181.

48 Denis Smith, *Gentle Patriot: A Political Biography of Walter Gordon* (Edmonton: Hurtig, 1973), 405.
49 D.S. Daly and S. Globerman, *Tariff and Science Policies: Applications of a Model of Nationalism* (Toronto: University of Toronto Press for the Ontario Economic Council, 1976), 50. How the problem is modelled vitiates the results. The tariff is assessed with only passing reference to foreign ownership, thereby assuming that the inefficient industrial structure is the consequence solely of the former and not the latter, though the two are hopelessly intertwined historically.
50 A.W. Jenkins, "Review" of D.S. Daly and S. Globerman, *Tariff and Science Policies,* in *Canadian Public Policy* 3 (1977): 386–7.
51 Wallace Clement, *Continental Corporate Power* (Toronto: McClelland & Stewart, 1977).
52 Gilles Paquet, "The multinational firm and the nation state as institutional forms," in Gilles Paquet, ed., *The Multinational Firm and the Nation State* (Don Mills, Ont.: Collier-Macmillan Canada, 1972), 17.
53 *Economic Nationalism in Old and New States,* 16.
54 Indeed, it may be, as Johnson was wont to argue in other contexts, that Breton was "rationalizing his local problem" and that Johnson is guilty of falsely universalizing to Canada and the Third World.
55 Clarkson, "Anti-Nationalism in Canada," 26.
56 In sharp contrast to the reductionism of the Breton-Johnson model is the richness of the class analysis by numerous writers on Quebec, for example, Herbert Guidon, "Social unrest, social class and Quebec's bureaucratic revolution," *Queen's Quarterly* 71 (1964): 150–62; Gilles Bourque and Nicole Laurin-Frenette, "Social classes and national ideologies in Quebec, 1760–1970," in Gary Teeple, ed., *Capitalism and the National Question in Canada* (Toronto: University of Toronto Press, 1972), 185–210; Denis Monière, *Le développement des idéologies au Québec: des origines à nos jours* (Montreal: éditions Québec/Amérique, 1977); Henry Milner, *Politics in the New Quebec* (Toronto: McClelland and Stewart, 1978); Pierre Fournier, *The Quebec Establishment* (Montreal: Black Rose Books, 1976), and "The PQ and the economic power of business," *Our Generation* 12(3) (1978): 3–15; and Stanley B. Ryerson, "Quebec: concepts of class and nation," in Teeple, ed., *Capitalism,* 209–27. There remains a tendency in this literature, notable in Bourque and Laurin-Frenette and wholly absent only in Ryerson, to reduce the national question to the class question rather than to recognize the primacy and fundamental interpretation of both.
57 Breton defines the middle class "to include managers, salaried professionals, sales people and office workers" ("Economics of Nationalism," 378).

To regard "white collar" as middle class and "blue collar" as working class is a distinction without merit; see Harry Braverman, *Labor and Monopoly Capital: The Degradation of Work in the Twentieth Century* (New York: Monthly Review Press, 1974).

58 As Garry Wills has wittily observed, "It would make policemen's work very easy if that maxim were truly the guiding one: they would automatically send to jail the principal beneficiary of any victim's insurance policy;" he sees those who work from that maxim as "acquiring the paranoid vision of politics" ("Heroic Darkness," *New York Review of Books* 25(5) (1978): 4).

59 Johnson's inability to understand how ordinary people could be rationally nationalist is reflected in his admitted puzzlement over the nationalism of Communist China. He is unwilling to concede that it may be an "expedient" means of mobilizing support for modernization but prefers, given "the internationalist philosophy of Communism," to see it as "clear evidence of doctrinal inconsistency." At best he is willing to admit that Chinese nationalism "raises some difficult conceptual problems ... which we have been unable to resolve in any useful fashion" (*Economic Nationalism*, viii).

60 For a general critique thereof, see Macpherson, *Democratic Theory*, 185–94.

61 "Anti-Nationalism in Canada."

62 Breton makes much of one poll for Quebec that "indicates that the probability of finding a separatist is higher in a high-income group than in a low-income group" ("Economics of Nationalism," 381); however, Carl Cuneo and James Curtis argue that, in 1968, working class support for separatism was comparable to that of the middle class ("Quebec Separatism: an Analysis of Determinants within Social-Class Levels," *Canadian Review of Sociology and Anthropology* 2 (1974): 1–29). At the moment there seems to be general agreement that a significant number of Québécois (and hence by necessity significant numbers of working class Québécois) support the PQ's demand for sovereignty-association but a significant portion of them may vote against it in a referendum because they fear the *economic* costs of not getting it.

63 Philip Resnick observes that "what is interesting is not that *some* bourgeois spokesmen supported nationalism but rather how few" (*The Land of Cain: Class and Nationalism in English Canada 1945–1975* (Vancouver: New Star Books, 1977), 112.

64 *Tariff and Science Policies*, 9.

65 Rotstein, *Precarious Homestead*, 21.

66 T.N. Guinsberg and G.L. Reuber, eds., *Perspectives on the Social Sciences in Canada* (Toronto: University of Toronto Press, 1974), 97.

67 Rotstein, *Precarious Homestead*, 13.

68 Vaitsos, *Employment Problems.*

69 James Petras, "New Perspectives on Imperialism and Social Classes in the Periphery," *Journal of Contemporary Asia* 5 (1975): 291–308.

70 "Integration and Disintegration." For a review of the Canadian literature see Mel Watkins, "The Innis Tradition in Canadian Political Economy," reprinted in this volume.

71 *Economic Nationalism in Old and New States,* 10.

72 The study is André Raynauld, Gérald Marion and Richard Béland, "La répartition des revenus selon les groupes ethniques au Canada," cited in Dale Posgate and Kenneth McRoberts, *Quebec: Social Change and Political Crisis* (Toronto: McClelland and Stewart, 1976). Perhaps Breton would now 'justify' this as proper, given the 'superiority' of English over French as a language of business (see Albert Breton, *Bilingualism: An Economic Approach* (Montreal: C.D. Howe Research Institute, 1978). But those less appreciative of the imperatives of transnational capital are entitled to have a sympathetic understanding of Quebec's language policies to the extent that they are intended to correct this "discrimination."

73 Rotstein, *Precarious Homestead,* 24.

74 Stephen Clarkson, "The Two Solitudes: Foreign Investment through the Prism of Canadian Economics," a paper presented to the annual meeting of the Canadian Economics Association, 1977.

75 H.A. Innis, *Political Economy in the Modern State* (Toronto: Ryerson, 1946), 78.

76 Nairn, *Break-up of Britain.*

77 *On Economics and Society,* 97, 80. Emphasis added.

78 *On Economics and Society,* 131.

79 *On Economics and Society,* 139.

80 Rotstein, *Precarious Homestead,* 25.

81 *Political Economy in the Modern State,* 100.

82 H.A. Innis, "The Teaching of Economics in Canada," (1927) reprinted in *Essays in Canadian Economic History* (Toronto: University of Toronto Press, 1956), 3.

83 *The Canadian Quandary,* 3.

84 Carl Berger, *The Writing of Canadian History: Aspects of English-Canadian Historical Writing 1900–1970* (Toronto: Oxford, 1976), 142–3, 146.

85 Significantly, Clement's *Continental Corporate Power* shows a persistent haemorrhage of Canadian-born managers to the United States consequent of the greater barriers to upward mobility in Canada. He finds that those who do migrate show strong ideological support for continentalism, notwithstanding the fact that it was the consequences of the latter

for Canadian social structure and economic opportunity that helped
to push them out in the first place.

86 *On Economics and Society*, 310.

87 *Continental Corporate Power.*

88 Zbigniew Brzezinski, *Between Two Ages* (New York: Viking, 1970).

89 Robert Collison, "Is there a Rockefeller conspiracy in your future?"
    Saturday Night (October 1977): 45.

90 Watson, "Harold Innis and Classical Scholarship."

91 Guinsberg and Reuber, eds., *Perspectives*, 85–6.

92 H.A. Innis, *Strategy of Culture*, 2.

93 *Political Economy in the Modern State*, xi.

94 Kuhn, *Structure*, 149.

95 *Political Economy in the Modern State*, 65.

13

The Innis Tradition
in Canadian Political Economy
(1982)

Although the name of Harold Innis is not a household word in Canada, it should be. He is without doubt the most distinguished social scientist and historian, and one of the most distinguished intellectuals, that Canada has ever produced. Successively he wrote pioneering works in Canadian history and in the history of civilizations, held together by the common thread of an intense, passionate concern for scholarship and for the future of his country; indeed, for Western civilization itself. As an economic historian or economist, writing on Canada, he was the central figure in creating an indigenous Canadian approach to political economy that transcended economic history and economics to embrace history, political science, sociology and anthropology. Yet the legacy of this "old political economy" has been in recent years to facilitate the emergence of a "new political economy," a new synthesis. That, at least, is what this paper will argue.[1] In the process it will seek to answer a number of questions: What was the nature of the old synthesis formed under Innis? How was its formation possible? Why did it fall by the wayside? Why is it now being revived? Why, in terms of creative work, is the new political economy mostly of a left – even Marxist – persuasion,

This is a slightly revised version of the paper by the same title which appeared in *Canadian Journal of Political and Social Theory* 6: 12–34.

though Innis was certainly not a Marxist and was very much opposed to the politics of his left-leaning colleagues?

Central to my argument, following the historian of science, Thomas Kuhn, is the power of paradigms to set the questions and to constrain the methods by which answers can be sought to a limited list of questions; that is, the powerful manner in which the disciplines discipline.[2] The phenomenon was familiar to Innis, who opposed monopolies of knowledge and schools. The practitioners of a discipline, as monopolists, set up barriers to the entry of dissenting ideas and so generally impose their will with the consequence, at first evident to the student but soon forgotten, that university departments are as much suppressors of creative thought as they can be its supporters, places of unfreedom as much as places of freedom. In Innis' arresting use of the language of orthodox economic theory to expose the reality of its practice: "Imperfect competition between economic theories hampers the advance of freedom of thought."[3] Intellectual modes of production are, in turn, related to real modes of production, so that the dialectic of paradigm change must be related not only to matters internal to the paradigm, following Kuhn, but also to the material reality. Concretely, we must be concerned not only with the hegemonic nature of the paradigm (in our case with the politics of economics) but also with the effect of the economy on economics, including economic history: Carl Berger's history of Canadian history might thus be better seen as notes toward an economic history of Canadian economic history.[4] As Innis put it: "We need a sociology or a philosophy of the social sciences and particularly of economics, an economic history of knowledge or an economic history of economic history."[5] Following Innis, the recognition of the narrowness of the margin for intellectual manouevre, or for creative freedom, can help us understand the bias of a discipline, and so overcome it.

Now Innis was an economic historian which means, in the North American tradition then as now, an economist who works on matters historical. The Innis tradition in economic history can properly be said to be embodied in the so-called staples approach, both in the concrete sense of the study of the great staple trades and industries and in the methodological sense that the study of staple activity broadly conceived was a unifying theme for the general historical experience at the periphery. In a paper written on the occasion of the quarter-century since Innis' death, the economic historian Hugh Aitken reminds us of "the golden age of Canadian economic history that accompanied the statement and elaboration of the staple theme," but he is critical of its legacy:

The fact of the matter is that, in Canadian economic history, Innis still dominates the field ... Elsewhere [meaning the United States], the last decade and a half in economic history has been one of the most exciting periods ever experienced in the history of the profession. Not so in Canada ... [A] reconstruction of the standard interpretation of Canadian economic history is still a long way off. That standard interpretation, enshrined in monographs and textbooks, is an interpretation of the Innis model. It is no compliment to Canadian scholarship that now twenty-five years after his death, it still monopolizes the field.

Referring to "developments in Canadian economic history over the last decade and a half – or rather, the relative lack of developments," he says "The strength of the Innis tradition may be one explanation."[6]

Aitken's evidence for "exciting" developments in the US is the emergence of the "new economic history" or cliometrics, forgetting Herbert Heaton's 1954 warning (significantly in the *Canadian Journal of Economics and Political Science*) that: "The American cult of quantities is no mere turning tide. It is a tidal wave, on which Clio's little craft seems likely to be sunk by the swarms of vessels manned by statisticians, econometricians, and macro-economists."[7] The new economic history now has a track record and not all observers are as impressed as Aitken. Paul Davenport observes that "the 'new' economic historians tend to take the position that if a technique is acceptable to the theorists it is acceptable for economic history." "The new economic history," he writes, "is sometimes described as 'the application of economic theory to economic history'; for too often it becomes "the application of history to economic history."[8] And the economic theory at issue is, of course, neo-classical theory. Ian Parker observes that after World War II "the gap between mainstream economic theory and economic history widened, despite Innis' argument that "Any substantial progress in economic theory must come from a closer synthesis between economic history and economic theory" and despite (and on occasion because of) recent attempts to apply simple neo-classical "cliometric" models directly to the explanation of complex historical situations.[9] The American economic historian Donald McCloskey says the theory in question is "especially the theory of price" and insists (properly) that it, and not counting, is "the defining skill of cliometricians, as of other economists." He recognizes that "the cliometric school is characteristically American" and, in a characteristically American way, writes "the frontier of cliometrics is the wide world beyond America."[10]

Predictably the technique has, in fact, spread to Canada, where it has been in part devoted to testing the staple theory. In a review of that literature I wrote that "to the extent it poses real questions it has upheld the validity of the staple's approach – though making little or no contribution to our theoretical understanding. The staple theory has survived the worst onslaughts of Americanization and for that reason alone must be as hardy and genuinely Canadian."[11] Aitken is excessively critical of the lack of developments in Canadian economic history while exaggerating the strength of the Innis tradition, at least in the sense of a holistic approach.

Only three years after Aitken, a new Canadian economic history textbook appeared (*Canada: An Economic History*[12]) which was largely successful in blending the best, or less fanatical, of the new economic history with some of the insights of both the old and the new political economy. A new textbook was possible precisely because, as Kenneth Norrie put it in a review: "There has been an explosion of research activity in the field over the last quarter century, from perspectives as diverse as cliometrics to the new political economy." But, as Norrie also points out, the limitations of a text reflect those of existing research. The Marr and Patterson book is "an economic history of Canada." It is not based on "a broader synthesis of economic with social and political history" because, writes Norrie, himself of the new economic history persuasion, "so few of us are ourselves involved in such broad interdisciplinary work."[13]

Norrie is here alluding to the nature of the paradigm, and there are deeper flaws in Aitken's argument that result from the superficiality of his analysis of economics as a paradigm and economic history as a field within that paradigm. Traditionally, economic history had been critical of economic theory and, to a considerable extent, prepared to generate its own analytical frameworks, loosely related to the prevailing body of theory. As well, under Innis, economic history was central to economics itself, and had, in turn, been the core for the broader synthesis that constituted the old political economy. Beginning in the '30s with Keynes, and greatly intensifying during the war and postwar period, economics became obsessed with the immediate and the short-run, and hence became ahistorical, falling victim to quantification and the reification of technique. In the United States, the new economics, or the so-called neo-classical synthesis, destroyed the surviving remnants of the institutionalism of Veblen and Commons; in Canada, it destroyed the Innis school as a dominant influence in economics and as the unifying theme for political economy. Innis survived within Canadian economic history because the new economics sees economic history essentially as a ghetto, and because those of the Innis tradition, particularly at Toronto under the influence of V.W. Bladen and W.T. Easterbook, were able to resist the inroads of the new economic history. In terms of influence over the profession, the successor to Innis was to be Harry Johnson located outside Canada at the University of Chicago and the London School of Economics and, as a happy prisoner of the orthodox paradigm, wholly committed to the obliteration of borders as impediments to the free movements of goods, capital and ideas.

Berger agues that Innis foresaw his fate and, in effect in his later work deserting the paradigm of economics, contributed to it:

Innis sensed that excessive specialization in economics, its presentist tendencies, and the desire for disciplinary autonomy implied a breakup of the political-economy tradition that had underlain his economic history of Canada ... The staple thesis linked the history of Creighton, the sociology of Clark, and the political economy of Innis. The common approach was weakened in the forties; there were complaints about the subordination of political science to political economy ... Changing fashions in economics also foreshadowed a very different style ... Innis's speculations on communications were partly responses to the conditions that were leading to a splintering of the "social sciences." Ironically, they were also his contribution to the dissolution of the political-economy tradition.[14]

It is difficult, however, to see how he could have avoided being read out of the paradigm, for quantification and Keynesianism represented everything he was opposed to as an economist. And in practice, Keynesianism – in the sense of state activity to facilitate economic growth so as to maintain full employment – was to mean for Canada in the postwar period a continuing if not increasing commitment to the export of staple products developed by and for foreign capital, that is, economic growth at the expense of deepening dependency. Keynesianism in Canada was grafted onto the "steady-growth" version of the staple thesis as articulated by W.A. Mackintosh, rather than Innis's dependency version.[15] Hence the influence of Keynes worked to erode the influence of Innis – though Innis' suspiciousness of Keynesianism, given his position within the profession with respect to academic appointments in Canada, tended to weaken Keynesianism in Canada.

The *prima causa* of the fate of Innis, and hence of Canadian political economy, lies with the nature of mainstream orthodox economics from the late 1930s onward, its monolithic character and the arrogance of its practitioners, and their intolerance of dissent. At the same time, however, some blame must be attached to those whom Drache calls "the launderers" of Innis.[16] It is, after all, in the nature of colonialism that at least some of the colonials are complicit; the essence of this comprador intellectual role (as we shall see below) consisted of rejecting the dependency-model of the early Innis and the anti-American imperialism of the later Innis.

The power of the neo-classical paradigm to kill reflects, of course, less its external verities as theory and more its deadly consequences as ideology, intensifying yet more powerful realities of global Realpolitik in the era of the waxing of the American empire. As I have argued elsewhere, Innis' capacity to develop a creative, indigenous approach to economics is in large part due to the sterility of discipline between the writings of Marshall and Keynes and the interregnum in Canada between the decline of British and rise of American imperial influence.[17] But the Toronto school declined as Canada inexorably shifted into the American empire. The era of the Cold War saw the Americanization of the social sciences as an aspect of the Americanization of everything, and the destruction of a unified political economy appropriate to a hinterland status. Canada became, for Canadian social scientists, a "miniature replica" of the US, a "peaceable kingdom," America in slow motion with less of both the good and the bad. Economics, with its pretensions to fine-tuning the economy, became relevant with a vengeance when secular prosperity was thought to have been "built-in". Canadian economics became a branch plant of US economics and, increasingly, of the Friedmanite orthodoxy of the University of Chicago. The subtlety and sophistication of Innisian political economy were replaced by the simplicity and banality of the doctrines of free trade and competition, notwithstanding the evident imperfections of competition that inhered in the now-ascendant, transnational corporations. Innis offered the general observation that "the success of laissez-faire has been paid for by the exploited areas of which we are one;" in the specific context of post-war Canada, Neill argues that the demise of Innis's influence was one of the costs: "By the nineteen-fifties Innis and those who would have seen the matter as he did were swamped by both the soft money Keynesian group and the continentalist free traders."[18]

The Department of Political Economy at the University of Toronto, once chaired with such distinction by Innis, grew quantitatively but, depending on one's point of view, not necessarily qualitatively. Sociology broke away and its assertion of discipline autonomy was followed, to some extent unavoidably, by pervasive Americanization. Economics and political science held together, but in the face of rising opposition from the economists that seems certain to triumph shortly. (In any event, they already operate as if they were separate departments and political economy as such is hardly taught.) The economists devote themselves to redefining political economy, on the one hand, by reducing politics to the narrowest margins of economic self-interest (for example, politicians exchanging policies for votes; nationalism reduced to a "taste for nationalism," the better to vilify it)[19] and, on the other hand, by equating political economy with the study of public policy. As the undergraduate Political Economy Course Union recently pointed out: "It is presently possible for a student to gain a four-year specialist degree in Economics at U of T without ever having read a word of Harold Innis." The University honoured Innis by naming a new college after him, but I am told that the opening line of the Innis College song is, "Who the hell was Harold Innis?"

If I have dwelt on economics particularly at the University of Toronto, it is because there is the situation I know best, not because I think that situation is unique. Nationally, the old Canadian Political Science Association combining economists and political scientists split in 1967; significantly, when a Political Economy section was created in 1976, it was not within the Canadian Economics Association (CEA) but rather the successor Canadian Political Science Association (CPSA). There is now more economic history, at least in the sense that Innis would have understood, to be found at the meetings of the CPSA than the CEA; the same is true with respect to the Canadian Historical Association and even the Canadian Sociology and Anthropology Association relative to the CEA.

Though this is what happened, it must be insisted that there is an important sense in which it did not have to happen that way, namely, that neo-classical theory could have incorporated Innis' staple economics. Innis, after all, was a liberal, albeit a liberal with a difference.[20] If he has been ignored, suppressed, and laundered, it has happened more for ideological reasons than from theoretical imperatives *per se*. The latter point is important not only in its own right but because it is suggestive of developments that may in due course take place within the beleaguered orthodox paradigm.

I have argued elsewhere that there *are* someways in which the staple thesis was relevant to neo-classical theory and the restatement of the staple thesis as a theory of economic growth in 1963 lent Innis respectability within the orthodox paradigm.[21] Subsequent literature has been mostly devoted to its quantitative testing or to theoretical elaboration narrowly focused and taxonomic in character. Nonetheless, it could have been effectively "modernized" by incorporating into the staple theory, as a resource-based theory of growth, the importance of economic rents for domestic capital formation. Innis recognized the tendency of rents to manifest themselves as profits, as well as royalties, taxes and license fees as government devices to capture rents. He also advocated using the tariff on machinery and equipment "to skim off a substantial portion of the cream by taxing equipment, raising costs of production and thereby reducing profits which would otherwise flow off into the hands of foreign investors"; suggested labour legislation "be designed to prevent exploitation of labour"; favoured "the investment of surplus by large companies in Canadian enterprises and the holding of stock by Canadian shareholders"; supported devices for increasing the prices of raw materials; and concluded, cryptically with the note "Government ownership as a means."[22] Serious attention to these matters would have forced the economic historian to address the issue of foreign ownership and Canada's role as a resource hinterland within the American empire, that is, with Canada's dependency, and offer an alternative to the sterility of the new economic history. For the orthodox paradigm, however, what could not be risked was the discovery of neo-colonialism.

The rationale for extending the staple approach to allow for the institutional fact of the transnational corporation transcends the matter of resource processing; at issue is the larger reality of the emergent global economy and polity. While historians have largely failed to do so, important work has been done of the contemporary phenomenon of foreign ownership and on the rise of Canadian nationalism as a reaction to it.[23] Against this, and particularly the latter, the neo-classicists wheeled out their heaviest cannon; it all smacked of economic nationalism, dangerous nonsense by second-rate Canadian academics in bed with second-rate Canadian businessmen.[24] The transnational corporations of the centre and the branch plant economy of the periphery were reduced by Canadian economists to the single equation: the Canadian tariff created inefficient industry. What could have been a promising approach was emasculated in the name of the most literal neo-classical orthodoxy; nature should copy art and Canadian secondary manufacturing could sink or swim on the tide of free trade. A less ideological response could have led to the writing of genuine industrial history – something that has still not been done. From the perspective of economic history proper, it would have been the most useful way to build on Innis – by blending the fact of dependent industrialization explicitly into the staple approach – and, by providing critical building blocks that the economist is best equipped to provide, would have given a firm foundation to the work of political, social and labour historians and led thereby to a new, but still orthodox synthesis.[25] "The surface of the economic history of modern Canada has barely been scratched, and until that task is taken up systematically it will be impossible to write a convincing new synthesis of our past."[26]

What was above all at risk was the discovery of dependency – a possibility that could not be tolerated, for to do so would risk legitimizing nationalism. The result was to strangle economic history of the Innis variety. This decline of economic history is evidence of the high cost of the evasion and suppression that inheres in the dominant paradigm. The staple theory was at best tolerated only within the context of the Mackintosh version where it could, by quantitative testing, provide work for economic historians deemed appropriate by economists. Nor were the historians proper guiltless; Paul Craven (who calls the Mackintosh version "the whig-staples view") writes with respect to J.B. Brebner's classic *North Atlantic*

Triangle: "Brebner's refinement of the whig-staples approach was to make it explicitly continentalist in scope. The staple's orientation of the Canadian economy was an expression of natural advantage, and the expansion of the turn of the century reflected a continental partnership between a highly industrialized United States running short of natural resources and a newly united Canada rich in them."[27]

If the early Innis was laundered, the later Innis was simply beyond the ken. Even those otherwise sympathetic to Innis (like Easterbrook) failed to see any message in Innis' later writings for Canadian economic history, and certainly not his recognition of Canada's increasingly satellitic status (contained in the now often-quoted phrase of "colony to nation to colony") nor his trenchant warnings against the newly intensified economic imperialism of the United States backed by the might of the military and the mass media. The costs of compartmentalizing Innis into the staples phase and the communications phase have been very high for Canadian economic history.

These matters cut deeply, for they tell us much about the colonial intellectual and the colonization of the mind. Writes John Watson: "It is Innis' colonial background which provides an explanation for his intellectual tragedy. It offered him the orientation and subject matter which eventually led, at the height of the Cold War, to his incisive critique of American imperialism. And yet, the same background dictated that his thought, though lauded, would not be fully appreciated and pursued."[28] Watson calls this "colonial myopia"; not to admit Canada's colonial situation was a way for the Canadian intellectual to avoid facing his own colonial situation.

A re-stated staple theory of growth in terms of the leading role of exports and in the context of an international economy powerfully influenced by transnational corporations was one possibility; another was (and is) the development of an Innisian theory of growth in terms of rigidities, monopolies, imbalances, radical instability, etc. Even a casual reader of Innis quickly becomes aware of his concern with constraints resulting from overhead costs, unused capacity, the burden of debt, and so on. Robin Neill was the first to systematically draw our attention to Innis' emphasis on the cyclonic nature of economic development in Canada. (The contrast with the Mackintosh conception is stark). Drache has now generalized these themes in Innis' writings into an Innisian theory of Canadian

capitalist development.[29] Orthodox economics offers an equilibrium model of capitalist growth through markets, linkages, harmo-
nies, etc. Innis offers us, Drache suggests, a disequilibrium model
of rigidities; in effect, a special, or limiting, case within the general
model, with the further critical feature that, unlike the neo-classical
equilibrium model, it is an open-ended, or dialectical, model. In
Drache's terms, "rigidities" result in "incomplete development" or
dependency. Watson independently makes the same point: "In the
'staples' period Innis was primarily concerned with 'cyclonics' or
radical instability' ... By definition, an understanding of the hinterland context revolves around a conception of imbalance, or disequilibrium or dependency."[30] Notwithstanding the sharp contrast
with the neo-classical model, Drache reminds us that Innis never
fully abandoned neo-classical economics. Rather, the neo-classicists
abandoned him. They have ignored and suppressed the essence of
Innisian theory because it was necessary to do so to avoid facing its
implications of inherent tendencies toward hinterland dependency.[31] Significantly, Drache shows us how Innis can be understood within the liberal paradigm, though he himself opts for the
perspective of the Marxists paradigm.

What actually happened was not the realization of any of these
possibilities, but rather the destruction of Innisian economic history; the latter being central to political economy, its destruction
contributed to the destruction of political economy. It is useful to
imagine what might have been. A central theme for Innis and his
school was the notion of "centre-margin"; in fact, I think we should
say the central theme in that, following Easterbrook, it is a unifying
theme for historical analysis. The terminology is Innis', from his
masterful "Conclusion" to The Fur Trade in Canada, where he
writes of "the discrepancy between the centre and the margin of
western civilization."[32] Others have rephrased the theme in the
more popular terminology of "metropolis-hinterland."

The theme is indeed pervasive in the writings of the old political
economy. Donald Creighton's Laurentian school of Canadian Historiography, the counterpart to Innis' staple approach, explored
the interaction of economics and politics in the creation of a transcontinental national economy, the empire of the St. Lawrence born
and reborn.[33] No one has shown as effectively as Creighton the
power of this theme to focus on the "separateness" of northern
North America. Canada as "hinterland" is explicit throughout. The

beleaguered St. Lawrence merchants face not only the competition of New York/Albany, but the indifference of the British Colonial Office to their grand (sub-) imperial designs. On the whole, thought, the metropolis-hinterland relationship within the British Empire is seen as a mutually beneficial rather than exploitative arrangement, at least in contrast to later experience within the American empire (a similar bias is evident in Innis' writing and is instructive in understanding the nature of his nationalism). The rise of the empire of the St. Lawrence in the British era is followed by its "decline and fall" in the American era and the successors to Sir John A. Macdonald become little more than puppets that dance to the tune of American imperialism; to read Creighton is never to be in doubt that Canada is now an American dependency.[34]

Where he errs is in exaggerating the nationalism of the National Policy, and in blaming Mackenzie King for a branch plant economy whose origins are to be found in the years immediately after 1879 and which was already fully evident by 1913 in the leading sectors of the Second Industrial Revolution.[35] Macdonald's National Policy politically had an aura of "home rule"[36] and "American industry in Canada" economically; the basis was fully laid for the "unequal alliance" of hinterland and metropole.[37] Indeed, even the St. Lawrence merchants of the early Creighton limited themselves to searching for a better deal within the British Empire; when it failed in the late 1840s, not a few of them sought to move fully into the American empire; they were a most colonial-minded group.[38] What follows, then, is that Canada has always been more of a hinterland or colony (subjected to, and its elites complicit in, metropolitan imperatives) than Creighton tells us – though none of this is to deny that Creighton deserves enormous credit for maintaining the focus on dependency.

In economic history based on the staple approach, the focus on the hinterland status of Canada was less firmly maintained. In part, the problem was the initial difference between Innis and Mackintosh, and their influence. Mackintosh's study for the Rowell-Sirois Commission constituted a general economic history of the years from Confederation to the 1930s (the impressive historical overview of Book I of the Report); it shows, in conjunction with Creighton on the immediate pre-Confederation period, how a national polity and economy were created but the problem of growing American influence (beyond reorientation of Canadian

trade patterns) is ignored. To Easterbrook, who clearly worked
out of the Innis tradition, Canada is characterized by a centralized, more controlled kind of growth ("a pattern of persistence"
appropriate to a "margin"), in contrast to the more vital and
diversified development of the United States ("a pattern of transformation" appropriate to a "centre"). The notion of Canada as a
satellite of the United States would appear inherent to such a
view, but Easterbrook's writing contains little that is explicit on
Canadian dependency.[39]

In the centre-margin/metropolis-hinterland framework, there is
not only an external dimension, but also an internal dimension of
internal metropolis (or sub-metropolis)/internal hinterlands. Innis' writings, notwithstanding his emphasis on the "naturalness" of
Canada in terms of geography (the St. Lawrence River and the Pre-
cambrian Shield) and the character of the great staple trades of fur
and wheat, always show a firm grasp of this (from the grievances of
the Western farmers against the CPR in his first book to those of the
Maritime Provinces against Central Canada in *The Cod Fisheries*,
and his appendix to the 1951 Royal Commission on Transportation).[40] In many ways, the most important writing in the Innis
tradition has been the development of this theme: for example,
S.D. Clark on the Canadian frontier, with its protest movements as
controlled margins; A.R.M. Lower on the forest frontier and the
"rip-off" by Toronto and, beyond, New York; W.L. Morton on the
West – regional history important in its own right and essential,
given the interplay of economic centres and subordinate areas, to
the writing of national history; George Britnell on the impact of
wheat on the West; Vernon Fowke on the exploitation of the western farmer by the National Policy; C.B. Macpherson on the political protest of Alberta wheat farmers and its limitation (emphasized,
in the same series on Social Credit, by J.B. Mallory's study of feder-
alism); A.G. Bailey on the culture of the Maritime Provinces as a
marginal area.[41]

The centre/margin or metropolis/hinterland framework is not
only two-dimensional; what is also critical is the interrelatedness of
the two. Again this was clearly understood by Innis, as is evident in
the following passage first published in 1937:

The end of the period of expansion based on the St. Lawrence and trade
with Great Britain coincided roughly with the achievement of dominion

status which followed the Great War and which was marked by the statute of Westminster. The end of the struggle for control over external policy has been followed by problems of internal policy; and the decline of the St. Lawrence as a factor contributing to the centralization of the Dominion has been accompanied by the increasing importance of regionalism evident in the growth of the powers of the provinces ... The extension of the American empire, the decline of its natural resources, and the emergence of metropolitan areas, supported capitalist expansion in Canada and reinforced the trend of regionalism. The pull to the north and south has tended to become stronger in contrast with the pull east and west.[42]

His later writings show a persistent concern with this issue of political disintegration and balkanization in the face of Americanization. Garth Stevenson refers to this as a "thin line of intellectual tradition, which ... has ... drawn attention to the relatedness of the internal and external threats."[43] Indeed, not all if Innis' successors have been able to keep their eyes focused to see both threats and their deadly interaction. Creighton powerfully analyses the external threat, but has no sympathy for "regionalism." "In all his works," Berger tells us, "Creighton concentrated on the centre, not on the periphery of the country ... He viewed with sarcastic disfavour both the growth of provincial powers and scholarly efforts concentrated on regional history."[44] Morton, on the other hand, in Berger's elegant phraseology, maintained "the delicate balance of region and nation."

In recent years, the Quebec question has increasingly intruded upon this matter. The issue is not central to Innis – indeed, there is little in his writings about Quebec which speaks to his limitations as an English-Canadian intellectual – but it has much exercised his successors whose responses starkly indicate the limitations, if not of Innis, then of the school. Creighton's rejection of the nationalist aspirations of the Quebecois are well known and consistent with his general stand on regionalism, but what may be more significant is the vehemence with which both Morton and Lower have taken the same position on Quebec, despite their general tolerance of regionalism (and Morton's long-standing sympathy with the rights of francophones as well as Lower's for the aspirations of Quebecers).[45] I do not pretend to know where Innis might have stood on the matter of Quebec, but it must be insisted upon that he was consistently suspicious of centralization. He wrote of "the lack of unity which has preserved Canadian unity" and of "the common basis of union (being) one of debt and taxes."[46] According to Neill: "He exposed the underlying forces both of unity and diversity, for the most part emphasizing the latter," and Berger adds: "Innis may have demonstrated the case for Canadian unity, but this dimension of his accomplishment was exaggerated by those who were either oblivious of, or chose to ignore, his own hostility to centralization of power and his concern with staples that had diverse effects on the country."[47] In the context of the recent use (that is, misuse) of national unity to put down the aspirations of the Quebecois, it is essential to insist that appeal to the old political economy need not lock us into a one-Canada, anti-Quebec position.

The discussion may also cast light on the argument by William Christian that Innis was not a nationalist.[48] It is, to say the least, an original position, the counter-position being held by such diverse people as Creighton, Brebner, Berger, Drache, Neill, Cook and others. In terms of the above, Christian makes two elementary errors. He fails to distinguish between the nationalism of the centre and the nationalism of the periphery; that is, between aggressive nationalism and defensive nationalism, the first being imperialist and the second anti-imperialist. Secondly, he shows no grasp at all of the two-dimensional character of the centre-margin dialectic and of the need, in the Canadian context, to distinguish between nationalism as "national independence" and nationalism as "national unity" (or what Drache has called, respectively, the nationalism of dependency or self-determination and the nationalism of domination.[49]) With a populist-like distrust of the Ottawa establishment, Innis did not relate well to the latter. This is not to deny the subtlety of Innis' position, particularly in his later works, nor the important point made by Watson (hinted at by Berger but which escapes Christian) that "Innis was not an anti-imperialism in the sense of having a prejudice against large-scale empires. On the contrary, he felt the balanced empire represented that which was best in human achievement."[50] This could have been Christian's strongest argument for the view that Innis was not a nationalist, but it was the fatal flaw – for Christian's argument – that is also explains why Innis was, in his later years, a Canadian nationalist. For, to again cite Watson, Innis "was an anti-imperialist in the modern sense of being committed to opposing the imbalance (in the form of military expansionism) of contemporary empires."[51] This shows the importance of relating ideas to the understanding of praxis. At the same time, it demonstrates the severe pitfalls inherent to textual criticism *per se*.[52]

Another major theme for Innis and the school was that of "the state and economic life." In the nature of the case, the theme linked economics (or economic history) and political science; it also stood out as a theme for historians (particularly Creighton) and for the sociologist S.D. Clark.[53] An argument central to Innis was that the hinterland state itself was almost a by-product of the exigencies of staple production as defined by the imperial state. Both the Act of Union and Confederation were essentially dictated by the need to create a larger state to provide security for foreign capital to build first the canals and then the railways to facilitate the movement of staples; Creighton's British North America at Confederation brilliantly documented the latter. Within economic history proper, Fowke and Aitken showed how "the state and economic life" could be a powerful unifying theme to the long sweep of Canadian history while Alfred Dubuc, in another seminal article, spoke directly of the post-Confederation period and the material basis for the erosion of federal authority.[54] In political science, Drache contrasts the older statist tradition of J.A. Corry (that is, the state actively engaged in the process of creating economic growth) with the new "social democratic" theorists (for example, Frank Scott and Eugene Forsey) and the role of the state as a housekeeper in an advanced capitalist economy. In the latter, dependency tends to drop away in a manner analogous to its fate in the Mackintosh approach (relative to the Innis approach). Political science, like economics, ceases to be political economy.[55] C.B. Macpherson has described how the search for discipline autonomy, in the context of American influence, worked to sever the link between the state and economic life:

Much ingenuity has been used by American political scientists, in the last twenty or thirty years particularly, in staking out a territory distinct from any other social science. The behaviouralists and systems analysts felt that they had to establish their claims to a 'new' political science. The way to escape from the confines of studying institutions was to see politics as an activity ... Not wishing to work with "the state" as the central concept, as the older political science had done, a formulation which had at least allowed some interest in the relation between the state

and economic life, the new men in effect built walls between the study
of the state and the study of the economy.[56]

A return to a central concern with the state and economy-building
is now evident in general and, in particular, in important writings
on the provinces. The relevant disciplines are more often political
science and history than economics or economic history, and the
authors are, to some extent, seen, by themselves and others, as part
of the new political economy and not merely as part of the established order of their disciplines.[57]

To return to the opening theme, I have argued that, post-World
War II, the dominant paradigm in economics suppressed Innis
while paying him little more than lip service. But the larger realities
of the world could not be indefinitely suppressed. In the world of
ideas, political economy in general and Marxism in particular have
revived in the United States and elsewhere, including Canada, in
the past ten to fifteen years; for Canada, this should be evident
from the bibliographic references presented so far in this paper.
This development can be presumed to reflect the greater contradictions of capitalism that manifest themselves in the new era of
economic crisis. The neo-classical paradigm is again in trouble. As
the Keynesian consensus broke down – in the face of persistent unemployment and permanent inflation, or so-called stagflation – it
was met, first and foremost, by a retreat to pre-Keynesianism called
monetarism. At the same time, Marxism, dormant since the 1930s,
experienced a major revival in the context of the antiwar and
student radicalism of the late 1960s and early 1970s, while Keynesianism, in the face of monetarism, transformed itself into a more
institutionalist, or Galbraithian, post-Keynesianism. In Canada, because of the central importance of dependency, these developments have been animated by a powerful strand of nationalism
inherent to dissent from the orthodox paradigm with its cosmopolitan, or pro-imperialist, bias toward free trade and free mobility of
capital. Hence, there has been a revival of interest in Innis precisely
because of his understanding of Canada's satellitic position, his
distrust of orthodox economics and, notwithstanding Christian, his
nationalism when it mattered. In the context of the revival of
political economy and the right-wing bias of the dominant
monetarist, or neo-conservative economics, Innis became, by

default, the property of the left. This is admittedly ironic given his own unwillingness to have any truck or trade with the intellectual left, particularly as represented by the League for Social Reconstruction in the 1930s.[58]

It is a tribute to the vitality of the new political economy in Canada – albeit more evident in political science, sociology, history and anthropology than in economics proper – that it would necessitate a separate paper to describe it with any justice.[59] Brief comments must suffice here.

Though I myself am not in doubt as to the legacy of the old political economy of Innis and his school, two qualifications are in order. The first is that there has been increasing interest in Innis by scholars who would, I presume, not wish to be seen as tainted either by the leftish or nationalist biases of the new political economy. The leading case in point would be William Christian, arguably the most productive of Innisian scholars.[60] One must also include under this heading an interest in Innis within orthodox writing that consists not merely in ignoring and neglecting him but in explicit attacks against him. The most important example here is William Eccles' "belated review" of Innis' *Fur Trade*: it is a tribute to the new political economy that this instantly produced an impressive defense of Innis and rebuttal of Eccles by Hugh Grant.[61] A recurring theme of this paper is the nature of paradigms; the issue between Eccles and Innis, and Eccles and Grant, then, consist of the contrast between the political economy paradigm of Innis and Grant and the orthodox Canadian history paradigm of Eccles with its enormous distrust of explicit theorizing and its tendency to see economic analysis as inherently deterministic (though it should be borne in mind here that other distinguished Canadian historian, Carl Berger, is mostly favourable to Innis).

The second qualification is that some within the new political economy who label themselves Marxist political economists the better to distinguish themselves from political economists in general are critical of the Innis legacy, holding it to be counter-productive to the development of Marxist political economy. The leading instances here are David McNally's just-published critique both of the staple theory and those of us who have written of the wedding of Innis and Marx.[62] At the risk of trying the patience of the reader, what is at issue is the nature of paradigms and so we so we should not be surprised that some new political economists are more rigid or doctrinaire than others. It cannot be denied, however, that what all but the most sectarian would regard as "political economy" has been influenced to some degree (and in some cases – such as my own – decisively so) by Innis and his school. As well, the use of the Innisian strand of political economy has the great virtue of being a protection against the mechanical application of Marxist models of Canada generated outside Canada, what Drache has called "metropolitan Marxism." Significantly, Innis explicitly warned against the limitations of imported theory when he himself set out to create an indigenous Canadian theory.[63]

Let me make two final observations on the Innis tradition that seem, to me, to be relevant to our contemporary situation. The first is that the later Innis deplored the militarism and irrationality he saw gripping the United States at the time of the origins of the Cold War. Once again, in the time of Ronald Reagan and the re-creation of the Cold War, there is surely much to deplore. The second seems to me, from reading Watson, to be Innis' most important message to Canadian intellectuals. It is that we must recognize, but refuse to accept, our lot as colonial intellectuals. This paper has been an attempt to describe the powerful constraints within Canadian scholarship. Innis' achievement is the proof that there is more room for manoeuvre than the orthodox pretend and we are today the stronger for it.

But the last word I will give to the person who is arguably the most distinguished contemporary Canadian intellectual, Northrop Frye (although I do so because his point in this quotation is particularly congenial):

Innis's influence, in Canada as elsewhere, will grow steadily, because with practice in reading him he becomes constantly more suggestive and rewarding. He was a curiously tentative writer, which may account for something of his rather spastic prose rhythm. He saw that every new form or technique generates both a positive impulse to exploit it and a negative impulse, especially strong in universities, to resist it, and that the former always outmanoeuvres the latter. But he had something of what I call the garrison mentality in him, the university being still his garrison for all the obscurantism in it that he comments on so dryly. Perhaps it is not possible to hold a vision of that scope and range steadily in one's mind without a more passionate commitment to society as well as to scholarship.[64]

NOTES

1 I am discussing the Innis tradition only in Canadian political economy and not in communications as well; this narrowing reflects my interests and competence. For one of the very few writers who is able to discuss both Innises with insight, see A. John Watson, "Harold Innis and Classical Scholarship," *Journal of Canadian Studies* (1977) 12(5): 45–61; and "Marginal Man: Harold Innis' Communications Works in Context," PhD thesis, University of Toronto (1981).

2 Thomas S. Kuhn, *The Structure of Scientific Revolutions* (Chicago, 1962).

3 H.A. Innis, *Political Economy in the Modern State* (Toronto, 1946), 100.

4 Carl Berger, *The Writing of Canadian History: Aspects of English-Canadian Historical Writing, 1900–1970* (Toronto, 1976); while Berger's book is most useful, it is the history of history rather than the economic history of history; it describes ideas with little or no reference to material circumstances and Realpolitik.

5 Innis, *Political Economy in the Modern State*, 83.

6 Hugh G.J. Aitken, "Myth and Measurement: the Innis Tradition in Economic History", *Journal of Canadian Studies* 12(5) (1978): 96–105.

7 Herbert Heaton, "Clio's New Overalls," *Canadian Journal of Economics and Political Science* (1954).

8 Paul Davenport, "Capital Accumulation and Economic Growth," (PhD thesis, University of Toronto, 1976), 342, 247.

9 Ian Parker, "Harold Innis, Karl Marx and Canadian Political Economy," *Queen's Quarterly* (19xx), 545.

10 Donald N. McCloskey, "The Achievements of the Cliometric School," *Journal of Economic History* (1978), 13–28.

11 Mel Watkins, "The Staple Theory Revisited," reprinted in this collection, xx.

12 William L. Marr and Donald G. Paterson, *Canada: an Economic History* (Toronto, 1980).

13 "Review," by Kenneth H. Norrie, *Canadian Historical Review* (1981) 339–40.

14 *Writing of Canadian History*, 191.

15 That there are (even within the liberal paradigm) two versions of the staple theory, see "The Staple Thesis Revisited" and Daniel Drache, "Rediscovering Canadian Political Economy" in Wallace Clement and Daniel Drache, eds., *A Practical Guide to Canadian Political Economy* (Toronto, 1978), 1–53. For Mackintosh's view, see W.A. Mackintosh, "Economic Factors in Canadian History" in M.H. Watkins and H.M. Grant, eds., *Canadian*

Economic History: Classic and Contemporary Approaches (Ottawa, 1993), 1–15.
On post-war economic policy, see David A. Wolfe, "Economic Growth and
Foreign Investment: A Perspective on Canadian Economic Policy, 1945–
1957," *Journal of Canadian Studies* 13(1) (1978): 3–20.
16 "Rediscovering Canadian Political Economy."
17 Mel Watkins, "The Dismal State of Economics in Canada" in Ian Lumsden,
ed., *Close the 49th Parallel, etc.: The Americanization of Canada* (Toronto,
1970), 205.
18 Innis, "Commentary," in The State and Economic Life (Paris, 1934), 289
cited in Robin Neill, *A New Theory of Value: The Canadian Economics of H.A.
Innis* (Toronto, 1972), 61; Neill, *A New Theory of Value*, 118.
19 For a critique of the latter, see my "The Economics of Nationalism and the
Nationality of Economics: a Critique of Neoclassical Theorizing," *Canadian Journal of Economics* (1978), S87–S120.
20 See Daniel Drache, "Harold Innis: a Canadian Nationalist," *Journal of
Canadian Studies* (May 1979), 7–12.
21 "The Staple Theory Revisited." Watson is critical of those who "use" Innis'
work rather than "understanding" it, but it is valid to translate from one
paradigm (Innisian) to another (neoclassical or Marxist) as a way of generating insights. As well, while every effort should be made to understand
Innis on his own terms (as Watson is doing), the ultimate test of the use of
anyone's work, including Innis', is putting it to use; otherwise, scholarship
bogs down in textual criticism.
22 Innis, "Snarkov Island," Appendix to Neill, *A New Theory of Value*, 146–9.
23 Aitken, *American Capital and Canadian Resources* (Cambridge, Mass., 1961);
Stephen Hymer, "Direct Foreign Investment and the National Economic
Interest" in Peter Russell, (ed.), *Nationalism in Canada* (Toronto, 1966),
191–202, and *The International Operations of National Firms: A Study in Direct
Foreign Investment* (Cambridge, Mass., 1976); Kari Levitt, *Silent Surrender:
The Multinational Corporation in Canada* (Toronto, 1970); Abraham
Rotstein, *The Precarious Homestead* (Toronto, 1973), and "Canada: The New
Nationalism," *Foreign Affairs* (October 1976), and "Is There an English-
Canadian Nationalism?" *Journal of Canadian Studies* (Summer 1978).
24 This is not overwriting on my part; vide Harry Johnson's vituperative comment on "the shallow and frequently near-psychotic writings of some Canadians employed in otherwise reputable economics departments, on such
subjects as American investment in Canada" ("The Current and Prospective State of Economics in Canada" in T.N. Guinsburg and G.L. Reuber,
eds., *Perspectives on the Social Sciences in Canada* (Toronto, 1974). An
elaboration on Johnson's views is provided in M.H. Watkins, "The

Economics of Nationalism and the Nationality of Economics: A Critque of Neo-Classical Theorizing," reprinted in this collection.

25 Labour historians, notable Clare Pentland, Bryan Palmer and Greg Kealey, have had to write industrial history themselves in order to write labour history, and with some tendency to get the former wrong. See H. Clare Pentland, *Labour and Capital in Canada 1650–1860*, edited by Paul Phillips (Toronto, 1981); Bryan D. Palmer, *A Culture in Conflict: Skilled Workers and Industrial Capitalism in Hamilton, Ontario, 1860–1914*; Gregory S. Kealey, *Toronto Workers Respond to Industrial Capitalism 1867–1892*. For a perceptive critique of Palmer and Keeley on this point, see the review by Leo Panitch, *Canadian Journal of Political Science* 14 (1981): 434–7.

26 Ramsay Cook, "History: the Invertebrate Social Science," in Guinsburg and Reuber, eds, 144.

27 Paul Craven, *"An Impartial Umpire": Industrial Relations and the Canadian State, 1900–1911* (Toronto: University of Toronto Press, 1980), 32. It should be noted that Craven's comments on industrial history are not subject to the critique made in note 31.

28 "Harold Innis and Classical Scholarship," 32.

29 Daniel Drache, "Disequilibrium economics and Canadian capitalist development: The Innis paradigm" (mimeo, 1979).

30 "Harold Innis and Classical Scholarship," 55, 54.

31 I have chosen to focus on the implications for dependency of Innisian theory as adumbrated by Drache for the purposes of this paper, but that is to do less than full justice to either Innis or Drache. In fact, a reading of Drache's paper suggests that Innis can be read as having a theory of capitalist growth and not simply of Canadian capitalist growth, albeit drawing primarily on the Canadian experience. Certainly a "disequilibrium model of rigidities" implies a more general relevance with the rigidities varying with the case. Also, Ian Parker has pointed out to me that the neo-classical theory of growth is, at least from any Marxist perspective, itself a special case of a general theory. In principle, Innisian theory may be at least as much a general theory as neo-classical theory and, since everything depends on where one stands, as Marxist theory. Hence, Parker himself shows (see note 9) that is not only helps our understanding of Innis to know our Marx, it also helps our understanding of Marx to know our Innis.

32 H.A. Innis, *The Fur Trade in Canada: An Introduction to Canadian Economic History*, rev. ed., (Toronto 1956).

33 D.G. Creighton, *The Empire of the St. Lawrence*, 2nd ed. (Toronto, 1956).

34 Creighton, "The Decline and Fall of the Empire of the St. Lawrence" in *Towards the Discovery of Canada: Selected Essays* (Toronto, 1972).

35 Creighton, *Canada's First Century, 1867–1967* (Toronto, 1970).

36 Drache, "The Canadian Bourgeoisie and its National Consciousness" in Lumsden, op. cit., 10.

37 This is the major theme of Wallace Clement, *Continental Corporate Power: Economic Linkages between Canada and the United States* (Toronto, 1977).

38 Tulchinsky goes so far as to argue that "the high drama of the annexation crisis, which passed so quickly, masks the fact that Montreal merchants had always been continentalists" (Gerald J.J. Tulchinsky, *The River Barons: Montreal Business and the Growth of Industry and Transportation 1837–53* (Toronto, 1977), 237. He also writes: "The merchants had never been nationalists and never would be – unless it was in their economic interest" (236) but fails to draw the inference that for a capitalist class not to be nationalist is to be colonial-minded.

39 W.A. Mackintosh, *The Economic Background of Dominion-Provincial Relations*, a study done for the Royal Commission on Dominion-Provincial Relations, Book I, "Canada, 1867–1939", Carleton Library, Toronto, 1963; Creighton, *British North America at Confederation*, a study done for the Royal Commission on Dominion-Provincial Relations, Ottawa, 1940; W.T. Easterbrook, "Long-Period Comparative Study: Some Historical Cases," *Journal of Economic History* (December 1957).

40 Innis, *A History of the Canadian Pacific Railway*, 1st ed., 1923; 2nd ed., Toronto, 1971; *The Cod Fisheries: The History of an International Economy*, 1st ed., 1940; 2nd ed., Toronto, 1954; "Memorandum on Transportation" in Report of the Royal Commission on Transportation (Ottawa, 1951).

41 S.D. Clark, *Movements of Political Protest in Canada, 1640–1840* (Toronto, 1959); A.R.M. Lower, *The North American Assault on the Canadian Forest* (Toronto, 1938); W.L. Morton, *Manitoba, A History* (Toronto, 1957); George Britnell, *The Wheat Economy* (Toronto, 1939); V.C. Fowke, *The National Policy and the Wheat Economy* (Toronto, 1957); C.B. Macpherson, *Democracy in Alberta: the Theory and Practice of a Quasi-Party System* (Toronto, 1953); J.R.Mallory, *Social Credit and the Federal Power in Canada* (Toronto, 1954); A.G. Bailey, *Culture and Nationality* (Toronto, 1972).

42 Innis, *Essays in Canadian Economic History* (Toronto, 1957), 209.

43 Garth Stevenson, "Continental Integration and Canadian Unity" in Andrew Axline *et al* (eds.), *Continental Community? Independence and Integration in North America* (Toronto, 1974), 195.

44 *Writing of Canadian History*, 235–6.

45 See, for example, Morton, "Quebec in Revolt," *Canadian Forum* (February 1977), 13; and Lower, "The Problem of Quebec," *Journal of Canadian Studies* (July, 1977), 93–97.

46 Innis, *Political Economy in the Modern State*.

47 Neill, *New Theory of Value*, 46; Berger, *Writing of Canadian History*, 261.

48 William Christian, "The Inquisition of Nationalism," *Journal of Canadian Studies* (Winter 1977), 62–72; and Christian's "Preface" to *The Idea File of Harold Adams Innis*, Toronto, 1980.

49 Daniel Drache, "The Enigma of Canadian Nationalism", Symposium on Creative Modes of Nationalism in New Zealand, Canada and Australia, *The Australian and New Zealand Journal of Sociology* 14:3 (Part Two), (October 1978), 310–21.

50 "Harold Innis and Classical Scholarship," 56.

51 "Harold Innis and Classical Scholarship," 56.

52 Christian also argues, even more improbably, that George Grant is not a Canadian nationalist "in any commonly understood sense" (William Christian, "George Grant and the Terrifying Darkness" in Larry Schmidt, ed., *George Grant in Process: Essays and Conversations* (Toronto, 1978). It is difficult not to conclude at some point that what is at issue is not the nationalism of Innis or Grant but the anti-nationalist bias of Christian who respects Innis and Grant but wants to wish away their nationalism. Because the writings of Innis and Grant are undeniably rich and complex, Christian apparently imagines that they cannot believe in anything so "simple-minded" (to him) as nationalism. A similar kind of (impoverished) reasoning presumably underlies as well John Muggeridge's denial of Grant's nationalism; see Muggeridge, "George Grant's Anguished Conservatism", in Schmidt, ed., *George Grant in Process*, 40–8.

53 Creighton, *British North America at Confederation*; S.D. Clark, *The Developing Canadian Community* (Toronto, 1962; 2nd ed. 1968).

54 Vernon Fowke, "The National Policy – Old and New" in Easterbrook and Watkins, *Approaches*; Aitken, "Defensive Expansion"; Alfred Dubuc, "The Decline of Confederation and the New Nationalism" in Peter Russell, ed., *Nationalism in Canada* (Toronto, 1966), 112–32.

55 Drache, "Rediscovering Canadian Political Economy." As well as Corry, Drache should have recognized the contribution of Alexander Brady, who writes that; "The role of the state in the economic life of Canada is really the modern history of Canada" ("The State and Economic Life in Canada" (originally published in 1950) in K.J. Rea and J.T. McLeod, eds., *Business and Government in Canada: Selected Readings*, 2nd ed. (Toronto, 1976), 28).

56 C.B. Macpherson, "After Strange Gods: Canadian Political Science 1973" in Guinsburg and Reuber, eds., *Perspectives on the Social Sciences in Canada*, 67.

57 See Nelles, *Politics of Development*; the collection of essays of a Marxist tendency edited by Leo Panitch, *The Canadian State: Political Economy and*

Political Power (Toronto, 1977); John Richards and Larry Pratt, *Prairie Capitalism: Power and Influence in the New West, Toronto* (Toronto, 1979). Also as evidence of the revival of this theme, the University of Toronto Press launched a new series in the late 1970s titled "The State and Economic Life," co-edited by Leo Panitch and myself.

58 On the latter, see Michael Horn, "Academics and Canadian Social and Economic Policy in the Depression and War Years," *Journal of Canadian Studies* (1978–79), 3–10.

59 For a bibliographic guide that is already dated see Clement and Drache, *Practical Guide* (1978). For a collection of essays on Innis that grew out of a symposium at Simon Fraser University on the occasion of a Quarter-century after his death, see William H. Melody, Liora R. Salter and Paul Heyer, eds., *Culture, Communication and Dependency: The Tradition of H.A. Innis* (Norwood, N.J., 1981).

60 As well as Christian's paper on Innis' nationalism and his editing of *The Idea File*, see his "Harold Innis as ... Political Science (March, 1977) 21–42 and *Innis on Russia: The Russian Diary and Other Writings*, edited with a Preface by William Christian (Toronto, 1981).

61 W.J. Eccles, "A Belated Review of Harold Adam Innis, The Fur Trade in Canada," *Canadian Historical Review* (1979), 419–41 and Hugh M. Grant, "One Step Forward, Two Steps Back: Innis, Eccles, and the Canadian Fur Trade," *Canadian Historical Review* (1981), 304–22. The latter also includes "A Response to Hugh M. Grant on Innis" by Eccles (323–9) which, in the customary tradition of academic rejoinders, adds nothing but vituperation to the discussion.

62 David McNally, "Staple Theory as Commodity Fetishism: Marx, Innis and Canadian Political Economy," *Studies in Political Economy* (Autumn 1981), 35–63. I am presently writing, at the request of the editors of SPE, a critique of this paper.

63 H.A. Innis, "The Teaching of Economic History in Canada" (1930) in his *Essays in Canadian Economic History* (Toronto, 1956).

64 Northrop Frye, "Across the River and Out of the Trees" in W.J. Keith and B.-Z. Shek, eds., *The Arts in Canada: The Last Fifty Years* (Toronto, 1980), 1–14.

14

Economics, Politics
and the Relevance
of Social Democracy (1989)

The 1930s is, in many ways, a long time ago. It is separated from the present by the great divide of World War II, which both rid the world of the twin scourges of fascism and the Great Depression and facilitated the building of the modern welfare state which had been called for by reformers in the thirties. This was to be followed, with only the slightest pause, by the launching of the Cold War; the welfare state was matched by the contemporary warfare state, and the restoration of economic normalcy accompanied by the new political pathology of the nuclear arms race that put all at risk. These developments fundamentally altered the agendas of economics and politics, both nationally and globally.

The result, it might be thought, is necessarily to render archaic the diagnoses and prescriptions of those earlier times. Indeed, to some extent this is true. Yet notwithstanding these most profound changes, there remain some striking similarities between the

An earlier version of this paper appeared in *A Long and Faithful March: Towards the Christian Revolution, 1930s/1980s*, edited by Harold Wells and Roger Hutchinson (Toronto: United Church, 1989), 73-81. The book is dedicated to "the vision, goals and achievements of the Fellowship for a Christian Social Order" and "gratefully commemorates" the publication of *Towards the Christian Revolution*, edited by R.B.Y. Scott and Gregory Vlatsos (1936).

thirties and the eighties. We are once again in a time of economic turmoil; some things that we would not mind seeing change, like the cyclical character of capitalism with its alternating waves of boom and crisis, are still with us. The orthodox economic and political ideas of the world of Herbert Hoover that were used to justify doing nothing then to alleviate the misery are tarted up in the garb of monetarism and supply-side economics to justify doing nothing now; if bad ideas can be recycled to our detriment, then the thought occurs: why not search for good ideas from the past that might still be used to our advantage?

Some of the few real policy achievements of the intervening years, like the welfare state, are under attack as the attempt is made, albeit most selectively, to roll back history. The extent to which the achievement has been less than reformers hoped – as in the limited extent to which income has actually been redistributed and inequality reduced – is seen, perversely, as cause to do less rather than more. Unemployment has come back to haunt us, but this time accompanied by inflation; that additional hazard is then used as the justification for policies that create yet more unemployment. Meanwhile, at the core of the capitalist system inequality and instability inhere as before: the ownership of the means of production is highly concentrated and planning for the public good eschewed. There is political democracy – and its existence and maintenance matters profoundly – but there is not the economic democracy that is also requisite of true social democracy.

I

Advice from an earlier time, perhaps particularly to the extent it was then ignored or only half-heartedly heeded, can have contemporary relevance. In 1936, nine members of the Fellowship for a Christian Social Order (FCSO) sought to marshal the "revolutionary resources" of Christian faith to address the "crisis in the Western world." The result, *Towards the Christian Revolution* contains two chapters on the economy by Eugene Forsey – "The Economic Problem" and "A New Economic Order – and one on politics by J. King Gordon titled "The Political Task." (Should any reader be in doubt, this Eugene Forsey is an earlier pre-Senatorial incarnation of the Eugene Forsey, now known for his acerbic letters to newspapers on constitutional matters; each ages in his own way). There are some specific features of these essays that merit passing comment (in a moment), but mostly they should be judged as part of a larger whole of indigenous left-wing writings in Canada in the thirties associated with the League for Social Reconstruction (LSR) – and particularly its massive and magnificent *Social Planning for Canada* – and with the CCF and the *Canadian Forum*. To a considerable degree the same people were involved, the interlocks which the left loves to expose in the corporate world not being confined thereto.

Forsey and King Gordon contributed to the LSR volume as well, and no less than four of the other contributors to the FCSO book (Eric Havelock, J.W.A. Nicholson, R.B.Y. Scott and Gregory Vlastos) were also members of the LSR. We can agree with Michiel Horn (the historian of the LSR) when he writes with respect to *Towards the Christian Revolution*: "Not surprisingly most of the economic analysis in the book was straight out of *Social Planning for Canada*."[1] Leonard Marsh, who was later to author the federal government's comprehensive and enlightened 1943 *Report on Social Security for Canada* – from whence came shortly family allowances – was both a member of the FCSO and on the editorial team of the LSR book. King Gordon ran three times as a CCF candidate for the House of Commons – even coming very close to being elected on one occasion – and Forsey twice. Forsey was a frequent contributor to the *Forum* and Havelock was on its editorial board. This should not surprise for they had, as we all know, J.S. Woodsworth himself to set an example. Methodist minister, honorary president of the LSR, first leader of the CCF (and a faithful reader of the *Forum*, it seems safe to presume).

The world was seen by these social democratic intellectuals as one where the competitive capitalism of small firms had been replaced by the monopoly capitalism of giant corporations. Once upon a time, capitalists had sought profits by expansion and by out-competing their rivals; this created jobs and, by keeping prices flexible, made the whole system more adjustable to crises. Now capitalists maximized profits by restricting output and by collusion, thereby destroying jobs at the same time as price rigidities lessened the adaptability of the system. Internationally, imperialists rivalries worsened and another world war threatened. The capitalist firms were productive and, in their own terms, efficient, but this was not because of private ownership. Indeed, within the corporations, which were not the dominant form of economic enterprise, control and management had been separated from ownership. Private ownership served only to reward a few, more for ownership than for effort, thereby worsening the distribution of wealth and income and exacerbating inequalities. The contradictions of capitalism – the phrase was used unflinchingly – were pervasive and worsening: capitalism had entered its final stages and was ripe for replacement.

The solution was to nationalize the means of production – at least much of it that was under private monopoly control – and create a government planning agency above it all that would replace capitalist "planning," which was really nothing more than the use of state power and public funds to shore up the capitalists, with socialist planning. Wherever possible, co-operatives should be encouraged as an alternative both to private and public ownership; this option had considerable appeal for farmers and hence for many CCFers, but was disdainfully dismissed by others in the movement, including Forsey in the FCSO book. The managers of the capitalist system were now the staffs of private corporations with no democratic accountability to the public; in the socialist society of the future, the central role would be exercised by planners in the public sector, accountable to parliament and hence to the people. Collective action would thereby be not an infringement upon freedom but the means of its attainment. The state would be used to create full employment and to put in place a greatly expanded system of social security. It would work for world peace and, though abhorring fascism, be chary of involvement in Europe's wars. The process by which this would take place would be by the democratic election of a party committed to creating the new co-operative commonwealth; given the nature of the old parties, with their ties to the capitalist class, this task required a new socialist party with broad support, particularly of farmers and workers.[2]

Such a summary does a great deal of injustice to the impressive detail with which an alternative vision was presented. It is often said by unfriendly critics that left-wing intellectuals are strong on criticisms of capitalism but short on concrete solutions. Perhaps such a charge sometimes has merit, but not in this case. While any group that included such skilful provocateurs as Frank Underhill and Eugene Forsey was bound to hit the capitalists where it hurt, to read *Social Planning for Canada* is to be impressed by its exhaustive description of a socialist plan for Canada; indeed, its thoroughness strikes one as excessive given the unlikelihood of immediate implementation.

It may also be alleged that those who engage in such writings as are here being considered are necessarily under the influence of alien modes of thinking and insensitive to the specific conditions of their own country. Now, something must be said (though, again, in a moment) about Marxism and Keynesianism as externally-generated systems of thought and how they affected these Canadian dissenters. But the point to be made here is the understanding they displayed, not only of the details of the Canadian economy, but of its special character as a staples economy. Harold Innis – the great Canadian economic historian – and others (including Irene Biss, later Irene Spry, who helped write the economic chapters in *Social Planning for Canada*) were busy fleshing out an indigenous school of Canadian political economy, with particular emphasis on the rigidities that flowed from the staples bias. Though Innis was himself highly critical of the LSR – insisting that academics should not be political activists – it learned to its advantage from his scholarly work. By any sensible criteria, the economic and political writings of the LSR and FCSO are a legitimate and creative part of Canadian political economy.[3]

A further and frequent charge is that clarion calls for a new economic order are the stock-in-trade of those who know no economics; in our time, the Catholic Bishops have been so pilloried. Though an economist myself, I have never seen much merit in this point of view. To be blunt about it: if economists know so much, then how come the economy is in such mess? There is also the tendency for the accusation mostly to be hurled about by politicians, businessmen and financial columnists who are themselves rarely professional economists. In any event, it would have no relevance to our thirties' band of sophisticated socialist intellectuals, many of whom had received graduate training in economics and political science, typically at the finest universities (English, of course!) and under the tutelage of the most renowned scholars, like Laski and Keynes.

II

How should these Canadian writers be judged vis-a-vis the broader state of economics? Prior to the Great Depression, the ruling paradigm was neo-classical economics; it reflected a faith in the market and in limited government familiar to us now in its contemporary guise as monetarism. But the bottom line on economics is that, in the crunch, it must meet the payroll, and the economic crisis of the thirties mercilessly exposed the limitations of the conventional wisdom. As the centre collapsed, there were new possibilities for dissent and creativity from the margins, including the left.

Even Marxism, which had never had much purchase amongst intellectuals in the English-speaking countries in spite of its origins in the British Museum, suddenly became fashionable as a mode of analysis the better to critique capitalist society. Note has already been made of the use of Marxist phrases and categories by the LSR; Norman Penner, who is an expert on these matters, sees in *Social Planning for Canada* "a Marxian interpretation … on problems of Canadian history and economy."[4] For whatever reason, what is probably the strongest endorsement of Marxism to be found in this literature is in Forsey's second chapter of the FCSO book, written in the purplest of prose: "This generation seeketh after a sign, and there shall be no sign given it but the sign of the prophet Marx" (139); the author he most frequently cites is the British Marxist scholar John Strachey. The horrors of the Great Depression radicalized people, particularly the sensitive and humane Christian. Actually existing capitalism was without appeal, while actually existing socialism was not yet discredited by the grotesque horrors of Stalinism.

Within the neo-classical paradigm itself, there were to be two great innovations in the thirties: Keynesianism (which everyone knows about) and also the theory of imperfect competition. Both reflected forces and sentiments that were in the air demanding to be breathed.

Take first the second matter, of markets and the degree of competition. Models of perfect competition, on which neo-classical economics centrally relied, had been untenable virtually since their elaboration – as the so-called Marshallian microeconomics – during the very years of the burgeoning merger movement of the late nineteenth century. Marxists always understood this; so too did American institutional economists – the most famous of whom was Thorstein Veblen – who were a powerful force within their profession in their own country and whose influence spilled over into Canada. The thirties made it possible to argue, as we have seen, that the monopolization of capitalism was at the root of the problem of too few goods at too high prices creating too much unemployment, and that the solution lay not in breaking up the monopolies but nationalizing them and operating them within a national plan. Intellectuals and politicians spawned a spate of studies, from Berle and Means' great classic on the large corporation in the United States to the exposé of corporate malpractice by Canada's Royal Commission on Price Spreads; both were generously cited by the LSR and FCSO.

There was a real cutting edge politically to this kind of writing because it confronted the distribution of power and proposed to do something about it. It was, however, to be incorporated into the neo-classical paradigm – as theories of so-called monopolistic competition and oligopoly – in ways that complicated economic analysis without radically altering economic policy; professional economists put it in a separate compartment of their brains, and have ever since kept it there, so as not to contaminate their long-standing commitment to unfettered markets. And, above all, it was finessed by Keynesianism.

III

Keynesianism was a big event – arguably the biggest in the discipline of economics in this century – that ramified widely and came to mean many things; we must digress to consider them. Within the corpus of economic theory, Keynes was able to show that rigidities in the economy, like the inflexibility of prices downward, made it possible to have an economy in equilibrium with unemployment, even massive unemployment – that being a possibility denied by neo-classical theory but demonstrably achievable in the real world. A major cause of the depression was the inadequacy of aggregate demand, evident in an excess of savings over investment. The neo-classical remedy for unemployment was a wage cut to increase the demand for labour, but the new Keynesian economics showed that this would be self-defeating since it would further reduce aggregate demand. The Keynesian prescription was rather to increase purchasing power by priming the pump: increase government spending, cut taxes, increase the government deficit, and pay for it by expanding the supply of money and credit.

The Keynesian revolution, as it has been called, was revolutionary from the perspective of the vested interests. It gave a powerful legitimacy to bigger government, to spend and to stabilize and in general to intervene. It provided a fresh rationale for the welfare state – that it would increase purchasing power and, by putting a floor on how far down the economy could go, act as a built-in

stabilizer – and that was good. But it also provided a fresh rationale for military spending – it was, as we know, the massive spending by governments in World War II that finally ended the Great
Depression – and that turned Keynesianism into military Keynesianism, and taught us something that was very, very bad and
counter-revolutionary.

The warfare state and the welfare state combined to permit an
unprecedented – and from the perspective of the thirties, wholly
unanticipated – postwar boom. Capitalism found a new lease on
life and the material circumstances no longer cried out in the same
way as in the thirties for radical solutions, or even, it seemed at
times, for all that much by way of reform.

In the spectrum of British politics, Keynes himself was Liberal
not Labour; not surprisingly, the implications of his writings for
social democracy were to prove problematic. Keynesianism (in the
broad sense we are using here) was embraced by social democracy,
and was its doing in terms of legitimizing it within mainstream
politics. But it was its undoing in terms of its radical component;
the Keynesian revolution, as John Kenneth Galbraith has put it,
"brought Marxism in the advanced countries to a total halt."[5] Full
employment became the legitimate goal of government, and the
state did become a welfare state and a more interventionist state.
From the perspective of the struggles of the thirties these were vic-
tories indeed for social democrats. But they were bought at high
costs. For the good life could now be achieved – or so it came to be
believed – without altering the private ownership of the means of
production and without a social planning agency that controlled
investment. Keynes had written in 1931: "the problem of want and
poverty and the economic struggle between classes and nations is
nothing but a frightful muddle, a transitory and unnecessary muddle;" social democrats allowed themselves to be seduced by this
sanguine diagnosis and its implicit technocratic prescription. The
central demands of democratic socialists in the thirties, and particularly of its more left-wing practitioners, were swept aside and nothing of much substance was put in their place.

When the long capitalist boom began to play itself out in the late
sixties and early seventies, the capitalist state responded by fighting
inflation – the new contradiction of capitalism – with unemployment, by dismantling the welfare state, and by escalating arms
spending. All of these ran contrary to the sentiments of serious

socialists, yet social democracy proved unable to mount a substantial response politically or even intellectually. Keynesianism as a progressive force has now been stood completely on its head; appropriated by the American far right, it has been recast as nothing more than military Keynesianism and (mercifully) renamed supply-side economics or Reaganomics. Having subscribed so fully to Keynesianism, social democracy has lost any sense of direction and stumbles about – and we are worse off for that.

And there was a further dark and costly dimension to the social democratic embrace of Keynesianism. Even at its most radical, social democracy aims to reform capitalism, not overthrow it. Keynesianism promised and, within limits, delivered on those reforms. In the Cold War that came to dominate everything after World War II, Keynesian economics became an instrument in the propaganda war with Communism.[6] Social democrats – who admittedly had good reason not to like communists – were now under the added thrall of Keynesianism; all too easily and too often they went too far and became avid cold warriors. On the issue that mattered, and matters most, that of war and peace, they risked coming down on the wrong side.

IV

We must now pick up the thread of the story of the social democratic intellectuals in the Canada of the thirties and relate it to these broad strands. *Towards the Christian Revolution* was published in the same year as Keynes' magnum opus, *The General Theory of Employment, Interest and Money*. Keynes' ideas were already circulating and were certainly known to the young British-trained intellectuals of the LSR and FCSO, and subsequent commentators invariably included Keynesianism among the numerous ingredients that went into the thinking of these people. Still, to read them now is to be struck by how pre-Keynesian they were – and hence, in one sense, how radical they could be. *Social Planning for Canada* has only two fleeting references to Keynes' writing, and neither is about the policies he advocated. There is no separate section on public works (in the sense of government spending thereon) – it is simply seen as part of the national plan – while taxation is treated as a transitional problem on the road to socialism when the government will be able directly to appropriate surplus. Forsey in the FCSO book notes that depressions have "a great deal to do with discrepancies between 'savings' and 'investment'," observes that "Precisely what capitalism should do about it is a matter of acute controversy among capitalist economists" – so much for Keynes! – and proceeds with his real concern which is to demonstrate that widespread nationalization is superior to the co-operative system.

The rest of the world mostly missed the Keynesian boat too, and Keynesian policies are about as scarce as hens' teeth in the thirties. In the dying days of World War II, there comes in Canada the commitment to full employment and some serious building of the welfare state, for which the left had so vigorously fought. Historians seem generally to give the CCF and the LSR and other forces for good, like the FCSO, much of the credit for this. We can all agree it is no small achievement and, in a world where political action has no certain payoff, is sufficient to justify the exercise. That these measures are brought in by the old line parties the better to destroy the CCF – and substantially succeed in doing just that – is an irony too well documented in numerous historical studies to need adumbration; though frustrating for the activists, from the viewpoint of the beneficiaries – which is what really matters – the achievement is real.

V

The CCF/LSR/FCSO grouping also missed another boat of particular salience to Canadians, namely, the American connection in general and foreign ownership in particular; to be fair, however, no one else in Canada really caught on to this issue until the fifties. The large corporation had been well and truly discovered in the thirties – indeed, its existence (as we have seen) was central to the critique of monopoly capitalism – but the fact it was multinational either eluded people or was thought not to matter. Foreign ownership is rarely referred to in the writings here under review and when it is, it is typical to insist that all capitalists are the same whether foreign or domestic; being equally bad, no case exists for replacing foreign with domestic capital, the proper solution being to nationalize the lot. In the postwar period, when the quantum leap in American ownership finally compelled recognition, the CCF was there but so, in their different ways, were the Diefenbaker Conservatives and the Walter Gordon Liberals; on this issue, the left was not ahead of the times.

The lack of foresight – that sin of omission that is by its nature detectable only in hindsight – extended to the Canadian-American relationship as a whole. The chapter on Foreign Policy in *Social Planning for Canada* includes the revealing sentence: "we may here neglect purely North American questions" (512). Mackenzie King and Franklin Roosevelt signed a reciprocal trade agreement that reduced tariffs in November 1935; historians have come to see it as an important step down that subsequent much travelled road towards Canadian-American integration.[7] The left in due course came to deplore that destination–and is today unanimous in its opposition to a Canada-US free trade agreement – but at that time I would infer support. In *Social Planning for Canada* we read: "If the United States ... were ready to offer us preferential entry to her market in return for special terms for her goods here, it might pay us to accept" – though, as always, it is hastily added that this would be in the context of a socialist Canada with national planning.

In some part this is because the LSR is explicitly anti-tariff, taking a clear position on the most perennially controversial issue in Canadian politics. It echoes the position of farmers and the West within the CCF but it does so, I would guess, less for that reason (though it would have affected Underhill) than because it here sees no cause to question a fundamental tenet – perhaps we should say the fundamental tenet – of neo-classical economics. Keynesian theory gave new credibility to the tariff as a way to create jobs (albeit under restrictive circumstances), and Keynes himself worried in the thirties that there was too much economic interdependence. But this was never central to Keynesian theory, and with Keynes himself soon forgetting such concerns the Canadian left had no reason not to stay with the older verities.

The generally complacent attitude adopted towards the United States may be taken as also reflecting the appeal of the New Deal – which was surely understandable when Roosevelt's progressive proclivities and energy were contrasted with Bennett's repressiveness and King's stodgy caution. As well, as the prospect of a European war loomed, it was hoped that the United States would remain neutral, and with it, Canada. But there were suspicions – and justifiably so – about American foreign policy. The LSR feared that the US policy of the open door in China risked war with Japan in the Pacific and was blunt in its advice: "The Canadian people as a whole have no more interest in this American imperialism than they have in British imperialism, and we must try to keep from getting entangled in its operation" (523).

There was, nevertheless, a certain innocence about imperialism, and about power generally, on the part of these Canadian socialists that needs to be noted. It was argued explicitly – not merely assumed implicitly as some social democrats have always been wont to do – that the capitalist class at home and abroad would permit the creation of a socialist society by a democratically-elected government. We now know, above all from the fate of Allende in Chile, that the capitalists within and without and the capitalist state from without – and American capital and its state in particular – preclude this happy option.

V I

Fifty years on, the FCSO and what it was related to – the LSR, the CCF, the *Canadian Forum* – should be judged as having served us well. In times as terrible as those of the thirties, when people cry out for help, the willingness to speak out is as important as what is concretely advocated; but we have seen that what was proposed in this case was imaginative and well-conceived. The LSR – and the FCSO – had their day and their members tended to drift into other things. Some, like Underhill and Forsey, ended up to the right even of the moderate NDP. This can, and should be, deplored, but it does not negate their achievements. The example they set for us stands; it is to give radical content to social democracy, now including its actually existing varieties.

NOTES

1 Michiel Horn, *The League for Social Reconstruction: Intellectual Origins of the Democratic Left in Canada, 1930–1942* (Toronto: University of Toronto Press, 1980), 63. The other contributors to *Toward the Christian Revolution* were John Line, R. Edis Fairbairn and "Propheticus" (Martyn Estall).
2 For the detailed blueprint, see League for Social Reconstruction, *Social Planning for Canada* (Toronto: University of Toronto Press, 1975; first published 1935). Summaries and commentaries are to be found in Horn, *The League for Social Reconstruction*; Gregory Baum, *Catholics and Canadian Socialism: Political Thought in the Thirties and Forties* (Toronto: University of

Toronto Press, 1980); David Lewis, *The Good Fight: Political Memoirs, 1909–1958* (Toronto: Macmillan of Canada, 1981); R. Douglas Francis, *Frank H. Underhill: Intellectual Provocateur* (Toronto: University of Toronto Press, 1986); Allen Mills, "The Canadian Forum and Socialism, 1920–1934," *Journal of Canadian* Studies (Winter 1978–79), 11–27; Norman Penner, *The Canadian Left: A Critical Analysis* (Scarborough: Prentice-Hall, 1977); the writings of Roger Hutchinson; and numerous entries in *The Canadian Encyclopedia* (Edmonton, 1985).

3 They are nevertheless oddly neglected in *The New Practical Guide to Canadian Political Economy*, edited by Daniel Drache and Wallace Clement (Toronto: Lorimer, 1985).

4 *Penner, The Canadian* Left, 245.

5 Galbraith, "How Keynes Came to America," in his *A Contemporary Guide to Economics, Peace and Laughter* (London: Houghton-Mifflin, 1971), 44.

6 I owe this point to a stimulating article by Josef Steindl; see his "J.M. Keynes: Society and the Economist," in Fausto Vicarelli, ed., *Keynes' Relevance Today* (London: Macmillan, 1985), 104.

7 For a fresh and engaging discussion of this, see Marc T. Boucher, "The Politics of Economic Dependence: Canadian-American Relations in the mid-1930s," *International Journal* (Winter 1985–86).

15

The Intellectual and the Public: A Neo-Innisian Perspective on the Contemporary English Canadian Condition (1994)

When I told my colleague Abraham Rotstein that I was speaking at the Concordia Conference on Innis on the theme of the role of the intellectual in contemporary Canada, he said, "It'll be brief, I take it." To ask an intellectual (I turn in a moment to what that word could possibly mean in English Canada) to discuss the role of the intellectual is to invite autobiography, if not compel it to avoid the charge of hypocrisy; one should, as it were, preach what one practices.

I

I am already older than Innis was when he died – a sobering thought given his extraordinary achievements – which has the virtue that I was born long enough ago to have taken a course from him in the academic year 1951–52, the last year he was alive. We celebrate his birth but I remember his death, on November 8,

---

An earlier version of this paper presented at the conference on "Harold Innis and Intellectual Practice for the New Century: Interdisciplinary and Critical Studies," Concordia University, Montreal 1994. I draw on occasion from my Innis Memorial Column in *This Magazine* (November 1994). Both the title and the sub-title of this paper were chosen by me before I wrote it; they now strike me as pretentious. This paper is more in the nature of personal reflections than they imply.

1952. I had graduated from college, was working in an accounting office, and already having doubts about my choice of career. I was shocked to see his obituary in the paper; we had known he was ill when he taught us but, being young, we had not grasped how ill.

I recalled the intellectual excitement of his course (those of us who teach at universities should bear that in mind), how he moved back and forth between ancient history and trenchant critiques of our times. Andrew Wernick, as well as recognizing Innis's "wild side" (it is a marvellous phrase), has written of how Innis "hid out in History."[1] As I read about what Innis had done with his life, I resolved to make something out of mine. I quit what I was doing to go back to university and do graduate work. I've been there ever since.

It is unlikely that Innis would want any credit for this, since in his time he strenuously opposed the leftish political activism that came to preoccupy me. So be it: Innis observed more than once that everything could be forgiven the founder of a school except his followers. But what I do know from his course, and from his writings that we read at that time, was that he did not flinch from using the phrase "American imperialism" and that he denounced the Korean War as an exercise therein.[2] This took courage in the context of the embryonic McCarthyism of the Cold War.

It also took an insight and prescience that was rare; nothing radicalized me – and, I would guess, many other of today's aging left intellectuals – like the Vietnam War, but Innis had seen the light (the darkness actually) a war earlier when few others had, and certainly no one of his eminence (a renowned scholar, the Chair of Political Economy, and Dean of the Graduate School). That is why I was frankly astonished and appalled later to learn how Innis had denounced the left intellectuals of the 1930s who were involved in the League for Social Reconstruction (LSR) and the CCF (the precursor to today's NDP). He labelled them "hot gospellers" and "pedlars of snake oil" and insisted more research had to be done before economists, or anyone else, could venture solutions for a Canada mired in the Great Depression. The huge public debt and the extraordinary openness of the Canadian economy tied the hands of government and ruled out for Innis the Keynesian ideas that were in the air.

This is only too familiar again in the 1990s. In fact, Innis's views merely strengthened the hands of those in power who then, as now, opposed anything potentially progressive, while his active discouragement of political activism by scholars is thought by both John Porter in the 1960s and William Christian in the 1980s to have had long-run adverse effects on the public involvement of the English-Canadian intellectual.[3] It is alright to sit on Royal Commissions as Innis did, thereby serving the established interest, but it is wrong to be otherwise involved in politics. The folly of such a stance is regularly made manifest: in the mid-1980s orthodox economists followed this prescription in droves by working for the Macdonald Commission and providing a legitimacy for free trade that had eluded both the business community and the Mulroney government.[4] We all now live (if that is the right word) with the consequences. John Kenneth Galbraith observes of the 1930s that: "No-one could look at capitalism in those years and think it a success. There was, accordingly, a choice between repair and revolt."[5] Innis knew capitalism was not a success, but by opposing both Keynesian and the left-wing social democracy of that time (ironically, they came later to coalesce) he rejected both; this was not helpful.

I can only say that I prefer the older, surely wiser, Innis who had studied the world's imperialisms, who did not like the American variant on offer where the media manipulated public opinion and the state had the Bomb, and said as much. In the 1930s he had attacked (counter-attacked is as accurate) his University of Toronto colleague Frank Underhill for his radicalism (though he submitted his resignation to the University to force it to back down on firing Underhill), but at the end, Underhill became the official curator of the Liberal Party and the defender of pro-American Cold War Liberalism and it was Innis who was the radical. Innis defied that powerful tendency as we age to give up the fight and make peace with the status quo.

A political activist he was not. But neither was he your run-of-the-mill academic, trapped on the treadmill in the ivory tower. Daniel Drache calls Innis an "intellectual activist": Innis actually believed that ideas mattered and it was the purpose of universities to nurture them. In 1946 he wrote, "With imperfect competition between concepts the university is essentially an ivory tower in which courage can be mustered to attack any concept which threatens to become a monopoly." Of course, most academics are happy prisoners of our paradigms and we do not even see the need to try to escape. Were we to try, and some of us have, we would find powerful forces arrayed against us, within the university as well as without.

Following Innis, ideas have roots, material and political. They come out of particular places and particular times and are disseminated by particular media and their particular monopolies. There are biases galore and it is the special duty of the scholar, who has been granted the time to do so, to search for those so as to try to transcend them. In the nature of things, ideas, no matter how lofty and abstract, tend mostly to represent the prescient concerns of the imperial centres and thus to be inappropriate to the needs of peripheral areas like Canada. Hence, Canadian intellectuals must develop their own ideas, hard though that is and not merely parrot those of others; this was, first and foremost, Innis's lifelong intellectual project. University professors in Canada must understand that they live at the margin of empire and of power, and must make of that necessity a virtue.

Innis, we know, practised what he preached. He was, throughout his adult life, that relatively rare phenomenon of a self-conscious intellectual; he always heeded the question that had been put to him as an undergraduate, "Why do we attend to the things to which we attend?" Those of us who are, as Innis was, members of social science disciplines with a notorious tendency to degenerate into social engineering – as Innis liked to put it, into pushing people around – need to pause each day and put that question. I return shortly to this matter with respect to my own discipline of economics where the costs of rote behaviour and unquestioning allegiance to dominant paradigms have proven to extraordinarily high.

It is likely, however, that Innis overestimated the potential of the university as a place from which to change the world for the public good. For all his understanding of the dark side of history, Innis exaggerated the role of ideas and of reason. Increasingly alienated from the world evolving around him, he seemed disinterested in the human agency that might make things better. Given the bias of my life, I am not a disinterested witness on these matters. But you have to believe Northrop Frye, that most distinguished and politically inactive Canadian scholar, when he wrote of Innis, "Perhaps it is not possible to hold a vision of [his] scope and range steadily in one's mind without a more passionate commitment to society as well as to scholarship."[6]

It is impossible, as an intellectual on the left, not to be ambivalent about the university. Alternative employment opportunities do not exactly abound, though some of English Canada's best left intellectuals work for the labour movement or for social policy groups. Having occasionally dabbled elsewhere, I would echo Lana Guinier, the law professor who U.S. President Clinton first nominated to head the Civil Rights Division of the Justice Department and then let hang out to dry. She says the epiphany occurred when she returned to her office at Penn Law School and blurted out to a colleague who welcomed her back, "It's so good to be back in the real world," a world where, she writes, "Ideas matter."[7]

With all their limitations universities are, relative to the corporate and bureaucratic worlds, islands of freedom in a sea of unfreedom. Edward Said states in the Preface to his brilliant book *Culture and Imperialism*, "In its writing I have availed myself of the utopian space still provided by the university."[8] Noam Chomsky, perhaps the greatest intellectual of the English-speaking world, has virtually no political podium except that offered by the university. All the more reason then why we must limit the influence on the university of those other worlds, and heed Innis's warning to the graduating students of McMaster University in 1945: "The descent of the university into the marketplace reflects the lie in the soul of modern society." That kind of sentence should also take care of the charge that Innis's writings are obscure and inaccessible; the problem is more that too many at the university, then and now, do not like his message.

Since Innis's time, there has been the further and relentless commodification of everything including knowledge – as in that dreadful term "intellectual property," now carved in stone under the NAFTA, which turns out to include the rights of tobacco companies not to sell death in plain packages. We must be wary too when a university like my own issues, as it did earlier this year, a document called *Planning for 2000* that is full of ringing phrases like "translation of research strength into problem-solving capacity" and "opportunities to bring knowledge and technology to bear on issues of concern within society."[9] There is nary a mention, however, that we take ideas seriously not by reifying the reigning ones and abetting their propagation by powerful corporate and state interests but by openly and publicly challenging them. We need to talk less about technology transfer and more about civil disobedience. It should be a matter of some concern that the University of Toronto document is silent on the matter of providing a haven for intellectuals as critics of society. Universities would not be tolerated if that was all they did, but our much-touted academic freedom has no social purpose, no real rationale, unless they do that.

II

We are in danger of taking ourselves too seriously; there is slight risk anyone else will. In common parlance, something is labelled "academic" in order to dismiss it as irrelevant; friends and family members even do so in my presence, apparently intending no offence. Admittedly, I teach at a university which is known, according to *The Canadian Encyclopedia*, for "the discovery of insulin and the development of Pablum." (In that same *Encyclopedia*, incidentally, there are two entries on "Intellectual History," one on "French Canada" and one on "English Canada"; is it not ironic that so many intellectuals, particularly in English Canada, imagine they transcend place? These entries are followed by one on "Intelligence and Espionage" which states forthrightly, "Intelligence is information gathered to enhance the security of the state.")

I have already invoked the name of Noam Chomsky. I showed a class the video *Manufacturing Consent*, where we see Chomsky marching with Martin Luther King, who was later assassinated, and there is a reference to the assassination of Robert Kennedy. In the discussion afterwards a student asks, "Why is Chomsky still alive?" and answers her own question: being a professor he was not taken *that* seriously. She does not say this disparagingly, her point being rather that intellectuals are not a threat to the contemporary order. I am compelled to agree.

Consider that figment of the media, Kim Campbell, where she was constantly referred to as an "intellectual." That was its way of saying that she was clever, smart, quick, argumentative, a point scorer, not that she was learned nor contemplative nor wise. She was labelled an "arrogant intellectual who felt that ordinary voters were incapable of informed debate." "Arrogant" and "intellectual" apparently automatically go together; as the wise Dalton Camp recently wrote about Jacques Parizeau, "He is clearly intelligent which, for editorial purposes, marks him as arrogant." We were also told that Campbell was cold, lacking in feeling, convinced that logic was everything. Campbell was presumably in deep trouble anyway, but being said to be like us did not help. The least that must be said is that intellectuals have a public relations problem on their hands.

Though it is arguable that politics is the first refuge of scoundrels, we are now expected to welcome the Campbells of the world into our academic ranks and we mostly oblige; though only Prime Minister for a day in a peripheral area she gets to teach at Harvard. During the Irangate affair, it was said of U.S. Secretary of State George Shultz, who had begun his life as an academic at MIT and Chicago, that "he has sounded very weary of late and many people expect he will return to academic life before the next two years are up." He did not but the point is made: when you cannot take the pace in the fast lane, try parking at a university. (I do not mean literally; thirty years ago there was a piece in the *New Yorker* on the University of Texas that said the main topic of discussion among faculty was parking.) We should, I suppose, be complimented that defeated politicians and retired civil servants see us as their fallback position. If it nevertheless leaves a bad taste in my mouth, it is because it negates that notion of intellectual activism, that commitment to an intellectual project, which Innis so much exemplified.

I risk making light of a larger issue which is the role of the intellectual in politics. Such is the magic of the Rhodes Scholarship that the American media sometimes describe Bill Clinton as being an intellectual and speculate that he is, as a result, too thoughtful for politics, too ready to see all sides of an issue – in short, indecisive. There is, however, a counter case, and that is that intellectuals in politics, whether elected or in the public service, are prone to insist that others take their ideas as seriously as they do. The risk is then the more serious one of fanaticism. Intellectuals played a large role in writing the foreign policy that led to the American atrocity of the War in Vietnam; one of my own MIT professors, Walt Rostow, who thought that countries had to march through his stages to attain affluence and maturity, danced on the White House lawn when President Johnson took his advice and bombed North Vietnam, the better to get it back on his growth path.

In Canada, we have, of course, the case of Mr. Trudeau. His intellectual reputation rested on his fanatical critique of Quebec nationalism which he blamed on the willful follies of other intellectuals; once elected, he relentlessly imposed his views on the country. The apparent result is that the issue of Quebec nationalism cannot be resolved but refuses to go away; this is, surely, the true triumph of an idea. Intellectuals in English Canada seemed only too ready both to buy into his views on nationalism and into his anti-intellectualism. Northrop Frye, no less, wrote that "Separatism in Quebec is an intellectuals' movement, a *trahison de clercs* ... As an intellectual's movement ... it may settle for a purely symbolic separation."[10] The power of intellectuals is exaggerated the better to clobber them; this seems like an odd task for the intellectual and is unlikely to persuade the public that *in toto* we play any useful role.

What of professors who become active not in politics *per se* but in advising governments? This too Innis deplored, though W.A. Mackintosh (the co-founder with Innis of the staple approach) did so to great effect, including writing the White Paper on Employment and Income of 1945 that came as close as his Minister, C.D. Howe, would permit to committing Canada to full employment. (Mackintosh wrote "full employment" in the first draft; Howe changed it to "a high and stable level"). There is another, and neglected possibility, which is that contact with power, and its corruptions, radicalizes the intellectual. My only sustained contact with the highest levels of the Ottawa government, when I worked for Walter Gordon in the 1960s, helped me to move left. It is said of the great John Maynard Keynes that "his recurrent immersions in the world of power disgusted him as much as they fascinated and fulfilled him ... It was the world of power than turned Keynes into a revolutionary, not the world of truth ... Practical experience was the grit without which there would have been no pearl."[11] I conclude that sometimes working for government is a risk that intellectuals should take. After all, the social sciences at least are inherently impure and much misused by those with power and there is virtue in observing that on the ground.

III

Innis wrote in 1941 that "the voice of the economist is heard throughout the land." It has since become a chorus, mostly stuck on a single note. As was Innis, I too am an economist; something needs to be said, in our discussion of the intellectual and the public, about that profession. Think of it as a case study; I urge those in other disciplines to do the same for theirs.

Innis was not simply an economist, he was a political economist, and his broad-gauged approach has fallen into disfavour in recent decades with the relentless division of labour with the academy, which has tended to hive off even holistic approaches (like Innis's communications work) into new disciplines. His work has been neglected and ignored within the economics discipline. By default, and because of his political economy bias, Innis's work in Canadian economic history has been incorporated, ironically, into the leftish New Canadian Political Economy that has flowered since the late 1960s. It has found its home in political science departments in particular, and also sociology, geography, history, and Canadian studies, but very rarely in economics. For my part, I now teach more in political science and Canadian studies than I do in economics, which is still ostensibly my main department.

The refusal of economics to tolerate political economy has not destroyed it, but it has meant that political economy is taught elsewhere in the university. The questions asked are too important to be ignored; where there is a demand there will be a supply. Still, economics has become the poorer and the economist increasingly narrow-minded and dangerous on policy, the latter being inherently matters of breadth.

Economics has become, in Innis's terms, a monopoly of knowledge. Economists preach competition but they do not practice it within the profession; they advocate choice, but not for students of economics. Economics is not a pluralist discipline, like political science or sociology or history, that admits of the possibility of different approaches. It is hopelessly present-minded, regarding all past theory as preparation for the present. Its truths are held to be universal, without respect to time or place. Economics floats free of reality. The point has been made by Galbraith and others that there is a negative correlation between the number of Nobel Prizes in Economics won by the citizens of a country and that country's rate of economic growth; Britain, the basket case of the developed world, has a number to its credit, Japan none. Here at home, since World War II there has been "an explosion in the output of Canadian economists but an implosion of Canadian economics;"[12] Innis's relentless struggle for the latter, which is ultimately a struggle for relevance, has been to no avail.

We can say of the orthodox economist what James Reston of the *New York Times* once said of Robert McNamara, the former US

Secretary of Defence: "He is tidy, he is confident, he has the sincerity of an Old Testament prophet, but something is missing: some element of personal doubt, some respect for human weakness, some knowledge of history."[13] The modern economist is congenitally unable to understand Innis's sensitivity to the bias that inheres in scholarship and is thereby a threat to himself as a scholar (most economists are men which is part of the problem) and to others as citizens. During the NAFTA debate in the United States, a reporter who phoned up the economics department of the University of Chicago and asked to speak to an economist on each side of the issue was told that there was no one in the department who opposed NAFTA. This may not surprise – we are talking, after all, about the home of the Chicago School of Economics – but it should appal. During the great free trade debate here in Canada in 1988, the tendency, particularly by the CBC, to represent both pro and con positions, led proponents like John Crispo to charge bias; their point was that error did not deserve the same air time as truth.

There is, apparently, free trade in everything but ideas; the much vaunted "market place of ideas" should be investigated by the anti-trust authorities. When there is unanimity on large questions we are dealing not with ideas but with ideology, not with creative competition but repressive monopoly. We need to recall what Innis once wrote to an American scholar on the limitations of the social sciences, that "We should keep raising our limitations." We also need to ask whose interest is being served, whose pockets are being lined, whose ox is not being gored; we need a cost-benefit study of economics; we need an economics of economics with particular reference to imperfections in market demand. These are, following Innis, proper, indeed essential, matters for economists to study. Those of us at the university might also study the effect on public understanding of economic issues of the media regularly quoting economists from the private sector, notably those who work for banks, as if they were disinterested economists, and regularly citing studies of the C.D. Howe Institute as if it was an independent non-partisan research body. Why do my orthodox colleagues no protest these travesties?

Disciplines discipline; unless checked, their discourse becomes one of dominance and exclusion. In fact, economics has become a weapon. At the public constitutional conference in February

1992 where interprovincial free trade was discussed, Carol Goar of the *Toronto Star* wrote of the women present, "They kept reminding the businessmen and economists who tried to dominate the debate that fairness matters as much as efficiency." Alice de Wolfe of the National Action Committee on the Status of Women said, "We feel a lot of distrust when we hear terms like dynamic, efficient markets. We need to develop a less threatening language of economic discourse."

The least we should know as intellectuals (it is our one permissible article of faith) is that words matter – they have consequences. We should derive some encouragement from the fact that this point has now crept into the economics literature itself, though so far to slight effect. A recent article by three Cornell Economics professors in the *Journal of Economic Perspectives* is titled "Does Studying Economics Inhibit Cooperation?" and answers "Yes."[14] It presents evidence from the literature that economists behave in more self-interested ways than others, and that the study of economics even for a single semester makes students more greedy and less caring.

A friend who majored in English literature because she loved to read says that, except for mystery stories, she no longer reads for pleasure. Literary criticism, she learned, takes no account of the reader's pleasure and now she derives none from reading. This is a damning story that reflects badly on professors – it is presumably the flip side of what Elias Canetti has in mind when he writes, "It amazes me how a person to whom literature means anything could take it up as an object of study" – but it is impossible not to wish that economics students, having studied greed, were no longer able to pursue it.

Part of the problem is that most economists are men and men behave less cooperatively than women, but economics still looks bad even after allowance is made for that. The Cornell authors conclude that "exposure to the self-interest model does in fact encourage self-interested behaviour." The bias is self-fulfilling; it is an intellectual disappearing act on a par with crawling up one's own dark unmentionable hole. They recommend that "With an eye toward both the social good and the well-being of their own students, economists may wish to stress a broader view of human motivation in their teaching." Neo-classical economics is a simple and powerful story but it is not a rich enough story of human behaviour to encompass the range of either history or contemporary experience.[15]

Nor, ironically, have those economists (and others) whose writings supported governments like those of Reagan and Thatcher that were obsessed by the economics of self-interest, necessarily got the reward to which they were, by the logic of things, entitled. Martin Anderson, an economist and former advisor to Republican Presidents, has written that, while in the Reagan White House, he never heard anyone refer to an article published in an academic economics journal. A reviewer of Margaret Thatcher's *The Downing Street Years*, writes, "It is some indication of the thoughtlessness of her politics that none of the intellectuals that wrote on her behalf and defended her policies both privately and publicly gets a mention in her book ... But that is not surprising. She had few ideas, and ideas as such clearly never interested her."[16]

The doyen of Canadian economists, Richard Lipsey of Simon Fraser University, deplores the lack of public involvement of economists (some might think the world is run according to orthodox economics and little else, and that if it is not it should be) and has implored his colleagues to get active. Consider, though, how he puts it: "Professional economists feel relatively at home giving evidence to parliamentary committees or advising politicians or civil servants in behind-the-scenes discussions designed to assess alternatives rationally. They feel much less comfortable – *and for very understandable reasons* – in the rough-and-tumble of public forum policy debates, where irrational arguments and emotional appeals are often more effective than rational analysis" (italics added).[17]

Perhaps we need a study of intellectuals and agoraphobia, which my dictionary defines as "a morbid fear of open spaces and public places." Innis, we know, longed for the oral tradition to correct the bias of the written. James Carey makes the persuasive point that in today's world that would mean more space and more time for civic, civil, discourse. If intellectuals would learn to write in a more accessible way, we might then find that we could speak that way as well. Moreover, we might be able to transcend the learned journal and the book to make use of the newer (hardly new) media. We need to escape the fusty image implied by Dalton Camp when he quoted a movie actress as having said that an intellectual was someone who read the morning paper.

Mind you, all of this is no necessary panacea. The one profession at the university in English Canada where the language of discourse is still English is history. This perhaps explains the frequency with which the media uses historians as commentators, notably on the constitution and Quebec/Canada. Their major role on the latter, however, has been to paint all compromise with Quebec as "appeasement" and pander to the worst of English Canadian sentiment. Though an economist, I suspect it is bad history; I certainly think it is poisonous politics. The bottom line is that there can be no substitute for decency and good sense.

It is economics that I have singled out because it is the profession I know best, but Innis's legacy for scholars generally is for us to have a perspective on our disciplines, to be aware of our limits and how much damage we can do, to understand the significance of time and place to ideas, to listen, to dialogue, to take ourselves seriously so that then perhaps others will.

NOTES

1 Andrew Wernick, "The Post-Innisian Significance of Innis," *Canadian Journal of Political and Social Theory* 10 (1986): 1–2.
2 Donald Creighton vouches for the latter point in *Harold Adams Innis: Portrait of a Scholar* (Toronto: University of Toronto Press, 1957).
3 "No one played a more important role in the depoliticizing of the higher learning in Canada than Harold Adams Innis ... It would probably be difficult to find another modern political system with such a paucity of participation from its scholars" (John Porter, *The Vertical Mosaic* (Toronto, 1965), 503). William Christian, who wrote the entry on Innis for *The Canadian Encyclopedia* (2nd ed. 1988) states, "To a considerable extent, the detachment of our contemporary Canadian academic community derives from Innis and his attitudes."
4 Richard Simeon, "Inside the Macdonald Commission," *Studies in Political Economy* (Spring 1987).
5 John Kenneth Galbraith, *A Journey Through Economic Time: A Firsthand Account* (1994), 84.
6 Northrop Frye, "Across the River and Out of the Trees" in W.J. Keith and B.-Z. Shek, eds., *The Arts in Canada: The Last Fifty Years* (1980).
7 *New York Times Magazine*, 27 February 1994.
8 Edward Said, *Culture and Imperialism* (1993), xxvi.
9 *Planning for 2000: A Provisional White Paper on University Objectives*, University of Toronto, 14 February 1994.
10 Northrop Frye, *Divisions on a Ground: Essays on Canadian Culture* (1982).

11 David Marquand, review of volume 2 of Robert Skidelsky's biography of Keynes in *Guardian Weekly* (22 November 1992).

12 Robin Neill and Gilles Paquet, "L'economie heretique: Canadian economics before 1967," *Canadian Journal of Economics*, February 1993, 11.

13 Cited in *New York Review of Books*, 22 April 1993.

14 Robert H. Frank, Thomas Gilovich and Dennis T. Regan, "Does Studying Economics Inhibit Cooperation?" *Journal of Economic Perspectives*, Spring 1993. This paper prompted many responses. See, in particular, Anthony M. Yezer, Robert S. Goldfarb and Paul J. Poppen, "Does Studying Economics Discourage Cooperation? Watch What We Do, Not What We Say or How We Play," *Journal of Economic Perspectives* 10 (1996): 177–86.

15 Hugh Grant, Comments on Economic History, Symposium on Innis at 100, Learned Societies, Calgary, June 1994.

16 Review by Alan Ryan, *New York Review of Books*, 2 December 1993.

17 Richard Lipsey, "A Crystal Ball Applied to Canadian Economics," *Canadian Journal of Economics*, February 1993.

Index

aboriginal peoples, in Canada: and aboriginal rights, 55; dispossessed of
land, 42, 56; and the FTA, 125; and
the fur trade, 19–20, 41, 54–5, 75; as
independent commodity producers,
55–6; as "lumpenproletariat", 42;
and northern development, 38, 61–
2; as redundant to capitalist development, 41; resistance of, 42; and resource mega-projects, 83; and self-
determination, 76; as wage labourers,
56. *See also* Dene
Aitken, H.G.J.: *American Capital and Canadian Resources*, 34, 45, 80; on economic history, 214, 215; on the staple
thesis, 6; on the state and economic
life, 227
Alaska, 51–2
Alberta: and farmers' protest movement, 224; and the FTA, 129
"American System" of the 19th century,
95–101
Amin, Samir, 186
Anderson, Martin, 261
Artistic Woodworkers strike, 133
Ashley, W.J., 174
Argentina, 73

arms race, 237, 244
Australia, 73
Auto Pact, 149, 152, 155–9, 160, 191;
and the FTA, 126; as part of Canada's
"special status", 81.
automobile: consumer spending on,
146, 150; insurance and the CCF/
NDP, 147; pervasive influence in
North America, 147, 159–61; and
regionalism, 14
automobile industry, in Canada: and
branch-plant industrialism, 147,
148; and Canadian-content rules,
152, 155, 158; importance to southern Ontario versus Quebec, 147,
158; labour process in, 146, 159;
and miniature-replica effect, 151;
and parts manufacturers, 149, 154,
157, 159; and trade policy, 106,
149–55.
Automotive Industry, Royal Commission on the (Bladen Commission),
154, and Saskatchewan Government,
154–5
Autoworkers, 159–60; and Canadian
Autoworkers (CAW), 133, 157, 159;
and United Autoworkers (UAW), 154

138; dispute resolution mechanism, 123; and employment, 122, 127; and energy, 125; and foreign ownership, 135–6, 138; and head offices, 138; and health care, 125–6; and industrial strategy, 126–7; and investment flows, 84; opposition of organized labour to, 125; opposition of the Left to, 246; political response to, 127–8; and public enterprises, 126; and Quebec nationalism, 84, 128–9; and rationalization of manufacturing, 138; and regionalism, 128; "right of establishment," 124; "right of national treatment," 124; and the service sector, 124; and social programs, 125–6; and socialism in Canada, 129; subsidy code, 123–4; and water, 129. *See also* NAFTA

Friedman, Milton, 217
Frye, Northrup: on ghost towns, 58; on Innis, 230, 253; on Quebec nationalism, 257
Fumoleau, Father Rene, 63, 69n2
fur trade, 12, 19–20, 21, 73; and aboriginal producers, 54–5, 63, 75; economic rents from, 58; and independent commodity production, 42, 74; mode of production, 55–6; and women, 76

Galbraith, John Kenneth: on automobile, 146, 162n7; on economics, 258; on Keynesianism and Marxism, 228, 244; on 1930s, 252; on poverty and affluence, 172
General Agreement on Tariffs and Trade (GATT), 122
General Motors of Canada, 145
Gilpin, Robert, 195
Ginden, Sam, 159
Goar, Carol, 260
Goodwin, C.D.W., 175
Gordon, Walter L.: on the auto industry, 155; and the Canadian capitalist class, 131, 194; and foreign owner-

ship, 78, 246; as target of Harry Johnson, 191, 199; and Watkins Report, 136–7, 257
Gordon Commission (Royal Commission on Canada's Economic Prospects), 199
Grant, George: interpreted by William Christian, 235n52; *Lament for a Nation*, 131, 188; on Ottawa mandarins, 137; on technology, 186
Grant, Hugh, 229
Gray Report (*Foreign Direct Investment in Canada*), 34, 140, 182
Great Depression: of 1873–96, 22; of 1929, 82
Guinier, Lana, 254

Hansen, Alvin, 170
Havelock, Eric, 239
health care in Canada: and the FTA, 125
Heaton, Herbert, 214
Helleiner, Gerry, 184
Heller, Walter, 170
highways: in Canada, 147–8; in the US, 146
Hirschman, Albert O., 9–10, 75
Historians: labour, 233n25; and the media, 262
Holmes, John, 159
Horn, Michiel, 239
Horowitz, Gad, 118
Howe, C.D., 257
Hudson's Bay Company, 37, 63; as real estate company, 56; surplus appropriated in fur trade, 58
Hurtig, Mel, 135
hydro-electricity, 73; from James Bay, 129; in Ontario, 37
Hymer, Stephen, 111, 182, 199n12, 204n11, 206n23

immigration to Canada: explained in staple thesis, 10, 12, 15, 17, 33; and the National Policy, 95, 97–8, 103, 105; in 19th century, 43; in post-WWII period, 80, 106

Kay, Geoffrey, 45
Kennedy administration: and econo-
mists, 171
Keynes, John Maynard: on economic
growth, 71; influence of Canadian so-
cialist intellectuals, 241; as Liberal,
244; on Marxism, 244; rescue of eco-
nomics, 170; as revolutionary, 257;
viewed by Harry Johnson, 197, 198
Kierans, Eric, 36
Kindleberger, Charles P., 14, 18–9, 187
King Gordon, J., 238, 239
King, Mackenzie, 246
Klondike Gold Rush, 82
Kondratieff, N.D., 72
Kuhn, Thomas, 181, 203, 213
Kuznets, Simon, 170

labour movement, in Canada: American origins of, 44; creation of a working class, 43; and foreign ownership,
140; growing nationalism in 1980s,
133; and international unions and
the NDP, 44–5; need for democratic
reform, 132; opposition to the FTA,
125; post-WWII capital-labour
accord, 81
labour movement, in US: opposition to
the FTA, 125
Laski, Harold, 241
Laurentian School, 176, 222–3,
234n38. See also Creighton, Donald
Laxer, Gordon, 78
Laxer, James, 148
League for Social Reconstruction
(LSR), Social Planning in Canada,
239–41, 245–6, 251; on American
imperialism, 247–8; on free trade,
246; ignores foreign ownership, 246;
Innis' hostility towards, 229; on mo-
nopoly capital, 240–2.
Levesque, Rene, 193
Levin, Jonathan V., 7, 10, 11, 16
Levitt, Kari, 34, 116, 137, 143n15
Lewis, David, 132
Lewis, W. Arthur, 18
Lipsey, Richard, 261

literary criticism, 260
long-waves of economic growth: 72, 79–
80; in Canada, 80–3
Lower, A.R.M., 176, 224, 225, 226

MacDonald, Ian R., 32, 40, 45, 48n29
Macdonald, Sir John A.: and Canada's
National Policy, 93, 95, 96, 97, 99,
105, 223
Macdonald Commission, 252
Mackenzie Valley: natural gas pipeline
proposals, 38, 51–2, 63
Mackintosh, W.A.: on Canada's cyclical
growth, 71, 72; on Canada's National
Policy, 93; and Canadian economics,
176; Economic Background on Dominion-
Provincial Relations, 223–4; "steady-
growth" version of staple thesis, 31,
32, 73, 217, 220, 221, 227; White
Paper on Employment and Income, 257
Macpherson, C.B.: Democracy in Alberta,
42; on economics and "political rigidities," 170; on economists, 181; on
Innis, 224; on the role of the state,
227–8
Mallory, J.B., 224
Malmgren, Harold B., 184
Manitoba: public auto insurance in,
147; resources industries in, 36
Marchard, Jean, 137
Marr and Paterson, Canada: An Economic History, 215
Marsh, Leonard, 239
Marxism: and individual choice, 196;
and Keynesianism, 244; "micro", 75;
and nationalism, 181; revival in
1960s and 1970s, 228; theory of economic growth, 71, 199n6, 120n15; in
the US, 173, 178–9
Marxism, in Canada: and the LSR, 242;
and the staple thesis, 31, 46n3, 38–9,
40–1, 45, 229–30; vulgar, 117; and
younger scholars, 38, 41. See also
Clement, Wallace; Macpherson, C.B.,
Naylor, R.T, Naylor-Clement thesis;
Pentland, H. Clare; political economy, new; Ryerson, Stanley